ROMAN GUERNSEY

ROMAN GUERNSEY

Excavations, Fieldwork and Maritime Archaeology 1980–2015

Guernsey Museum Monograph No. 9

HEATHER SEBIRE, PHILIP DE JERSEY AND JASON MONAGHAN

With contributions by T. Arnison, B. Dickinson, G. C. Boon†, V. Ferneyhough, B. R. Hartley†, C. E. King, J. Le Huray, J. Rackham, C. Salter, R. S. O. Tomlin, T. Walls and A. M. Wood†

OXBOW | books
Oxford & Philadelphia

Published in the United Kingdom in 2018 by
OXBOW BOOKS
The Old Music Hall, 106–108 Cowley Road, Oxford, OX4 1JE

and in the United States by
OXBOW BOOKS
1950 Lawrence Road, Havertown, PA 19083

Paperback Edition: ISBN 978-1-78925-068-8
Digital Edition: ISBN 978-1-78925-069-5 (epub)

A CIP record for this book is available from the British Library

Library of Congress Control Number: 2018951272

Typeset in India by Versatile PreMedia Services. www.versatilepremedia.com

For a complete list of Oxbow titles, please contact:

UNITED KINGDOM
Oxbow Books
Telephone (01865) 241249
Email: oxbow@oxbowbooks.com
www.oxbowbooks.com

UNITED STATES OF AMERICA
Oxbow Books
Telephone (800) 791-9354, Fax (610) 853-9146
Email: queries@casemateacademic.com
www.casemateacademic.com/oxbow

Oxbow Books is part of the Casemate Group

Contents

List of figures

List of tables

Acknowledgements

The excavations described in the following pages were undertaken in often difficult circumstances, and with very limited resources. The authors are therefore grateful above all to the volunteers who gave freely of their time and effort, over many months, to rescue the first significant evidence of the Romans in Guernsey.

We are grateful to the Garenne Group for their generous support of the publication of this volume. We would also like to thank Barbara McNee, who drew the pottery and other finds in a series of visits to Guernsey, and Paul Le Tissier, Design and Development Officer at Guernsey Museum, who produced the publication drawings of the Bonded Store excavation. The image from the Legge Report of 1680, used in Fig. 18, is reproduced by kind permission of the Royal Court, Guernsey.

I

The excavations

1

Introduction: the archaeological evidence for the Romans in Guernsey and the other Channel Islands

Excavations in Guernsey between 1980 and 2000 provided evidence that the Romans not only visited and traded with people in Guernsey and the other islands, but also built settlements that lasted over several centuries. Before the 1970s Roman discoveries in Guernsey consisted of a few chance finds of coins, including small hoards from Jerbourg and St Sampson's, plus a handful of sherds of samian pottery from St Peter Port harbour and from prehistoric megaliths. By 2000, however, the accumulated evidence from many rescue excavations and underwater discoveries provided enough information to show that the islands were Romanised and indeed played a role in the transportation of goods from various parts of the Roman world to northern Gaul and Britain.

The state of knowledge around the millennium has been summarised by Sebire (2005, 107ff.), but discoveries continue apace. Ongoing fieldwork is starting to reveal more evidence for the Roman period in Sark and Jersey, whilst Alderney has the extant remains of a late Roman small fort (Monaghan 2011–12) with the suspicion this also had an adjacent settlement and a military presence from the late 1st century onwards (Monaghan and de Jersey 2014–15). The Gazetteer in this volume includes all Roman find-spots in Guernsey, Herm and the surrounding waters up to 2015.

By the late Iron Age period, *c.*120–50 BC, finds of Mediterranean amphorae and other pottery show that the Channel Islands were already part of a significant trading network (see p. 69), involving both regional and long-distance interaction. It is not certain whether the Iron Age occupants of the islands were part of one of the Gallic tribes of Armorica, perhaps the Unelli from the Cotentin or the Coriosolites from northern Brittany. Jersey has yielded a huge number of coins of the Coriosolites – almost 80,000, predominantly in hoards, compared to just a handful from Guernsey – but this does not necessarily mean they were normally in control of that island, or that Guernsey had the same rulers.

The two islands appear to have had different settlement densities. This was perhaps at least partly a consequence of the fact that Guernsey, with a good natural harbour, provided a more favourable shelter than could be offered by Jersey. Guernsey thus presented an ideal stop-off point between the ports of northern Gaul and southern Britain (McGrail 1983). It is possible, although as yet unproven, that the two islands had very different political allegiances in the late Iron Age and early Gallo-Roman period, with Guernsey adopting a more 'pro-Roman' attitude and Jersey remaining closer to its Gaulish allies on the mainland; this could have influenced the very different archaeological records which we see today.

Throughout the last decades of the 1st century BC, wine amphorae were exchanged on mainland Britain for slaves and animal hides, and for raw materials such as tin. Exchange goods passing via Guernsey may have included corn, hides, wool and hunting dogs (Cunliffe 1987, 340–2). The most common amphora in circulation in the Late Iron Age was the type known as Dressel 1A, principally carrying Italian wine, which dates from the first half of the 1st century BC. Sherds of Dressel 1A are present in the assemblages of the sites at both La Plaiderie and the Bonded Store. They have also been found at Nacqueville and Coutances in western Normandy (Cunliffe 1986) and Brittany, particularly from shipwrecks off Les Sables d'Olonne and the Île d'Yeu (Galliou 1986). They are also present at Hengistbury Head and other sites in central southern Britain, which suggests that the wine trade was well established before Caesar's abortive campaigns to the British mainland in 55 and 54 BC. Other sites on Guernsey where sherds of Dressel 1A amphora have been found include Les Tranquesous, St

Saviour's and King's Road, St Peter Port (see Gazetteer, this volume). At King's Road and La Plaiderie, four of the sherds were in a distinctive 'black sand' fabric; this has been shown to originate in the Pompeii-Herculaneum area of Italy (Williams 1996). In Jersey, a sherd of Dressel 1A was found during excavations at Old Street in St Helier, on the south coast (Wood 1989). These trade routes are likely to have been disrupted during Caesar's Gallic campaigns, but after the defeat of the Veneti at sea in 56 BC and a concurrent land offensive against the Armorican tribes, north-western Gaul was also taken into the Empire. Mainland Britain, however, remained outside full Roman control until the Claudian invasion of AD 43. For a fuller discussion of trade routes see p. 69, below.

We do not know at which point between the Roman victories over the Armorican Gauls in 56 BC and the invasion of Britain in AD 43 Guernsey fell under the control of the Empire, but the balance of probability was that it fell in with its neighbours on coastal Gaul at a relatively early date, certainly before the end of the 1st century BC. As mentioned above, Guernsey may indeed have been more Romanised than Jersey, or become so at an earlier date, simply on the back of its maritime connections. Roman material has certainly occurred more widely in the archaeological 'background' of both formal excavations and casual finds in Guernsey than in Jersey.

The modern names of the islands all have Viking origins. The Roman name for Guernsey as given in the Peutinger Table is thought to have been *Lisia* (Kellet-Smith 1962; Coates 1991), with Herm possibly *Sarnia* and Sark, *Caesarea* (Ridel 2014); Alderney was certainly *Riduna,* and Jersey probably *Andium*. The name *Lisia* may have Gallic origins and might imply that late Iron Age Guernsey was marshy (Ridel 2014). The Channel Islands as a whole were known as the *Insulae Lenuri*, but there have as yet been no inscriptions found to verify any names. It is not known from where the islands were administered but the likeliest candidates are *Constantia* (Coutances) on the nearby Armorican coast, tribal capital of the Unelli, or possibly *Fanum Martis* (Corseul), the capital of the Coriosolites. It is conceiveable that Guernsey and Alderney fell under the former, and Jersey under the latter.

The imposition of Roman rule possibly saw a formalisation of proto-St Peter Port as a town, with a shift of activity to there from the high ground at King's Road, which had been important in the late Iron Age. We have no indication of what the town was called, if indeed it had a name distinct from that of the island. The Gazetteer in this volume lists almost 100 sites at which Roman material has been found, indicating that Roman material culture was widely spread across the islands, even if thinly. Roman-style buildings with tiled roofs, employing flat bricks/floor tiles and box-flue tiles certainly existed in St Peter Port and at the Castel Church. An extensive settlement may also have existed on Longis Common in Alderney, though the island is excluded from this work. Significantly, the burial grounds of Guernsey have not so far been located.

Evidence for Roman military activity comes chiefly from Alderney, commencing by the late 1st century AD. The 4th/5th-century small fort known as the Nunnery may have been the base for naval patrols at a time of growing uncertainty. On Waganeur's map of 1550 this fort is referred to as *Castrum Longini* or 'Castle of Longinus'.

It can only be assumed that the islands may have changed rulers during the revolts of the 3rd century; the breakaway 'Gallic Empire' of AD 260–74 is a possible context for the counterfeit coin production at La Plaiderie. The late 3rd century also saw the sinking of the Romano-Celtic vessel at the mouth of the harbour, which remains the best-preserved Roman ship outside the Mediterranean. Its contents show continued trading links with Algeria, Spain, western Gaul, and southern and eastern England. Ceramic evidence ashore demonstrates links to the Rhineland and the Mediterranean well into the 4th century. On the mainland, *Fanum Martis* certainly came under attack in the upheavals of the 4th century. The islands are presumed to have remained under at least nominal Roman control until the fall of northern Gaul to the Franks in AD 486.

New evidence from excavations since 1980

La Plaiderie

The excavations at La Plaiderie, described below, were the first on Guernsey to indicate Roman settlement of any substance. Building foundations on the site give evidence of Guernsey's role as an entrepôt or stopover for the Roman entrepreneurs making their way on the trade routes between southern Britain and Gaul, and ultimately the rest of the Empire.

La Plaiderie is situated at the northern end of what would become medieval St Peter Port, and possibly also at the northern limit of the Roman settlement. Excavations revealed building foundations, which suggest that two wooden structures were later replaced by stone buildings with thick low granite walls. The upper walls would likely have had wooden studwork with plaster and wattle partitions above. The roofs were tiled and the outside yards had well-made stone drains. Various pits and gullies were found associated with the buildings, which stood close to the high water mark (slightly inland today), and so were ideally situated to take advantage of the gently sloping beach where vessels could be unloaded with little difficulty. Broken coin moulds were discovered which suggest that a small smelting complex was used for coin counterfeiting in the later 3rd century AD.

The evidence from coins and pottery suggests that the site was in use from the early 2nd century until the late 4th century AD. The ceramic evidence in particular indicates that there might have been a military or naval presence at the site, when considered alongside pottery types from northern France and the Picardy region, and also from further east in Germany (see p. 62). This may represent the *Classis Britannica* (the Roman fleet) calling into the islands in search of shelter and raw materials. Over 6000 sherds of pottery were recovered, of which nearly 400 were samian ware. The pottery originated from Gaul, particularly the Pas-de-Calais and Picardy, but also from Spain, the Rhineland and Britain, strongly suggesting that there was movement of goods both north and south, as well as along the Channel. Samian from La Plaiderie ranges from the Tibero-Claudian period to the 3rd century AD.

A human cremation burial in an earthenware urn was excavated in the southern part of the site. Large areas of burning and apparent rapid demolition of the buildings give an indication that use of the site may have come to an abrupt close.

The Bonded Store

Excavations in advance of the development of the town markets in St Peter Port in the late 1990s and early 2000s added to the growing corpus of Roman material from Guernsey.

The Bonded Store is situated in the heart of modern St Peter Port, very close to the parish church, at the bottom of one of the two valleys that border the town. In the Roman period the site would have been 100m or so from the waterfront. It is approximately 400m south of the site at La Plaiderie.

Structural remains of Roman buildings were located under later medieval walls. There was evidence of metalworking in the higher part of the site, and part of a small clay-lined furnace was excavated. Not enough vitrified furnace-lining fragments were found to confirm this as a smithing furnace, but the evidence suggested there must have been one nearby. In another area of the site a building appeared to have burned down *in situ*, leaving traces of burnt timbers and quantities of roof tile lodged vertically in the layer.

At the Bonded Store, some 5000 sherds of pottery were recovered, of which approximately 450 were samian ware. Other pottery came from a wide variety of sources in southern, central and eastern Gaul, plus some from Britain and the Rhineland. The main bulk of the finds from the excavation were from the 2nd century AD, although the pottery dated from the later 1st century through to the 3rd century AD. The assemblage indicates that Guernsey was receiving high percentages of products from eastern Gaul, which is unusual as this is not generally the case on sites west of the Seine in France, or in south-western Britain (see p. 69). Coarsewares also show strong links with areas of the Rhine, the Argonne and northern France. The traded pottery assemblage resembles more what might be expected in London than in south-western England. A considerable number of tripod bowls were found with blackened surfaces, which may suggest their use as portable cooking pots or holders of oil for lamps (p. 67).

Along with the sherds of Dressel 1A amphora, Dressel 20 olive oil amphora sherds from Spain were also present. Other amphora sherds indicated the import of wine, fish sauce or fruit from the Mediterranean. Mortaria for preparing food were also found, although in relatively small quantities. Glass fragments were retrieved including several pieces of vessel handles and a tiny fragment of a polychrome pillar-moulded bowl (see p. 104).

Although there was no Roman coin evidence from the Bonded Store, a single Iron Age coin of the Baiocasses tribe (from the region around Bayeux) was recovered from one of the earlier phases. There were several more exotic finds, including an intaglio or engraved gemstone, of cornelian, showing a three-headed figure (*gryllos*), plus another – of glass – showing Prometheus creating man. Both date from the 2nd century AD (see p. 107). As at La Plaiderie, religious observance is suggested by parts of two Venus figurines. The site is in an area of known fresh water and indeed one of the neighbouring streets is now called Fountain Street. A stream runs through the site and the parish church of St Peter Port is very close by, so it is not unreasonable to assume that a temple might have been in the area (McCormack 1986, 157).

The results of the major excavations of La Plaiderie and the Bonded Store indicate that the Roman presence in Guernsey was both substantial and long lasting, and that Roman St Peter Port was not just a trading outpost but a lively, bustling town. The evidence from almost 100 sites elsewhere in Guernsey and Herm (presented in the Gazetteer) supports the view that this occupation was spread widely across the islands, even if represented by only a few sherds or coins on many of these sites.

2

Excavations at La Plaiderie, 1983–1985

by Philip de Jersey

Introduction

The excavations at La Plaiderie between 1983 and 1985 provided the first real evidence of a significant Roman presence on the island of Guernsey. Excavations in the previous decade – notably at the Tranquesous (St Saviour's), and at King's Road (St Peter Port) – had revealed tantalising glimpses of Gallo-Roman occupation, and chance finds had been recorded at least since the mid-19th century, such as the occasional scraps of samian re-deposited in the island's megalithic tombs (see Gazetteer). Richard Keen's discovery of the Romano-Celtic vessel nicknamed 'Asterix', on Christmas Day 1982, and its subsequent excavation in 1984–85, provided a convincing maritime aspect to the Gallo-Roman period in Guernsey, and the Plaiderie investigation at last provided a suitable counterpart on the land.

Background to the excavation

In November 1983 the States of Guernsey Ancient Monuments Committee was given permission to excavate the large rear garden of Plaiderie House, in the northern part of St Peter Port (Fig. 1), in advance of a major redevelopment of the site by Langlois Ltd. It was anticipated that the excavation would shed more light on the medieval history of the town, not least because of the presence of the medieval courthouse of La Plaiderie adjacent to the site. Nonetheless, in 1980–81 a small quantity of Gallo-Roman material had been unearthed at 18/20 The Pollet, just 100m to the south, suggesting that there might also be more concentrated Gallo-Roman occupation in the vicinity.

Excavation at the Plaiderie began on 19 November 1983, directed by Bob Burns, Assistant Curator at Guernsey Museum, and thanks to the co-operation of Langlois Ltd continued intermittently until 2 October 1985. The entry in the site notebook for the first day of excavation records the discovery of a sherd of samian pottery, and by mid-February 1984 it was apparent that there were Gallo-Roman structures to accompany a wealth of pottery and other finds of the era.

Despite the full co-operation of the developers, the excavation did not always proceed smoothly. Work at the Plaiderie had to be slotted in alongside Bob Burns's other museum commitments, not to mention other archaeological work going on in the island. As for the site itself, the site notebooks provide a revealing testimony to the foul weather which repeatedly stopped work, damaged exposed surfaces and led to frequent baulk collapses. The excavation was carried out almost entirely by volunteers from the Guernsey Museum Archaeology Group, who could have been forgiven for losing heart at the need to clean up the mess repeatedly but who stuck it out for the best part of two years, enriching the island's history in the process.

The excavated area

The garden behind Plaiderie House was split into two parts: a lower section to the north, of approximately 27m east/west by 17m north/south, and an area of higher ground, 20m by 25m, immediately behind the house (see Fig. 1). The garden sat astride the 10m contour, and lay just 75m west of the current quayside. The land to the west of the site rises quite steeply, but the garden itself appeared essentially level, apart from the artificial change in height between the upper and lower parts.

Excavation began with a small L-shaped trench (Trench 1) on the east side of the lower part of the garden. This was gradually enlarged over the next 18 months to cover an area of approximately 12.5m by 16.6m, or some 230m^2, all

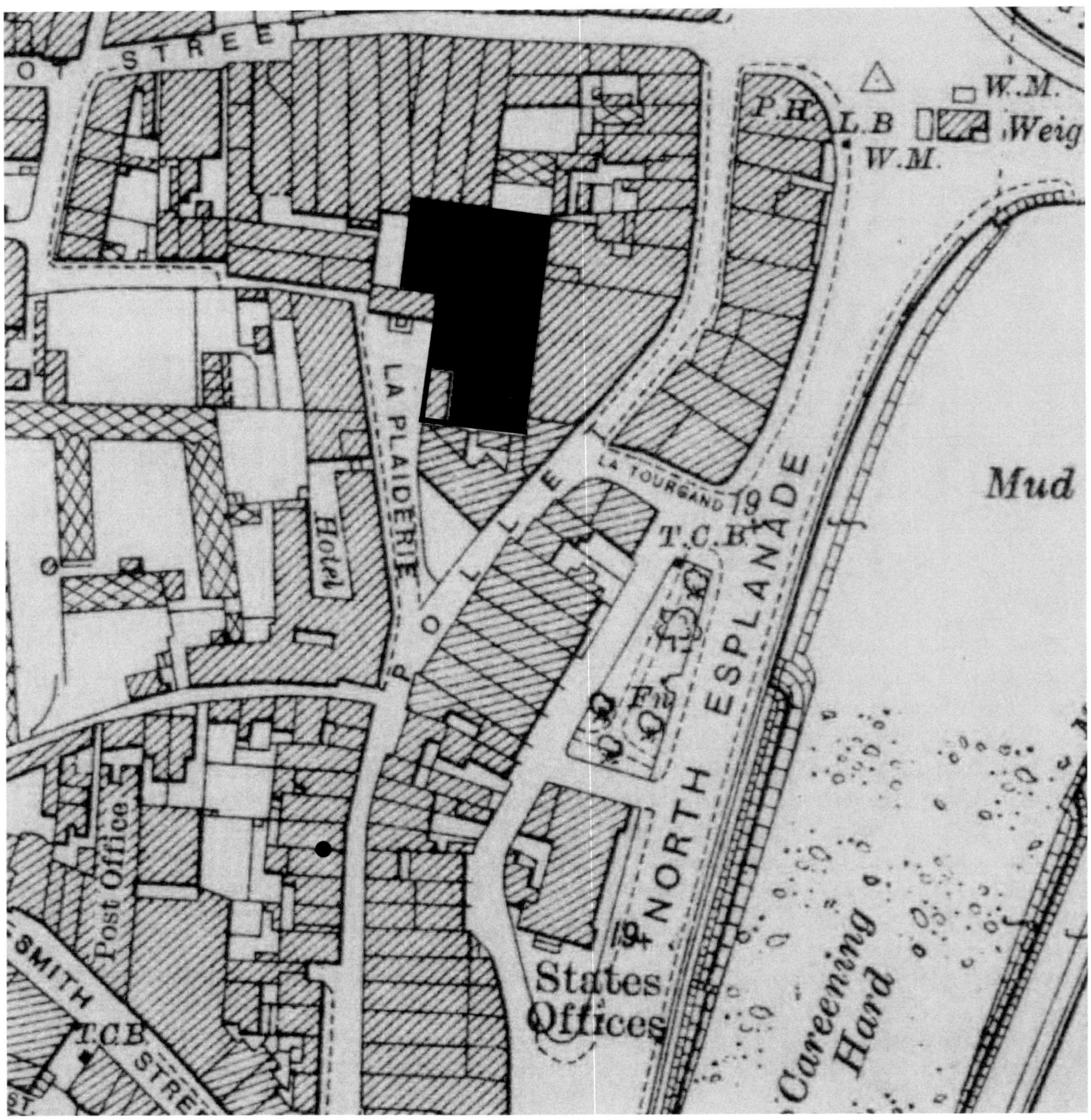

Figure 1 The garden of La Plaiderie House (in black), on the 1938 OS map. The dot marks Gallo-Roman finds at 18/20, the Pollet.

within the lower area of the garden (Fig. 2). Work in Trench 1 continued until 21 May 1985.

Trench 2 was laid out in the upper part of the garden on 13 July 1985, in the form of a rectangular area 11m by 6m, located approximately 1m from the southern edge of Trench 1 (see Fig. 2). Excavation continued here until the close of the work in October 1985.

Phasing and key features

There are four main periods of activity at La Plaiderie: prehistoric, Gallo-Roman, medieval and post-medieval/modern. The evidence for the medieval and later periods will be considered elsewhere. The following discussion concentrates on the Gallo-Roman phases with a brief consideration of the prehistoric. Residual Gallo-Roman material – found in medieval or later contexts – is not examined in detail here but is incorporated into the pottery report (see p. 58).

Within all of the four main periods it is sometimes possible to suggest further refinements to the phasing, but in general the excavation records are not sufficient to allow for the construction of a detailed site matrix. In the case of the Gallo-Roman occupation of the site, which is arguably its most important element, it is possible to identify at least three distinct episodes of activity, which are described below as Phases 1–3. There are, however, a number of Gallo-Roman features, or at least features which appear likely to have been Gallo-Roman, which cannot be dated any more precisely within that period or which are very difficult to

Figure 2 La Plaiderie: trench location plan, superimposed on 1979 air photograph.

relate to the more clearly defined elements of the site. These difficulties are discussed more fully below.

Period 1 Prehistoric

Only a few features certainly of prehistoric date were identified at La Plaiderie. Approximately 900 pieces of flint were found on the site, almost all residual in later contexts; a report by David Lane is held in the Guernsey Museum archive.

The main surviving area of prehistoric occupation lay in the south-west of Trench 1, where the natural land surface sloped upwards towards the west and where later occupation had not disturbed the prehistoric soil horizons. In this area of *c.* 6m × 2m there were some 29 postholes and four stakeholes, the whole group labelled as F.75 (Fig. 3). One posthole contained a single sherd of prehistoric pottery and the remainder were devoid of finds.

Two other features were recorded as prehistoric at the time of the excavation: a rectangular pit (F.86), approximately 0.4m × 0.25m, near the southern edge of Trench 1, which had been largely truncated by medieval pit F.14; and an unlocated pit of uncertain form cut into L5 (F.97) containing 12 prehistoric sherds and nine flints. The fill of F.86 contained three sherds of Roman pottery, perhaps intrusive, as well as seven prehistoric sherds so it cannot certainly be regarded as prehistoric.

The group of postholes (F.75) was recorded as cut into the natural and sealed by L5, initially identified in the site notes (14 September 1984) as a 'dark soil overlying natural, containing only Bronze Age material and flint'. Later entries refer to this layer as 'the prehistoric soil inside Building 2' (27 November 1984) and 'a stone free mid-brown loam beneath Roman occupation levels, on natural yellow clay, containing Neolithic and Bronze Age artefacts' (undated).

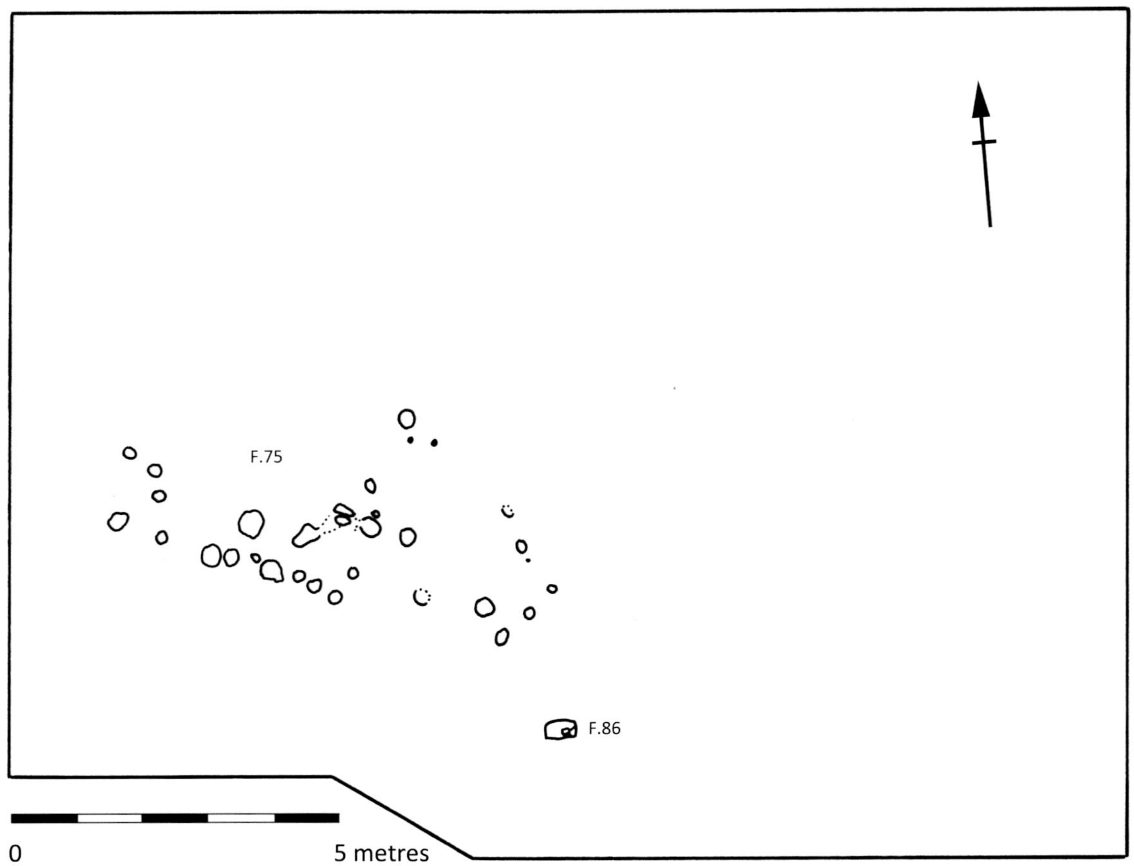

Figure 3 La Plaiderie: prehistoric features.

The L5 designation was used for deposits of soil in several areas across both trenches, and although some of these yielded only prehistoric finds there are others which are clearly contaminated by later activity. Material ranged from a *petit tranchet* arrowhead (small-find 199), 148 prehistoric and 15 Roman sherds to eight medieval sherds and some Roman tile.

Period 2 Gallo-Roman

At least three different phases of Roman activity were present at La Plaiderie, conveniently summarised as an Early Phase (1), Buildings Phase (2) and Kiln Phase (3).

PHASE 1: EARLY PHASE

The earliest phase of identifiable Gallo-Roman occupation consisted of a small number of features mostly sealed by Building 2, the Phase 2 building which occupied the central southern area of Trench 1, or by the Phase 3 kiln complex set within the walls of the building. Among these were a large clay-lined pit (F.90), sealed by the east wall (F.20) of Building 2, and several gullies or trenches (including F.76, F.84 and F.87, and possibly F.15/11) which perhaps represent the remains of robbed-out walls from an earlier phase of building. In addition there are a number of smaller pits in the same general area (Fig. 4).

a) F.15/11, F.73, F.76, F.81, F.82, F.84, F.87, F.95, F.123

F.76 was a shallow U-shaped trench running approximately north/south from the south baulk of Trench 1, extending northwards for 7m and varying between 0.3 and 0.4m in width. It was cut into the natural and also (at its southern end) into a pit of approximately 0.9m diameter with a dark charcoal fill (F.73). Identification of F.73 on the site plans is not certain, however, and its dimensions are not clearly recorded. Two other pits (F.81 and F.82), both roughly circular and 0.5m and 0.7m in diameter respectively, seem to have been cut by F.76 within the area of Building 2, but in both cases it is not absolutely clear from the site records whether the gully cut the pits or vice-versa. F.76 was not traced to the north beyond the north wall of Building 2 (F.71) but is likely in any case to have been disturbed by Phase 2 structures in this area.

A gully (F.123) ran from the north-west corner of Trench 2 in a south-easterly direction, extending for about 6.5m in

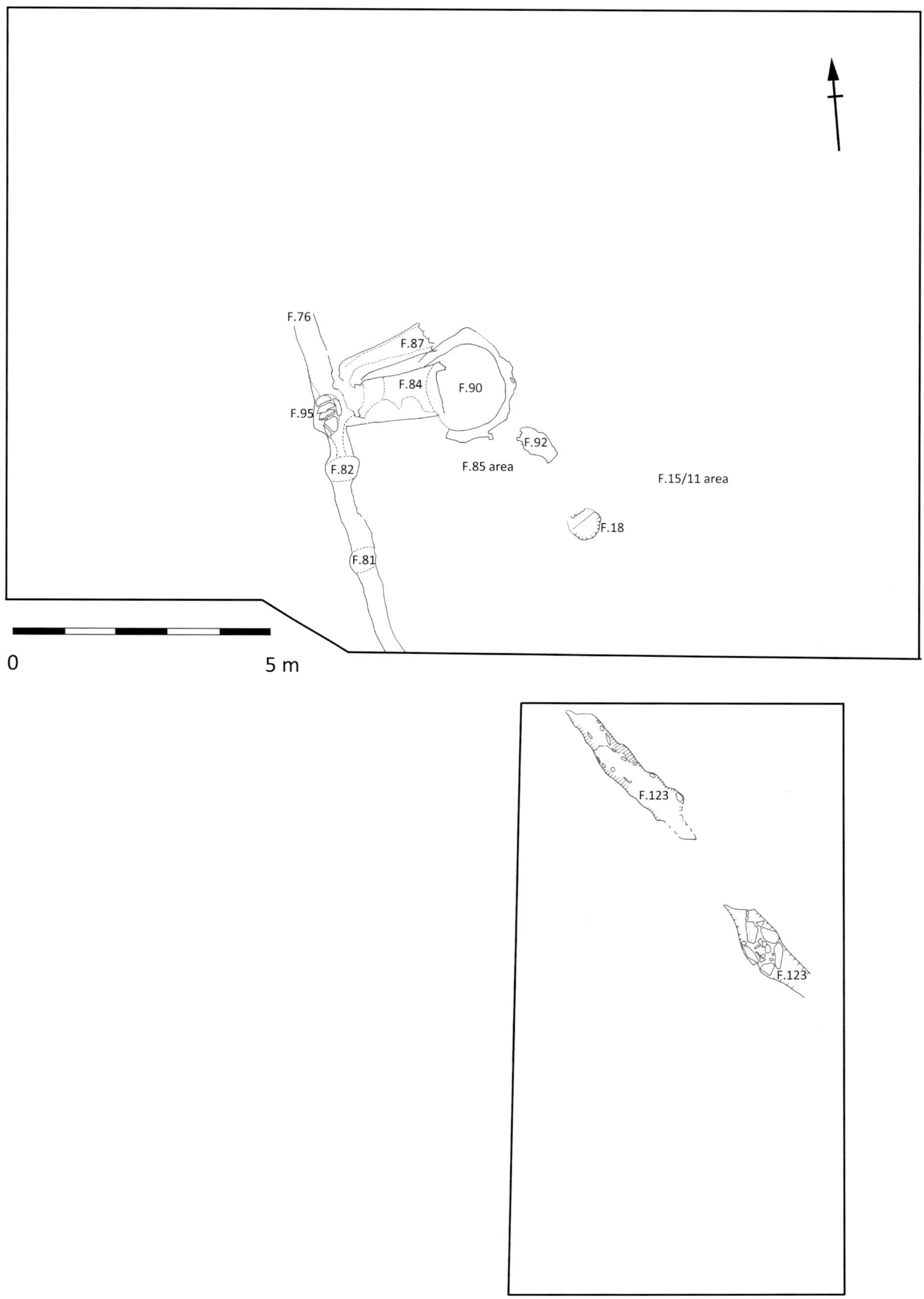

Figure 4 La Plaiderie: Gallo-Roman features, early phase 1.

total. Of this, 3.2m lay to the north of the medieval drain F.121, 1.5m was destroyed by the drain, and 1.8m lay south of the drain into the east baulk. Its width north of the drain averaged between 0.3 and 0.4m, widening to 0.7m south of F.121, before narrowing again towards the east baulk. There were some large stones (up to 0.45m) in the southern part of the gully and it may perhaps have been stone-lined along part of its length. When Trench 2 was excavated it was considered that gully F.123 might represent the southern continuation of F.76, but the combined plan of the two trenches indicates that this is unlikely (Fig. 4).

In Trench 1, two shallow trenches (F.84 and F.87), possibly representing robbed-out walls, were identified running approximately at right angles to F.76. The former, with a maximum width of *c.* 0.9m near the east wall of Building 2, extended approximately 1.8m to the west, narrowing slightly to *c.* 0.8m. It contained large pieces of granite and a small quantity of ceramics. At the junction of F.76 and F.84 was a posthole (F.95) with several large (up to 0.3m) packing stones, the whole measuring approximately 0.7m north/south and 0.5m east/west.

F.87 lay about 0.25m north of F.84, extending for 1.7m south-west from the inner face of F.20. It varied in width between 0.6m (in the east) and 0.4m (in the west) and contained a dark, silty fill with some small (60–80mm) stones. The fill also included a lump of jasper, which was presumably intended for use in the manufacture of jewellery or an intaglio. There are some suggestions in the site records that this feature could be detected outside (i.e. to the north-east) of F.20, but if so it was not planned as such. It appears to have been cut by the clay-lined pit F.90.

A substantial quantity of Roman pottery was recovered from this phase, tabulated in the pottery report, plus tile which was not all retained. F.76 yielded a copper alloy ring (small-find 135). F.73 included six sherds of medieval pot which may be contamination from F.14, the adjacent medieval pit. The relatively large quantity of bone recorded from this Roman context might also include some intrusive medieval material. F.95 included an east Gaulish samian Dr.37 sherd, indicating a late 2nd-century date at the earliest. Likewise F.123 included Cologne colour-coated ware and a possible iron fibula fragment. Residuality was high, including prehistoric pottery and flints, plus 1st-century Roman material.

The area lying roughly equidistant between the south-east corner of Building 2 (formed by F.12/F.20) and the west wall (F.8) of Building 1 was initially identified as 'an area of stones' or 'Roman tumble' and labelled as F.15. In the site records it is used primarily in conjunction with F.11 (a small area of medieval cobbling against the south baulk), i.e as F.15/F.11, to describe an apparent robber trench between these two features. The feature can be clearly seen on the August 1984 site photograph (Fig. 5) but it is difficult to say exactly how it relates to either Building 1 or Building 2, or whether it might also be part of the group of robber trenches described above. The finds labelled as F.15/11 are predominantly early, and so it seems appropriate to include this feature here. These included an *as* or *dupondius* of Trajan, of the early 2nd century AD (small-find 22). Pottery amounted to eight prehistoric, 21 Roman and four medieval sherds, including central Gaulish samian Dr.31 (Maternianus die 2a) and a Dr.37 sherd possibly of Cettus.

b) F.90

F.90 was a large clay-lined pit, approximately 1.5m in diameter at the surface (excluding the clay lining, which adds 0.2m each side) and 1.25m at the base; the depth was approximately 1.1m. The bottom half of a rotary quern (small-find 214) had been carefully set into a scoop in the gritty natural gravel at the base of the pit. Two courses of stones survived in the base and there may originally have been more courses higher up, indicated by the 'corrugated' clay sides. The clay lining was absent from about one-quarter of the surface circumference of the pit (Fig. 6).

The fill consisted of four layers (Fig. 7). The earliest deposit was a dark soil with large numbers of small pebbles, in the bottom 0.25–0.3m. Above this was a layer of 0.1–0.15m of a clayey orange soil with occasional streaks of charcoal. Above this lay approximately 0.2–0.25m of a dark soil with a few pebbles and charcoal streaks, and over this a layer of up to 0.4m of a dark soil with orange patches and more frequent charcoal. The feature as a whole was sealed by approximately 0.1m of L4 (see below) and above that by the wall F.20.

The finds were not recorded with reference to the four layers within the pit, but included 20 prehistoric, 81 Roman and 12 post-Roman sherds (presumed intrusive). Small finds included a pierced lead counter (small-find 139 Fig. 68.1), a folded lead strip (small-find 210) and a 'Frontinus' bottle base (small-find 209, Fig. 72.1).

The presence of Alice Holt/New Forest sherds is indicative of a later Roman date, with high residuality in the remainder.

c) F.18, F.85, F.92

F.18 was a roughly circular pit, diameter approximately 0.55–0.6m, mostly outside Building 2, but lying partially beneath the south-east corner (F.12) of the building. It was filled with a fine, dark silty soil.

In the south-east corner of the building was an irregular pit (F.85) and an associated feature which may have been a hearth (F.92). The pit extended for approximately 1m by 1.3m, although it is not clearly marked on the site plans and some doubt remains about its precise location. On its eastern edge an area of reddened soil and charcoal was identified as a hearth of about 0.8m × 0.4m. Both features were probably sealed by F.20, although the wall in this area had been robbed and it is not impossible that the pit and the hearth post-dated the robbing of the wall. However, they are perhaps better associated with the phase of the clay-lined pit

Figure 5 La Plaiderie: site photograph, August 1984. Taken from the west, looking east.

Figure 6 La Plaiderie: F.90 after excavation. Scale one metre.

F.90, which F.85 abuts on its northern edge. Ten post-Roman sherds in the contents list are presumably intrusive from the levels above. There were no finds recorded from F.92, but F.18 again included Alice Holt/New Forest greyware. F.85 included an east Gaulish Dr.33, plus west Normandy micaceous ware and BB1, both considered to be later Roman in Guernsey. Small finds in F.85 amounted to a copper alloy tag end (small-find 136) and the neck/shoulder from a blue/green glass flask or jug (small-find 188).

PHASE 2: BUILDINGS PHASE

Two main groups of features are associated with this phase: Buildings 1 and 2, and a complex of gullies located to the north of Building 2, probably associated with buildings beyond the northern and western boundaries of the site (Fig. 8). At least one of the gullies (F.44) may have run beneath the north-east corner of Building 2, and is thus almost certainly earlier than the building, although as described below the evidence is inconclusive. Another short stretch of gully (F.80) stops just short of the north wall of Building 2 and would make little sense in this position if either contemporary with or post-dating the wall, so this too is likely to be earlier than Building 2. For the sake of argument, then, all the gullies are considered here as Phase 2a and the buildings as Phase 2b, but it should be borne in mind that not all of these features can be stratigraphically interrelated – in particular the gullies lying at the northern edge of the trench.

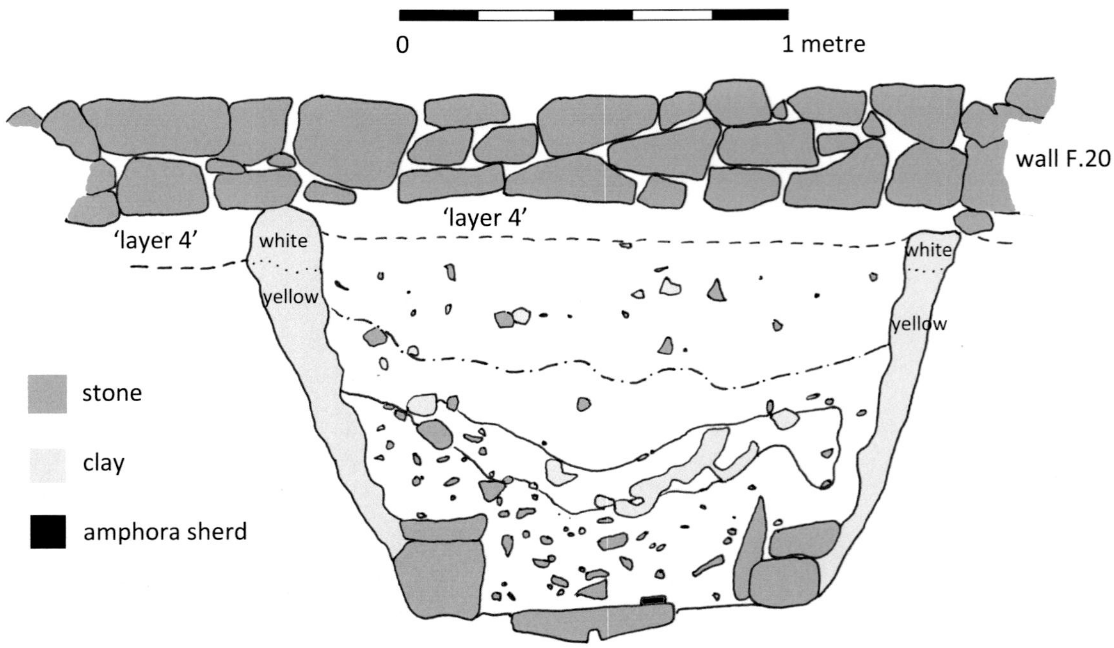

Figure 7 La Plaiderie: section drawing of F.90.

Gully Complex (Phase 2a)

In the northern third of Trench 1 the remains of at least two or three substantial stone-built gullies were identified. The records in the site notebooks for these features are confusing and inadequate, and it has proved impossible to establish a satisfactory reconstruction of the gullies and the relationships between them. The site plans are of little help, since some parts of the gullies were not planned and none was labelled. As a consequence, even some of the most basic elements of the following descriptions must be regarded as tentative at best.

a) F.44/F.102, F.31, F.31a, F.62, F.108

F.44 was originally identified as a large area of tile and rubble in the north-east portion of Trench 1, which – after further excavation – was observed to have a more linear aspect, and eventually identified as a stone-built gully, which 'might run beneath the east wall [F.20] of Building 2' (site notebook, 23 October 1984). No further mention is made in the site notebooks of whether it genuinely did run beneath Building 2. In the east of the trench, F.44 is said to have been cut by the robber trench F.8a for the surviving wall F.8 of Building 1, but this area was not planned and it is obscured on site photographs by collapses of the eastern baulk. A further complication in the identification of the gully is introduced by the comment (site notebook, 7 November 1984) that the pig burial F.91 was cut into the 'upper fill of F.44', followed two months later (site notebook, 5 January 1985) by the following:

> Commenced investigating the 'gully' in which the pig skeleton was found. I had originally assumed that this was associated with F.44 the tumble filled gully but it appears that this is not so. Allocated a new F. no. F.100.

The obvious implication is that there were two gullies in this area and yet only one – with the cut for the pig burial – is clearly visible on the plans. There is perhaps some evidence on the final site photograph (Fig. 9) that a gully did lie between F.99 (see below) and (approximately) the north-east corner of Building 2, and it may have continued for at least 1–2m further east, but it is by no means clear. Nor were two gullies shown in this area on the interim report on the Roman features (Burns, unpublished MS). To all intents and purposes F.100 would appear to be the same feature as F.44, but there remain numerous problems with this interpretation, not least the assertion quoted above that there were two separate features, or the observation that F.44 might have run beneath the wall of Building 2.

The picture is complicated still further by the association of F.102 with F.44. In the western part of Trench 1, the gully F.102 was initially identified as the continuation of F.44 (site notebook, 24 March 1985). It was described as containing 'much large stone' in the upper fill, and was sealed by F.99, a loosely assembled boulder wall running approximately north/south, north of Building 2. The final site photograph suggests that there are two candidates for this feature: one is very clearly the continuation of the gully which contained the pig skeleton (i.e. F.100, which as we have seen may be the same feature as F.44), which is perhaps just sealed by the

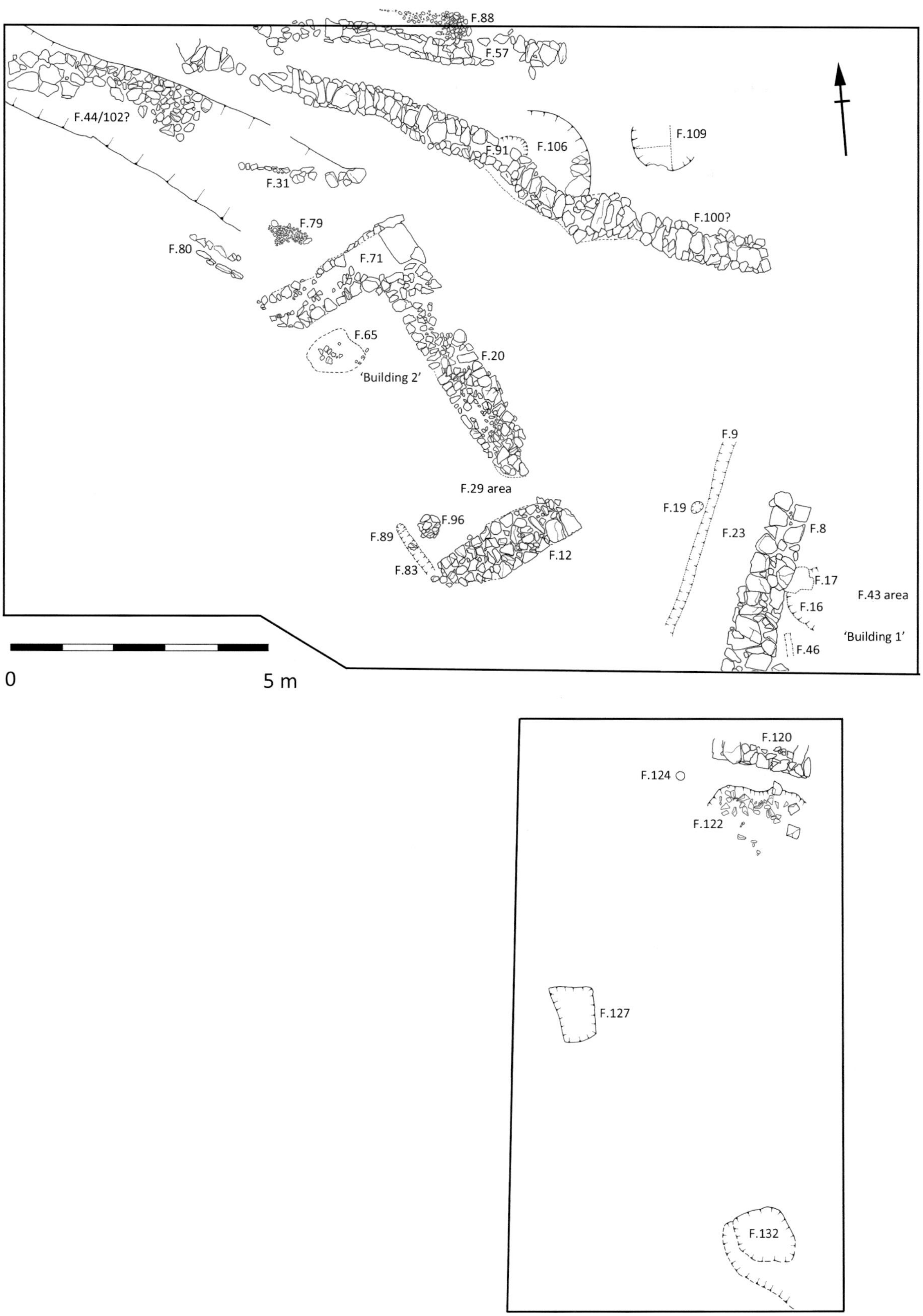

Figure 8 La Plaiderie: Gallo-Roman features, buildings phase 2. Undated features (F.122, F.124, F.127 and F.132) are also shown on this plan.

Figure 9 La Plaiderie: site photograph, April 1985. Taken from the west, looking east.

northern end of F.99. The other possibility – which seems on balance to be preferable – is that F.102 lay about 0.5m south of F.100. The photograph (Fig. 9) confirms the presence of much large stone in the fill and the feature is certainly sealed by F.99. There is also a small test-section visible on the photograph, cut against the southern side of the feature, which appears to match a sketch in the site book (20 March 1985) with the section labelled as F.102. It appears, however, as though the full contents of F.102 were never completely removed; there are no further mentions of it in the site book before the end of the first phase of excavation, and there are fewer finds than one might expect (see list below).

Boulder wall F.99 was believed to be Gallo-Roman when Burns (unpublished MS) produced the interim plan of Gallo-Roman features on the site, but when it was dismantled at the close of the first phase of excavation (site notebook, 16 May 1985) it was shown to contain Normandy stoneware and other post-medieval sherds in its make-up.

If the gully described above is correctly identified as F.102, it raises again the possibility that F.44 – which it is supposed to continue westwards – is *not* the same as F.100, the gully containing the pig burial. In that case F.44 to the east of the north/south boulder wall F.99 must, after all, have run either beneath or very close to the north-east corner of Building 2. Between F.99 and Building 2 it is perhaps represented by F.31, an alignment of stones initially identified as a wall, lying within a larger area of tumbled granite (F.62, no finds recorded). This insubstantial feature was visible for approximately 2m, with a width between 0.1–0.3m, consisting mostly of small (up to 0.15m) stones with a couple of slightly larger (0.35m) stones in the west. There are a few references in the site notebooks to another small linear feature (F.31a) which is said to have run directly beneath F.31, on the same axis; this was perhaps an earlier cut of the same gully. F.62 is not shown on the site plans, but from the description of its position in the site notebook (18 June 1984, 23 October 1984) it must have occupied the area immediately north of Building 2.

As we have seen, the location of F.44 further east was not clearly recorded, but the fact that it was said to have been cut by the robber trench for F.8 indicates that it must have been identified at the eastern edge of the site.

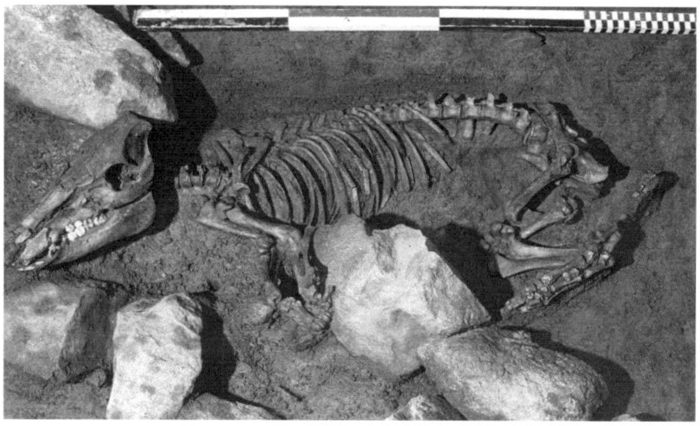

Figure 10 La Plaiderie: pig skeleton in F.91. Scale marked at 10cm intervals.

In view of these difficulties in identification, it is not possible to provide more detailed dimensions of F.44/F.102. Furthermore, it seems likely that many of the finds listed as F.44 probably came from more general areas of disturbance – the large area of tile and rubble initially identified in the north-east of the site – rather than from the secure context of the gully.

At the western end of F.44/F.102, the gully cut a large shallow pit identified as F.108. The exact dimensions of this feature were not recorded but on the evidence of the site photograph it extended for at least 1.4m by 1.5m, although it does not appear to have been completely excavated. Some of the finds from this area were recorded as 'F.108 associated with F.44'.

F.44 contained abundant finds, including some 870 Roman sherds and 1261 retained pieces of tile. The presence of *céramique à l'éponge*, New Forest colour-coated and greywares, and Oxfordshire red/brown colour-coated ware take the date into the 4th century. Small finds included a pipe clay figurine (small-find 130, Fig. 69.1), a 'black' glass finger ring (small-find 131) and a dark green glass finger ring (small-find 128), and a glass cup/flask base, small-find 127 (Fig. 72.4); There were also 21 sherds of medieval pottery, indicating how disturbed this feature was. F.108 included *céramique craquelée-bleutée* (east Paris basin) and *Eifelkeramik* as well as six post-Roman sherds.

b) F.91, F.100, F.106, F.109

If gully F.100 is correctly identified on the plans and photographs – and with the presence of the pig burial F.91 along its course, it is more readily identifiable – then it ran in total for some 8m, approximately east/west, with an average width of 0.6–0.7m. Each side of the gully was lined by small (up to 0.15m) stones, with larger capstones (up to 0.4m) as cover. The capstones had remained in place for at least two significant portions of the gully's course.

F.91 consisted of a small circular pit, approximately 0.5m in diameter, with a fill of dark soil containing the complete articulated skeleton of a small pig (Fig. 10). The pit had been cut into the northern edge of F.100, removing a couple of stones from the edge of the gully in the process.

A circular pit (F.109) of approximately 1.2m diameter was recorded about 0.6m north of F.100, at the eastern edge of Trench 1. It was sealed by F.105, a medieval or post-medieval wall. Its date is uncertain but it could be a Gallo-Roman feature contemporary with the nearby gully. F.106 appears to have been a large pit, lying alongside the gully F.100 for about 1.8m immediately east of the pig burial (F.91) and extending up to 1m north-east from the gully. It contained many large stones and 'large body sherds of an amphora' (site book, 12 May 1985; but not recorded in the pottery report for this feature). It presumably post-dates F.100 but may be broadly of the same period.

c) F.57, F.88

Another stone-lined gully (F.57) lay almost against the northern baulk of Trench 1, running for approximately 6m east/west. At its western end it disappeared beneath the baulk and at the eastern end it was cut by medieval pit F.94 (also labelled as F.110). The gully was formed of two lines of edging stones, up to 0.3m in size, with rather larger (up to 0.4m) pieces as capstones, although most of the latter had been disturbed. The gully contained a fine, silty fill, with a relatively high number of fragmentary iron objects, but little pottery.

In the restricted space excavated between F.57 and the northern baulk there was a very small area of cobbling (F.88) which did not appear to the south of the gully. It consisted of small stones or pebbles, typically 0.1m or less, and covered an area of 1.4m west/east by a maximum of 0.5m north/south. It was presumably contemporary with F.57, although it did not contain any finds.

d) F.80

A short stretch of stone-lined gully was observed immediately north of F.71 (the north wall of Building 2), running for approximately 1.4m north-west/south-east with a width (including the stones forming the two sides of the gully) of 0.3–0.4m. On the interim report on the Roman features (Burns, unpublished MS) this feature was associated with two other short stretches of stone further to the west, F.78 and F.98, but in fact these latter structures are more likely to have been part of post-medieval boundary wall F.10. There were no finds from any of these three contexts, F.78, F.80 or F.98.

Buildings 1 and 2 (Phase 2b)

a) Building 1: F.8, F.9, F.16, F. 17, F.19, F.23, F.43, F.46, F.120

The eastern (F.8) and southern (F.120) walls of 'Building 1' were located in the south-eastern corner of Trench 1 and the north baulk of Trench 2 (see Fig. 2). F.8 consisted of large (up to 0.5m) granite stones (including beach stones) with yellow clay bonding, extending approximately 3.6m north-north-east from the south baulk of Trench 1, and averaging 0.9m in width. The wall survived for two or occasionally three courses. It had been robbed at its northern end, but to judge from the associated drip gully (F.9, about 0.15m wide and lying 1m west of F.8) it originally continued for at least a further 0.5m in this direction. Both F.8 and F.9 were cut into a hard, yellow-brown 'surface' designated as F.23; this extended about 3.5m south-west/north-east but was heavily disturbed west of the drip gully by medieval features. One other feature possibly contemporary to Building 1 was identified immediately west of the gully: F.19, the base of a truncated pit or posthole, with a maximum diameter of 0.2m.

To the south, F.8 presumably extended for another metre, through the unexcavated baulk between Trenches 1 and 2, and was then exposed (as F.120) in the north baulk of Trench 2, where it turned to the east, extending 2.1m to the east baulk. This section of the wall lay on the natural, and survived to a maximum height of 0.6m in three courses (Fig. 11). At a much later stage this wall formed the foundation for one of the 18th-century garden walls.

A small portion of the interior of Building 1 was excavated in the south-east corner of Trench 1, although this area had to be abandoned at an early stage because of repeated collapses of 19th- and 20th-century rubbish pits in the baulks. A possible hearth (F.17) of approximately 0.6m by 0.4m was identified adjacent to F.8, although it is unclear whether this feature butted up to F.8 or was cut by it. The hearth cut into the western edge of an earlier pit (F.16) of estimated diameter approximately 1–1.2m within the building.

The general area within Building 1 (i.e. east of F.8) was later designated as F.43, described in the site notebook as a 'sooty' area of multi-coloured soil with much evidence of burning, and incorporating some crushed tile. This is likely to represent a later phase of use of the structure, or indeed the demolition of it. Finds labelled F.43 are, however, likely to come from several different phases – possibly predating F.16

Figure 11 La Plaiderie: south wall of Building 1 (to right of 2m range pole), in north baulk of trench 2.

and F.17, as well as levels contemporary with the walls F.8 and F.120, in addition to the posited destruction level (which included significant quantities of post-Roman pottery). F.43 should not therefore be regarded as a secure context.

Within F.43 a blackened area with a straight edge was identified as a possible carbonised plank 0.1m wide (F.46), extending for approximately 0.3m from the south baulk.

Roman finds associated with this phase included sherds of black-burnished ware, *Eifelkeramik* and *céramique à l'éponge* in both F.8 and F.43, indicative of a 4th-century date. *Eifelkeramik* was amongst four sherds in F.17. Several features (F.9, F.16 and F.43) also included post-Roman sherds. There was a worked piece of slate in F.43 (small-find 341).

b) Building 2: F.12, F.20, F.29, F.30, F.65, F.71, F.79, F.83, F.89, F.96

Building 2 consisted principally of a largely intact eastern wall (F.20) and robbed northern (F.71) and southern (F.12) returns (Fig. 12). F.20 survived in the form of two or three courses of stones, typically between 0.2–0.3m in size, with smaller rubble in the core and clay bonding. It ran for 6.8m (length of outer face) on a north-west/south-east orientation and the width averaged 0.7m. A small part of the south-eastern end had been robbed out.

At the northern end of F.20 was a large (0.8m × 0.5m) flat stone forming the cornerstone of the building. The northern wall extending from this point, F.71, survived for approximately 3.2m at an average width of 0.9m. The robbed line of F.71 marked the northern edge of a roughly circular hearth (F.65) which had presumably been in use when the wall was still upstanding (although it might also be associated with the Phase 3 kiln complex). The hearth measured approximately 1.1m east/west by 0.85m north/south; it was constructed on a bed of broken tile and at the centre was about a dozen small stones, up to 0.15m in length.

At the southern end of F.20 the return wall F.12 ran for approximately 2.5m, average width 0.8m, before being cut by the large medieval pit F.14. Both north and south return walls were constructed in the same fashion as the east wall.

There was no trace of any western wall of this building, which had presumably been robbed out in antiquity. Internal features were difficult to discern but probably included at least one pillar base (F.96). This consisted of small pieces of granite (maximum 0.2m) set in a yellow clay matrix of diameter approximately 0.45m, and located about 0.6m inside the southern wall of the building. There were no finds within this feature.

In the south-east corner of Building 2 (at the junction of F.20 and F.12) was an irregularly shaped pit (F.29) of approximately 0.7m by 0.5m. The pit is not clearly marked on the site plans and there are some inconsistencies in its description, and in the details of the finds, in the site notebooks: in particular it is unclear whether it extended beneath F.20. The site book entry for 18 March 1984

Figure 12 La Plaiderie: excavation within Building 2, looking east.

reads: 'In the SW [sic] angle of F.20 (Building 2) there is a pit with a charcoal/sooty deposit F.29. This has produced large quantities of pottery plus the 2 finger rings and bronze coin.' A few days before (13 March 1984) the two rings are recorded as 'found on the inside of F.20 (inside building). These were in the soil which is stratified below the wall levels – there was a good deal of pottery in this area including a large flagon-base.' This implies that the pit extended beneath the wall F.20, but the site photographs of this time seem to indicate that this deposit may have lain entirely within the building walls; it is difficult to see how these objects could have been found at this relatively early stage of the excavation below the wall levels, since the general site photograph of August 1984 shows that only the surface course of F.20 had been revealed by that point.

Pit F.29 thus probably post-dates the construction of Building 2 but may be earlier than the kiln complex. As noted in the site book entry quoted above – although listed as F.20 – it included one bronze sestertius of the late 2nd or early 3rd century AD (small-find 10), and two copper alloy finger rings, one (small-find 9; Fig. 68.4) inscribed VALE and the other (small-find 11; Fig. 68.5) with a blue glass intaglio possibly depicting a cupid.

Other minor features which were perhaps contemporary with the original development of the building included a circular posthole (F.30) of diameter 0.15–0.2m, recorded (but not planned) north of F.29. A small area of 'flooring' (F.79), approximately 0.8m east/west by 0.3m north/south, was outside Building 2, about 1m north of F.71. A shallow scoop (F.89) of 0.2m × 0.2m was perhaps levelled when the building was constructed. Another feature (F.83) was possibly a continuation of F.89 for a further 1m to the south.

Feature F.20 included a piece of slate and five post-Roman sherds. Finds designated as F.20 were presumably retrieved in the general vicinity of this wall. Some finds were listed as F.20/F.12. As noted above, the two finger rings (small-finds 9, 11) and the coin (small-find 10) were ascribed to F.20 rather than F.29, and may have come from the general area within the south-east corner of Building 2. Other finds said to be from F.20 are also likely to have come from F.29, but it is not now possible to separate them out. F.65 produced a sestertius of Marcus Aurelius, AD 161–80 (small-find 112) and a small piece of incised copper alloy (small-find 113), pl us two post-Roman sherds. F.79 included Alice Holt, BB1 and six post-Roman sherds.

c) 'Layer 4'

'Layer 4' was used in both Trenches 1 and 2 as a general designation for a putatively Gallo-Roman layer, defined in the site notebook as:

> a somewhat arbitrary layer which commences at the lower level within Building 2. The soil is a compact grey/pale brown loam with an admixture of sand in the matrix. The level commences approx 8cm below the tops of the stones in the wall of Building 2 ... Sealed by L3 [see below]. Roman soil. Cut in several places by the forges – hearths and other late features.

The site notebook records that L3 'has been applied to areas where no medieval pottery has been found and where no Roman structural remains present', implying a late or post-Gallo-Roman – but pre-medieval – date for these contexts. However, in practice it appears that most of the contexts recorded as L3 contained substantial quantities of medieval and post-medieval material, and for the Gallo-Roman period at least there is little to be gained from attempting to analyse the L3 assemblages in more detail.

The section drawing for the large, clay-lined pit F.90 (attributed here to Phase 1) shows a deposit of approximately 0.1m of L4 sealing the pit, above which is the wall F.20 (see Fig. 7). This evidently shows that L4 post-dates the first phase of occupation, but was at least partially formed before the construction of Building 2 (even if it was also used to designate deposits which lay within the building, which cannot have been formed until after the construction of the walls). On the assumption that L4 post-dates Phase 1, but certainly pre-dates the kiln complex (Phase 3), it seems appropriate to include finds from various contexts labelled as L4 here, with the remainder of the Phase 2 material. To a large extent the contexts are free of intrusive post-Roman material. Trench 1 'L4' included 75 prehistoric, 167 Roman sherds as late as New Forest colour-coated ware, a copper alloy 'foot' (small-find 413, Fig. 68.2), 41 post-Roman sherds and part of an iron tool that is almost certainly post-medieval. Small finds included an iron split ring fixing (small-find 133), a hone fragment (small-find 132; Fig. 70.3) and a stone rubber (small-find 419; Fig. 70.6). L4 in Trench 2 included 38 prehistoric sherds, 103 Roman and 13 post-Roman sherds.

PHASE 3: KILN PHASE

At some time after Building 2 had gone out of use, the remains of this structure formed a shelter for several kilns and related features. At the centre of this small complex of features lay two stone-lined kilns (F.69, F.72), with three teardrop-shaped kilns (F.66, F.67 and F.68) around the outer edges (Fig. 13).

a) F.37, F.66, F.67, F.68, F.69, F.72

The relationship between F.69 and F.72 is not altogether clear in the site records. F.69 was initially identified as a charcoal-rich area linking all the other kiln areas, but was eventually recognized as a (partially) stone-lined kiln in its own right. It extended approximately 1.4m north-east/south-west, with a width of up to 0.7m. At the south-west end there were several courses of roughly placed stones, reddened by intense heating. There was some evidence of clay lining which had been replaced on more than one occasion, with layers of charcoal between the linings. The stones removed from the fill were not noticeably reddened, leading the excavator to suggest that they may have been part of a roof structure which had collapsed into the kiln. Adjacent to the south-west end of the structure was a complete (though broken) tegula, lying flat.

The fill of F.69 was recorded (site book, 1 September 1984) as possibly running 'beneath the reddened soil of F.72', suggesting that the latter feature might be associated with a later phase of use of this area, 'inserted into the centre of the forge complex.' It is, however, difficult to identify the precise relationship between these two features from the existing records. F.72 was roughly circular, stone-lined (on the edges and in the base) and approximately 0.6–0.7m in diameter. At its base were interleaved lenses of buff-coloured clay and more reddened clay. Finds were scarce.

To the north (F.66) and south (F.67, F.68) of the central kiln area were three teardrop-shaped kilns, all of very similar form and dimensions, and oriented in the same north-east/south-west direction (Fig. 14). F.66, the northernmost of this group, was 1.2m in length and a maximum of 0.4m wide at the bulbous, south-western end. It narrowed to approximately 0.25m in width before widening again to 0.4m, and then tapering to 0.17m at the north-eastern end. The maximum depth within the kiln was 0.2m. The fill consisted of approximately 0.15m of a black, charcoal-rich soil, sealed by 5cm of a grey/brown loam.

F.67 lay in the south-west corner of this group of features. The form was again essentially teardrop-shaped: 1.1m in length with a more bulbous head to the south-west, up to 0.25m in width, narrowing and then widening out to a maximum of 0.45m for the body of the kiln, before tapering again to 0.25m at the north-eastern end, marked also by several stones set around the edge. The fill consisted primarily of a very dark, charcoal-rich soil, about 0.15m in depth, with a few centimetres of silt on the surface at the south-western end.

The third kiln, F.68, differed from the other two in having a pillar near the south-western end, roughly circular in form (diameter 0.15–0.18m and height 0.12–0.18m). The overall form of the kiln was again teardrop-shaped, 1.18m in length and 0.35m wide at the south-western end, widening to a maximum of 0.45m before tapering to 0.15m and then widening slightly (to 0.2m) at the north-eastern end. The fill was a dark charcoal-rich soil, up to 0.18m in depth, with a few centimetres of silt towards the north-eastern end.

F.37 was not fully recorded, but appears to have been a large spread of mostly flat stones (generally 0.15–0.2m in length, but with occasional stones of 0.4m) and tile immediately north-east of F.69, measuring approximately 2.1m south-west/north-east by 1.2m north-west/south-east.

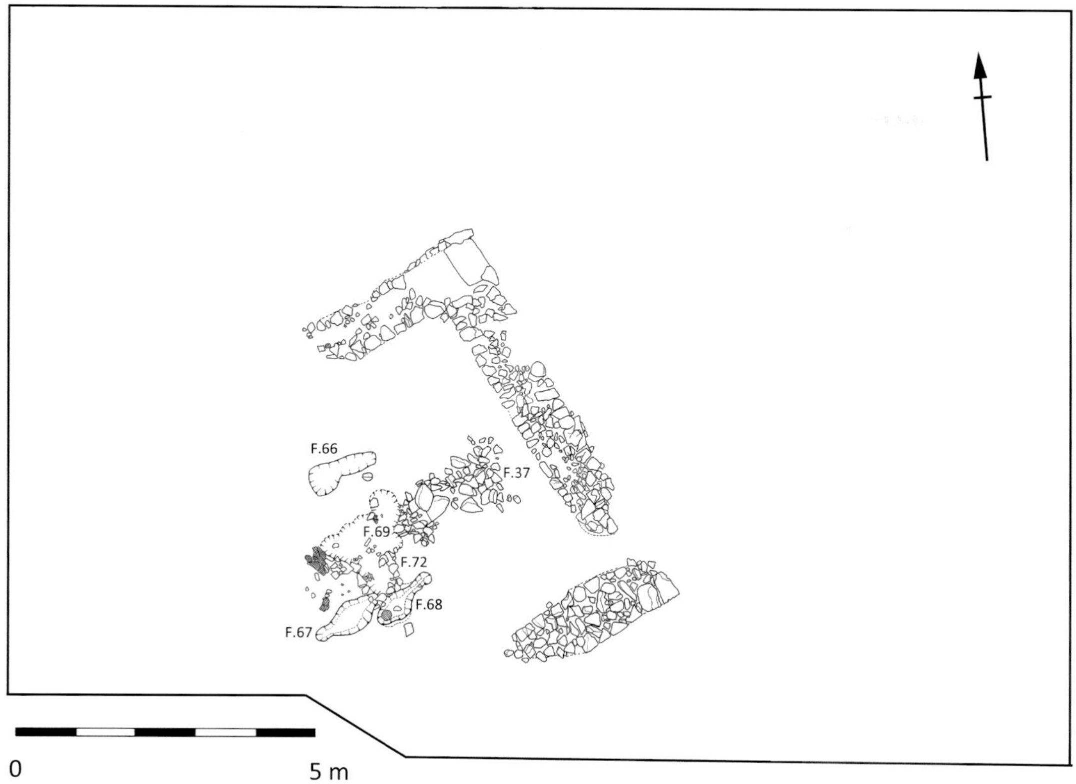

Figure 13 La Plaiderie: Gallo-Roman features, kiln phase 3, within the walls of Building 2.

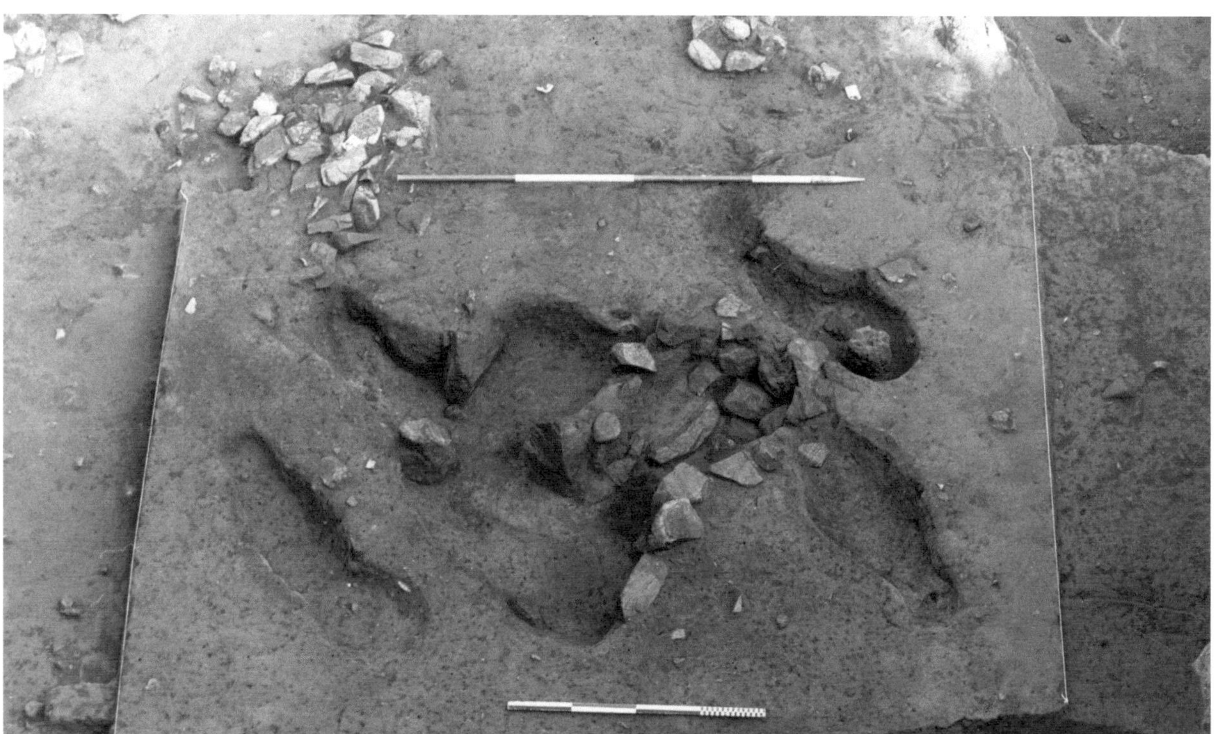

Figure 14 La Plaiderie: kiln complex during excavation, viewed from the west. Upper range pole 2m.

Finds associated with these kilns were mostly residual, with the latest pottery being black-burnished ware, *céramique à l'éponge*, *céramique craquelée-bleutée* and *Eifelkeramik*. Presumably intrusive material included fragments of slate, brick, glass and 15 post-Roman sherds.

PHASE UNCERTAIN

There are a few Gallo-Roman features at La Plaiderie which cannot be directly correlated to the three phases described above, all of them in Trench 2 (see Fig. 8). They are listed as a group here, but principally for convenience's sake. In most cases they probably correspond to the Phase 2 or 3 occupation of the site.

a) F.122, F.124, F.127, F.132

In the north-east corner of Trench 2 was a large irregular pit (F.122), approximately 1.9m east/west and 0.6m north/south, cut into the natural. The southern and western boundaries of the pit were unclear, as it had been partially cut by medieval or post-medieval features F.119 and F.121. The fill was described as a dark silty soil, containing some large (up to 0.15–0.2m) stones.

A cremation urn (F.124) was located approximately 0.6m south-west of the corner of Building 1 (the point where F.120 stopped in the north baulk of Trench 2). The pit into which it had placed was indicated by a few centimetres of burnt soil and charcoal, mostly on the western and northern edges of the pot (Fig. 15).

A sub-rectangular pit (F.127) in the south-west corner of Trench 2 was cut into the natural and filled with a dark soil; it was cut by a ?medieval pit, F.126, in its north-east corner. The pit extended approximately 1.05m north/south and 0.8m east/west, with a maximum depth of 0.28m. Some 25 fragments of moulds for the manufacture of counterfeit coins were recovered from these pits. Four were listed as finds from F.126 (small-find 386, no designs visible), five from 'F.126/F.127' (small-find 386a; no designs visible, but 'antoninianus rather than denarius?'; Boon, pers. comm.), and 16 from F.127 (small-find 387; very small, with no designs visible). It is assumed here that all the fragments were originally deposited in the Gallo-Roman pit F.127, though some were presumably disturbed by the later pit F.126.

Figure 15 La Pladerie: cremation urn (F.124) during excavation.

F.132 was a roughly circular pit in the south-east corner of Trench 2, possibly dug in two phases with a shallower 'tail' in the south-east. The deeper (up to 0.5m) part of the pit measured approximately 1–1.2m in diameter, with the shallower area (up to 0.3m) extending another 0.5m to the south-east. The pit was cut into the natural, and sealed by a thin layer of sand, above which turf or occupation layers had developed. It contained seven prehistoric sherds and 31 Roman, including black-burnished wares and *céramique à l'éponge*, which are typically later 3rd and 4th century in Guernsey.

ROMAN FINDS FROM LATER CONTEXTS

Table 1 provides a summary of small-finds of the Gallo-Roman period which were found in later, medieval or post-medieval contexts at the Plaiderie. Further details of the coins and coin mould fragments are provided below (p. 99).

Summary

The somewhat confusing mass of detail presented above should make clear the difficulty of refining the chronology of the Gallo-Roman site at La Plaiderie, beyond the simple threefold distinction into early, buildings and kilns phases. There are fundamental problems in the accuracy of the site record, and the presence of considerable quantities of late or intrusive material, even in contexts which must be stratigraphically early, creates some significant problems in interpretation. As a case in point, the large, clay-lined pit F.90, which was apparently sealed by Building 2 – and consequently must be one of the earliest features on the site – is said to have included in its fill a dozen post-Roman sherds, plus two sherds of Wood's western Normandy micaceous ware (WNMW), dated to the 4th or 5th century AD, and other sherds (fabrics AQR and Alice Holt/New Forest?) almost equally late. One possible implication of this late material in an 'early' feature – that the chronology of the whole site should be shifted several centuries later – is really not tenable, since it would push the construction of the buildings and the use of the kilns into the post-Roman period, and there is no positive evidence to support quite such a late chronology. Similarly, although this pit could evidently have been filled some considerable time after it was dug, it is difficult to accept that the lapse between excavation and backfill could have been in the order of centuries. Some late material could certainly be intrusive,

Table 1 La Plaiderie: Gallo-Roman small-finds from later contexts.

Context	*Small-find no.*	*Description*
T1, L2	17	coin mould fragment
T1, L2	18	coin mould fragment
T1, L2	21	silver denarius, Salonina (AD 253–68)
T1, L2	27	fragment of probable Roman coin, stolen
T1, L2	83	sestertius, Antoninus Pius (AD 161–80)
T1, L2	407	fragment of clay statuette? (24 × 20 × 6mm)
T1, L3	216	long oval green bead, narrow perforation
T1, 'L3 block 2'	124	fragment of stone hone (Fig. 70.2)
T1, F.41	38	iron hobnails (13)
T1, F.47	125	coin of Victorinus (AD 268–70)
T1, F.47	141	dark blue hexagonal bead, two wide sides, narrow perforation, worn at ends; Roman?
T1, F.48	71	coin, possibly 4th century AD
T1, F.48	85	rim and neck of glass unguent bottle (Fig. 72.1)
T1, F.48	91	copper alloy finger ring; oval bezel with plano-convex disc of dark glass with pale blue spots (possibly medieval?)
T2, L3	256	copper alloy cleaning utensil (Fig. 68.6)
T2, L3	262	copper alloy cauldron foot in form of paw (Fig. 68.7)
T2, L3	281	copper alloy foot in form of paw (Fig. 68.3)
T2, L3	363c	glass vessel rim, Roman? (Fig. 72.5)
T2, L3	381	fragment of green/colourless ribbon handle with folded attachment, from a jug?
T2, F.121	264	sestertius, Marcus Aurelius (AD 163–64)
T2, F.121	273	fragment of Frontinus bottle base in blue green glass, two concentric rings and pontil mark, letter F facing right between rings

and the intensive medieval and post-medieval occupation of the site no doubt contributed to the general mixing up and disturbance of the Gallo-Roman features. But the fact that even a supposedly well-sealed context such as F.90 contains what must surely be much later material does not encourage confidence in the reliability of much of the site record. Table 2 gives some indication of the mixing of ceramic material across contexts which in theory belong to quite different phases of the site.

All this being said, it is nonetheless possible to outline the broad aspects of development on the site. Prior to the Gallo-Roman occupation, there was evidently prehistoric settlement in this area. Although structural remains certainly of prehistoric date are few, the presence of significant quantities of re-deposited prehistoric material in many of the Gallo-Roman features suggests that a greater density of occupation once existed than was archaeologically visible, before being largely erased by the Roman development. Most of the re-deposited prehistoric material consists of abraded, non-diagnostic body sherds, probably spanning both Bronze Age and Iron Age in date, but there are a couple of fine rims which are likely to be from the end of the prehistoric period.

While there are not insignificant quantities of early Roman ceramics from the Plaiderie (see p. 59), it is not possible to identify any structural evidence which can be securely dated to the 1st century AD – or indeed the late 1st century BC. Some of the 'early phase' features tentatively identified as robbed-out walls could be from this period, but if the robbing took place in the 2nd century AD then it is not surprising that the fill of these features generally includes rather later material. Despite the problems with the contents of the large clay-lined pit, F.90, described above, it is difficult to avoid the conclusion that this must belong among the group of early features of the site, given its stratigraphic relationships. There is no good reason to believe that the wall (F.20) which seals the pit could be medieval, and so account for the late material. Indeed there is evidence to support a Roman date for F.20 as there was no indication of a foundation trench cut through the Roman layers, and the deposits inside the building – notably the complex of kilns – seem to have built up within the confines of its walls.

Much of the earliest Roman occupation of the site must have been damaged or destroyed by the structures identified here as the 'Buildings Phase'. This consisted principally of the surviving walls of two buildings in the

Table 2 La Plaiderie: contexts with joining sherds of pottery.

		Early phase								*Gullies/buildings phase*								*Kilns phase*		
		F.15/11	F.18	F.73	F.76	F.84	F.85	F.90	F.95	F.20	F.20/12	F.29	F.31a	F.44	F.102	F.108	F.109	F.66	F.66/69	F.69
Early phase	F.15/11								■								■			
	F.18							■												
	F.73							■						■				■		
	F.76							■		■		■								
	F.84								■	■				■						■
	F.85													■						
	F.90		■	■	■					■		■								
	F.95	■				■											■			
Gullies/buildings phase	F.20				■	■		■				■		■						
	F.20/12													■						
	F.29				■			■		■										
	F.31a													■						
	F.44			■		■	■			■	■		■							
	F.102																		■	
	F.108																			■
	F.109	■							■											
Kilns phase	F.66			■																
	F.66/69														■					
	F.69					■										■				

Table 3 La Plaiderie: summary of dating suggested by samian sherds.

Early phase a)	Second half of 2nd century; nothing later
Early phase b)	Second half of 2nd century; nothing later?
Early phase c)	Second half of 2nd century
Buildings phase (gullies)	Mostly second half of 2nd century; some early 3rd century
Buildings phase (buildings 1 & 2)	Mostly second half of 2nd century; nothing definitely later
Buildings phase (layer 4)	Mostly second half of 2nd century; some early 3rd century
Kilns phase	Late 2nd century/early 3rd century

centre and south-centre, and the complex of gullies in the north. Many of the gullies probably served structures lying beyond the confines of the site, and there are indications in the stratigraphic record that some may have lain beneath elements of the buildings. In general the information available is not sufficient to refine the chronology beyond the broad phasing given here. However, the analysis of the samian pottery from these various contexts (summarised in Table 3) does suggest that these structures may date from before the end of the 2nd century AD, with occupation probably persisting into the early 3rd century.

The function of these buildings remains unclear. Burns (unpublished MS) suggested that they may have been warehouses, situated just a few metres from the shore in the Gallo-Roman period, but there is no evidence among the finds to support this proposal. The gullies may have served other buildings of a similar nature, immediately to the north-west of the excavated site, but they have long-since been lost beneath the medieval and post-medieval development of this part of the town.

The central 'warehouse' building at the Plaiderie gained a second lease of life perhaps in the early or mid-3rd century AD, when a series of kilns were dug into the deposits within the structure. The walls presumably provided a convenient shelter; they were eventually robbed and considerably reduced in height, although this may have occurred as late as the medieval period. The precise purpose of the kilns is uncertain. The largest, F.69, contained many iron nail fragments, but there was no clear evidence that these had been manufactured in the kiln. Burns (1986, 96) suggested that the kilns may have been used for coin counterfeiting, because of the discovery of numerous fragments of coin mould in Trench 2 and two relatively intact pieces (small-finds 17, 18) in Trench 1, but no such fragments were found directly in association with the kilns, so the relationship remains unproven. If the coin moulds can be reliably associated with the kilns then the presence of counterfeits of Severus Alexander (AD 222–35) and Philip I (AD 244–49) would support a mid-3rd-century date for this phase of the site. The small, two-handled flask (Fig. 62.98) from F.69 is dated by Wood to the mid- or later 3rd century, again supporting this chronology.

Although its stratigraphic relationship to other features is somewhat unclear, the cremation urn (F.124) in Trench 2 (Fig. 63.104) is dated to the late 3rd century AD, and it may well have been deposited at the period when the kilns were in use. A couple of the pits to the south of the cremation burial are likely to be from the same period of occupation, including F.127, which contained some 25 fragments of coin moulds. In general the Gallo-Roman evidence from the more southerly part of the site was poorer, perhaps largely because of medieval and post-medieval disturbance rather than because there was necessarily less evidence there to begin with.

As Wood indicates in the pottery report, there is enough late material to suggest occupation into the second half of the 4th century AD, or even into the 5th; and there are a few sherds (e.g. of Palestinian amphorae) which could be 5th or 6th. But there is no structural evidence which can be unequivocally linked with this late period, and really no clear indication of when occupation ended. It seems unlikely though that there was very significant activity on the site after the mid- or late 4th century AD, until the medieval development of the town.

3

Excavations at the Bonded Store, 1996–2005

by Heather Sebire

Background to the excavation

The Bonded Store lies beneath the Victorian market buildings of St Peter Port, Guernsey, immediately to the west of the parish church of St Peter, known locally as the 'Town Church' (Fig. 16). The market buildings and the area of the Bonded Store are bounded to the south by Fountain Street, and to the north by Market Place, leading up to Mill Street.

The St Peter Port market buildings were constructed over a period of approximately a century, on the site of what was originally the rectory garden behind the Town Church. The first phase, built in 1780 on the classic European model, included the Market Hall with assembly rooms above (Brett 1975, 32). In 1822, John Wilson added a Doric Market Hall, with a south-eastern addition in 1830. Wilson then redesigned Fountain Street; John Newton added the fish and meat markets; and in due course the lower vegetable market and the Bonded Store beneath it, which were finished in 1879. The Bonded Store was used to store temporarily alcohol and other bonded goods coming into the island.

In advance of the redevelopment of the market buildings, permission was granted by the Board of Administration of the States of Guernsey for an archaeological excavation to be carried out within the floor area of the Bonded Store, prior to any work commencing. The excavation began in January 1996, directed by Heather Sebire, then Archaeology Officer of Guernsey Museum, with the assistance of the volunteer Guernsey Museum Archaeology Group and later by several temporary paid staff. The majority of the floor area of the Bonded Store was examined, as were various other areas within the market buildings, particularly once the development had begun. It had been anticipated that buried archaeology relating to the medieval town of St Peter Port might be found, but in fact most of the medieval layers had been truncated. However, rather unexpectedly, there was survival in places of up to 3m of Roman deposits, which are the principal subject of this report; the medieval and post-medieval phases will be published elsewhere.

The Bonded Store was built on massive foundations, between which the archaeological layers had survived relatively intact. Contemporary drawings of the foundations provided a useful, although not entirely accurate guide to the degree of disturbance likely to be encountered (Fig. 17). The conditions for archaeological excavation were difficult, with little or no natural light, lack of space for spoil, and frequent flooding of the lower levels of the trenches when the water table rose (to about 6.5m OD) after heavy rainfall. The stream of La Charroterie, draining down the valley to the south-west of the market buildings, now runs beneath Mill Street and Market Place, on the north-west side of the Bonded Store. The name of Fountain Street, to the south-east, also implies the presence of water in the immediate vicinity.

Geology

The Bonded Store is located on St Peter Port gabbro, which is made up of several types of hornblende-bearing gabbro with pronounced layering at various scales (Roach *et al.* 1991, 45). In the Roman period the original land surface and underlying geology consisted of a fertile loess soil, which was deposited after the last glacial maximum by cold easterly winds carrying silt material from beneath the ice sheets. Below the loess lay material that formed when powerful glacial streams eroded the plateau which became the Channel Islands. Rock fragments from exposed outcrops were broken off and moved down the surrounding slopes. The ensuing mixture of silt and loess formed the characteristic orangey-yellow rubble deposit known as 'head', which is visible in the eroding cliffs of Guernsey today.

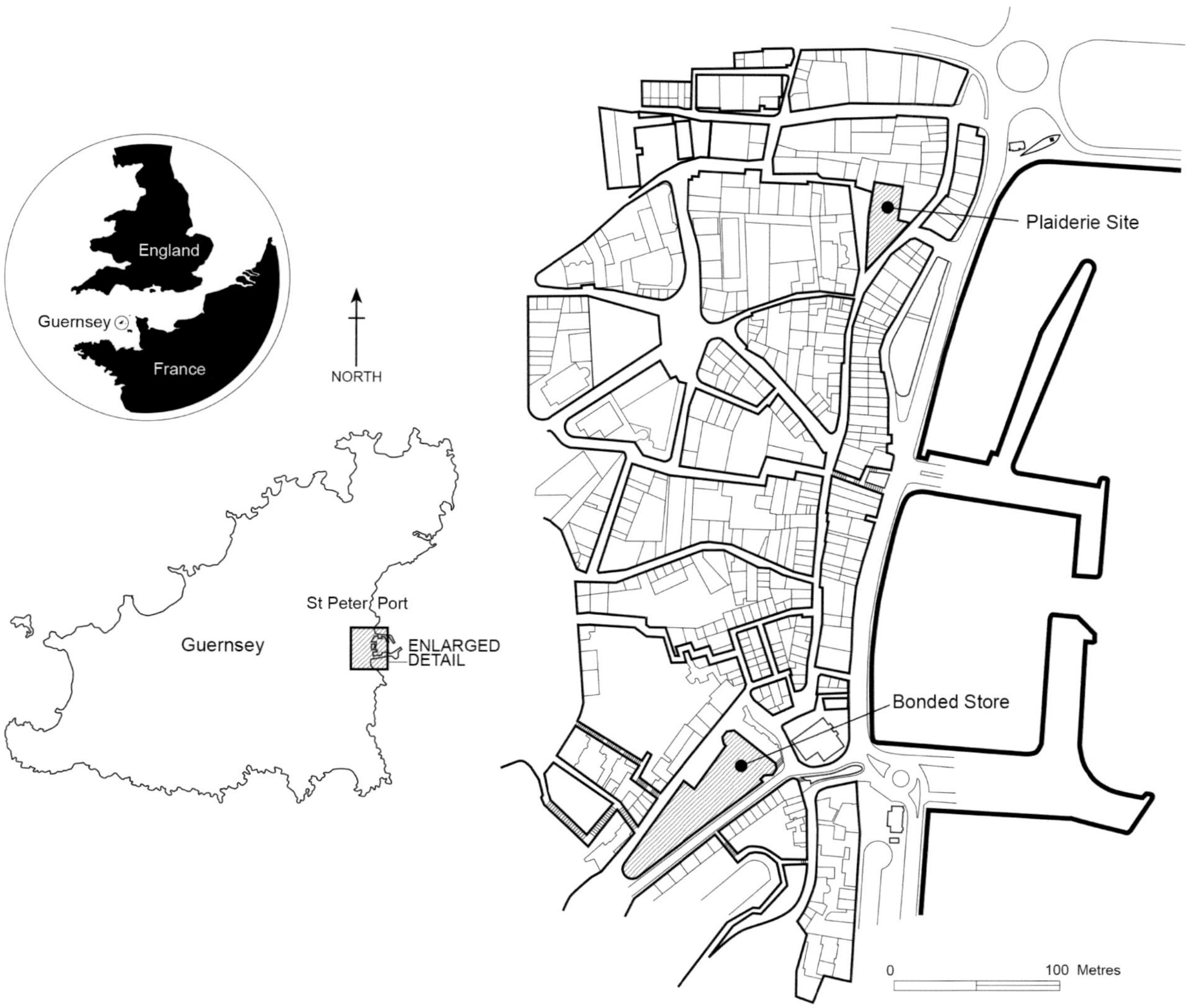

Figure 16 Location map of the Bonded Store, St Peter Port, Guernsey.

Topography

The topography of the area on which the Bonded Store was built was difficult to establish precisely, since so much of the area had been truncated in the medieval and post-medieval periods. Although a considerable quantity of documentary evidence survives it was difficult to accurately position some of the main features, such as the course of the millstream (now beneath Mill Street and Market Place) and the natural valley bottom. Glimpses of the natural topography were encountered in some of the trenches, however, particularly in trench A1 in the north-east, and trench B2 in the south-west, which gave an approximate indication of the level of the valley sides. The market buildings were erected on a shelf created in the bedrock, which had evidently destroyed much of the overlying deposits of head and loess. An illustration from the Legge report of 1680 (Fig. 18) shows some of the topographical features that were obscured by later development.

Environmental background

Environmental conditions were examined at various stages of the excavation. Dr Robert Jones identified deposits from the lowest levels of the valley floor (*c.* 3.9m OD), in trench A1 as consistent with damp woodland, with alder, birch, willow and a fern understorey. The latter also had grass and one or more members of the lily family growing there. The stream had water starwort, water lily, and pondweed, and was thus likely to have had a slow to moderate flow. Crucifer, chenopod and plantain species are indicative of saline influence. Heather was probably growing in cliff-top heath. Higher in the profile (at 4.44m, 4.69m and 4.99m OD), woodland was poorly represented, but with the same components. The valley floor now had mainly herb-rich vegetation but was still damp, with sedges and umbellifers in addition to its earlier flora. Cereal pollen indicates cultivation close to the site, and there are numerous weed and ruderal members of the *Compositae* family, in particular, to support the suggestion of farming

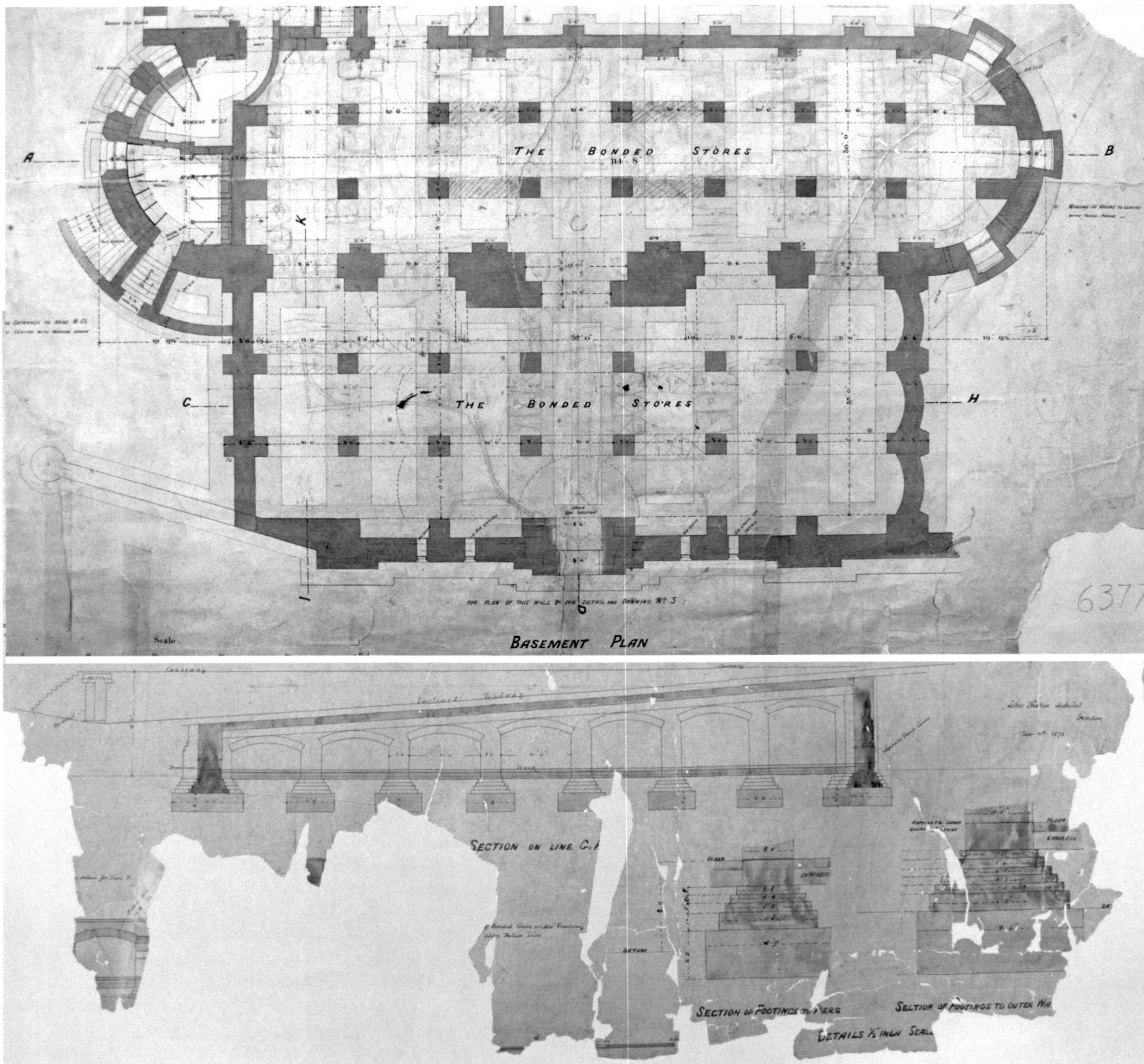

Figure 17 The Bonded Store: contemporary drawings of the foundations (compare with Fig. 19). The lower drawing shows (at bottom right) the massive concrete footings in section. Images courtesy of States Property Services and the Island Archives (6377, 6377/03).

activity. Charcoal in the pollen samples implies burning of vegetation, in this context likely to have been associated with clearing areas perhaps on the cliff-top plateau, for agriculture. A more detailed environmental report is provided below (Chapter 5).

The excavations

The excavation began in the lowest part of the Bonded Store, in the north-east of the site, as this area was due to be redeveloped first. In order to identify the trenches excavated each area was designated by A, B, C, *etc* (Fig. 19), as it was unclear at the beginning how much excavation would be needed or possible. Trenches within each area were numbered AT1, AT2, *etc* and context numbers begin with the area letter. Modern features were removed in order to examine potential earlier deposits.

Modern features and features associated with the building of the Bonded Store

The modern features consisted primarily of several layers of rubble build-up, replicated throughout the floor area of the Bonded Store. The surface of the floor of the building used as a bonded store (i.e. for goods that were 'bonded', or taxable, which were in transit in and out of the island) was covered in fine dust, and artefacts from the period of the industrial use of the buildings. These included railway sleepers and a barrel-run, which took up the main area of the central doorway and which was used to move barrels of spirits in and out of the store.

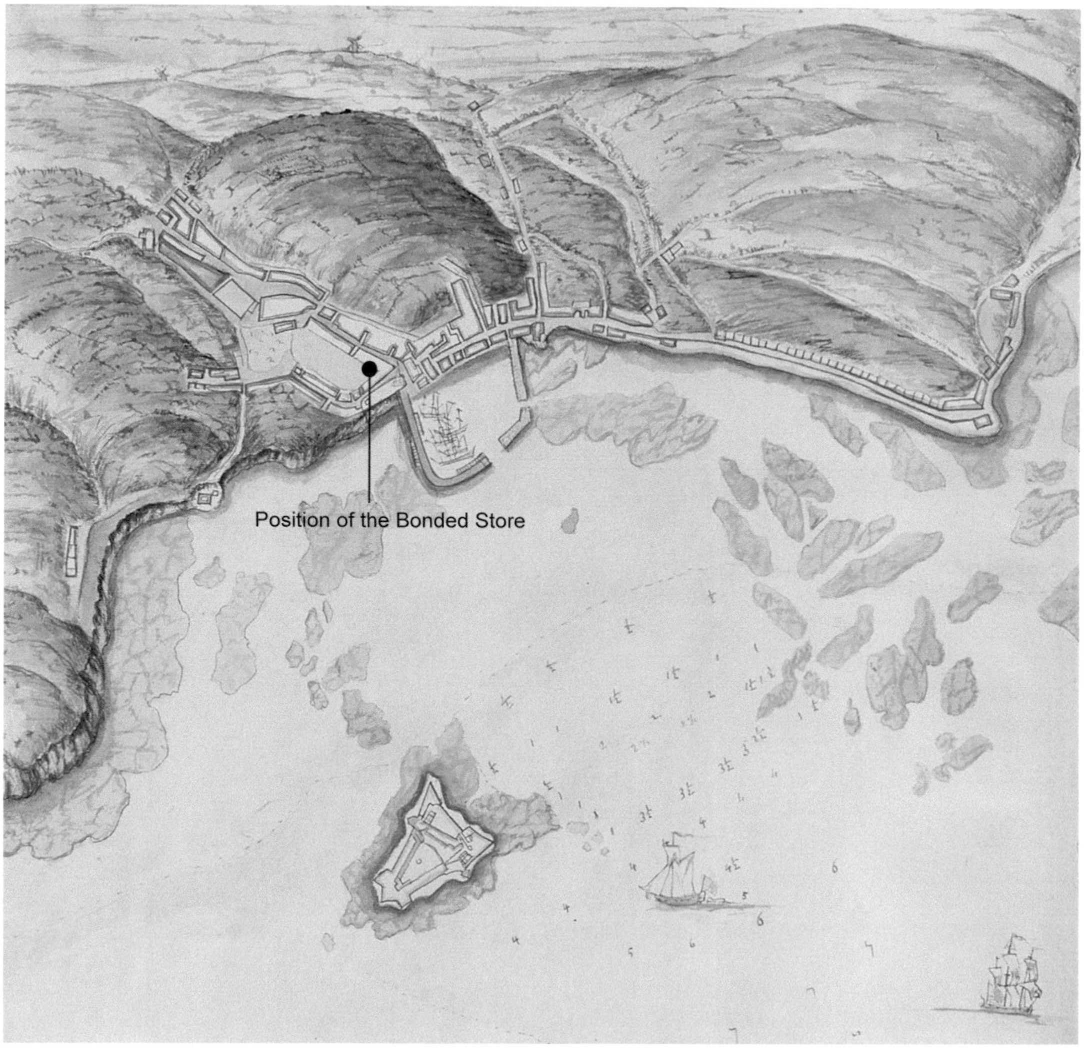

Figure 18 The area of the Bonded Store as shown in the Legge Report, 1680.

The floor of the Bonded Store was made up of a layer of compacted chalk material, which does not occur locally and which was presumably brought in by ships as ballast. It was present in a layer up to 0.2m thick across all the trenches. Below the chalk, the foundations of the Bonded Store itself were visible, consisting of stone rafts on which stood massive brick pillars (see Fig. 17). These pillars held up both the upper storeys of the market buildings and the road above (Market Street, removed as part of the redevelopment work). Construction trenches for the rafts were not clearly visible on both sides so it was surmised that the rafts were constructed right against the deposits that remained on one side, with a small construction trench – cut by hand – on the other side. Below the stone rafts was a layer of about 0.3m of an aggregate-type material. The archaeological deposits that survived were cut by these massive foundations and in some cases it was possible to leave archaeological material still adhering to this aggregate after excavation, making it a useful device for protecting thin sections through the archaeological deposits.

Below the chalk there was a hard-packed rubble layer with a patchy beige mortar and a brown gingery soil, with small amounts of demolition rubble. This deposit contained a range of finds indicating the long-continued use of the area in general. Mortar, tile, and brick were found in abundance along with prehistoric, Roman, medieval and post-medieval pottery. There were also considerable quantities of modern china and glass, and fragments of shell and bone. Amongst the rubble layer in Area A, at the very beginning of the excavation, a sherd of samian ware with a potter's stamp (Cobnertianus, see p. 83) was found which was instrumental in the decision to continue with the excavations. Prior to this find, but after the clearance of the modern layer to gain access to the lower levels, it was felt that very little buried archaeology might survive.

Roman deposits did survive to varying degrees within the site, however, and several phases of occupation could be distinguished. Interpretation was made more than usually complex by the nature of the deposits, lying in between the massive piers of the Bonded Store construction. The type

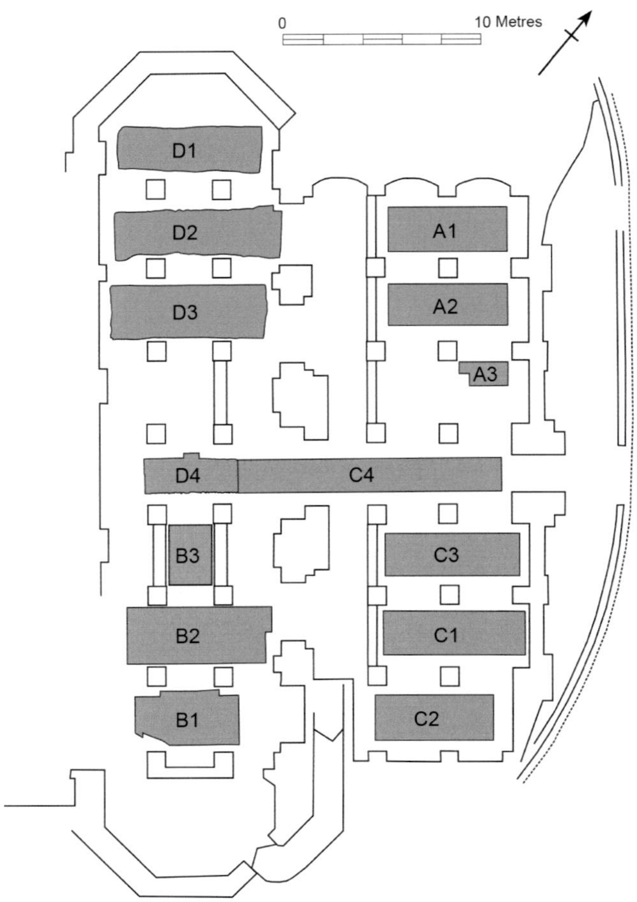

Figure 19 The Bonded Store: trench location plan.

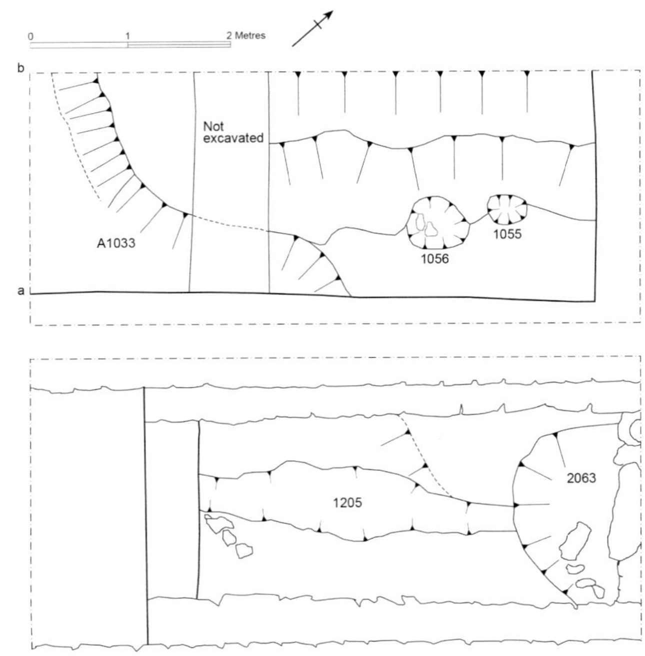

Figure 20 The Bonded Store: area A, lower levels of trenches 1 (above) and 2 (below).

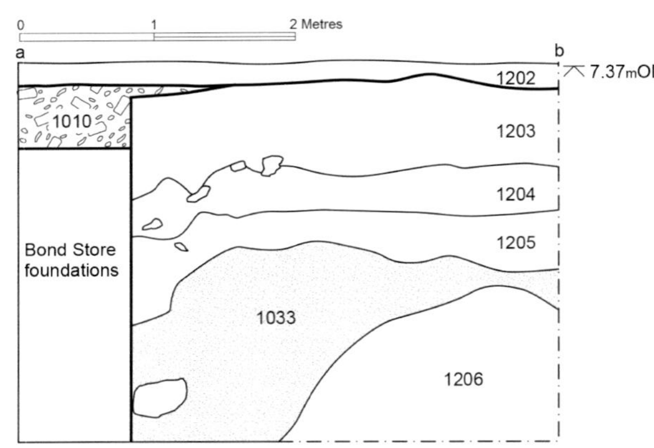

Figure 21 The Bonded Store: area A, west-facing section in trench 1, showing the ditch A1033 at an oblique angle.

of 'keyhole archaeology' that ensued meant that it was particularly difficult to follow the stratigraphy from trench to trench, although it was possible to link some deposits across the trenches.

Area A

The excavations began in Area A, which was located in the lowest-lying area in the north-east of the Bonded Store. (Fig. 19).

Natural bedrock was identified at approximately 2.2m (5.03m OD) below the floor level of the Bonded Store. Above this lay the natural head deposit (context A1206). Several features were cut into this layer, including a ditch (A1033), which was traced for about 7m across both trenches in Area A (Figs 20–22). In AT1 this feature measured 0.83m wide by 1.73m deep and was filled by very sticky, grey clay with some evidence of silting at the bottom. Finds included several minute sherds of prehistoric pottery and fragments of iron-pan, presumably geological in origin. The ditch may have formed some sort of boundary.

The ditch cut into the bank which represented the surviving valley side on the north of the site (Fig. 20). Scoops and other prehistoric features (A1055 and A1056) had also cut into this bank. A1055, measuring *c.* 0.5m by 0.32m by 0.13m deep, contained a few small angular stones and traces of very degraded prehistoric pottery in its gritty, brown clay fill. A1056, at 0.58m by 0.49m by 0.14m deep, with a similar fill, contained two stones which may have been used as potboilers.

These features were sealed by context A1205, a dark brown, gritty soil, which contained mainly prehistoric finds, including a spindle whorl (small-find 80, at 6.07m OD). A fibula of Langton Down type was also recovered from this layer (small-find 41, see p. 99).

The layer A1204, lying above A1205, consisted of a gritty orange-brown soil with lenses of grey clay, ranging between 0.17m and 0.24m in thickness. It contained Roman pottery, slag, and considerable quantities of roof tile. It was sealed by a mixed layer of re-deposited material and modern (19th-century) finds in a brown soil with some rubble (A1203).

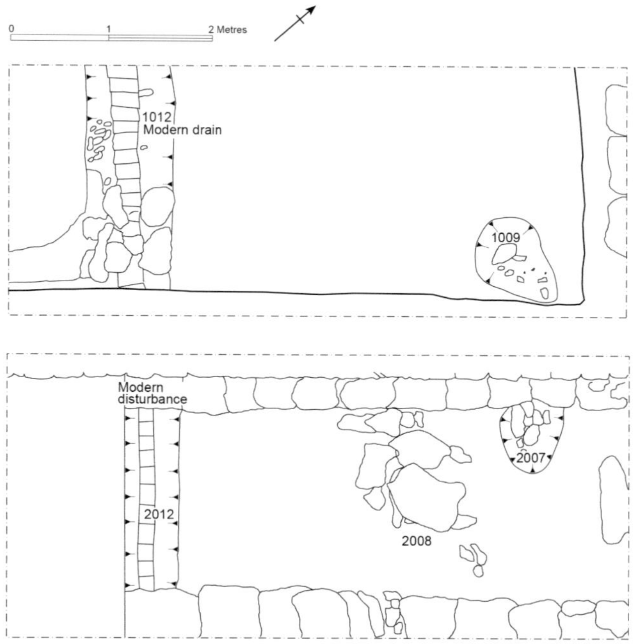

Figure 22 The Bonded Store: area A, upper levels of trenches 1 (above) and 2 (below).

Within A1203 were two clusters of stones (A2007 and A2008) (Fig. 22). The former, measuring *c.* 0.4m × 0.25m and 0.12m deep, contained large quantities of re-deposited Roman material in a dark grey clay fill. The latter, measuring between 0.22m and 0.48m × 0.66m, also contained Roman pottery. Nearby a truncated, semi-circular pit (A2063) represented one of the few distinct medieval features on the site; it contained large stones, some of which had been incorporated into the footings of the Bonded Store.

Environmental samples were taken from the lowest levels of trench AT2 (see p. 112). A third trench (AT3) was opened in Area A but was abandoned as no archaeological deposits remained.

Area B

The second area to be opened up for excavation was Area B, in the upper level of the south-east part of the Bonded Store (see Fig. 19). The chalk surface here was significantly higher than in Area A, at 8.15m OD. The first trench (BT1) in this area was abandoned because of particularly large quantities of aggregate, although the rubble layers did yield the usual mix of multi-period finds.

The second trench (BT2) was more productive, revealing Roman structural features with Iron Age deposits below. The lowest archaeological deposit in this trench, context B1205, was an orange gritty layer sealing the natural head material. This contained Iron Age pottery, including shell-tempered wares. Above it, a truncated U-shaped ditch (B2085; Fig. 23) was traced for 1.48m across the lowest part of the trench, at 6.02m OD. Examination was difficult because it lay below the water table, but it resembled a small field boundary

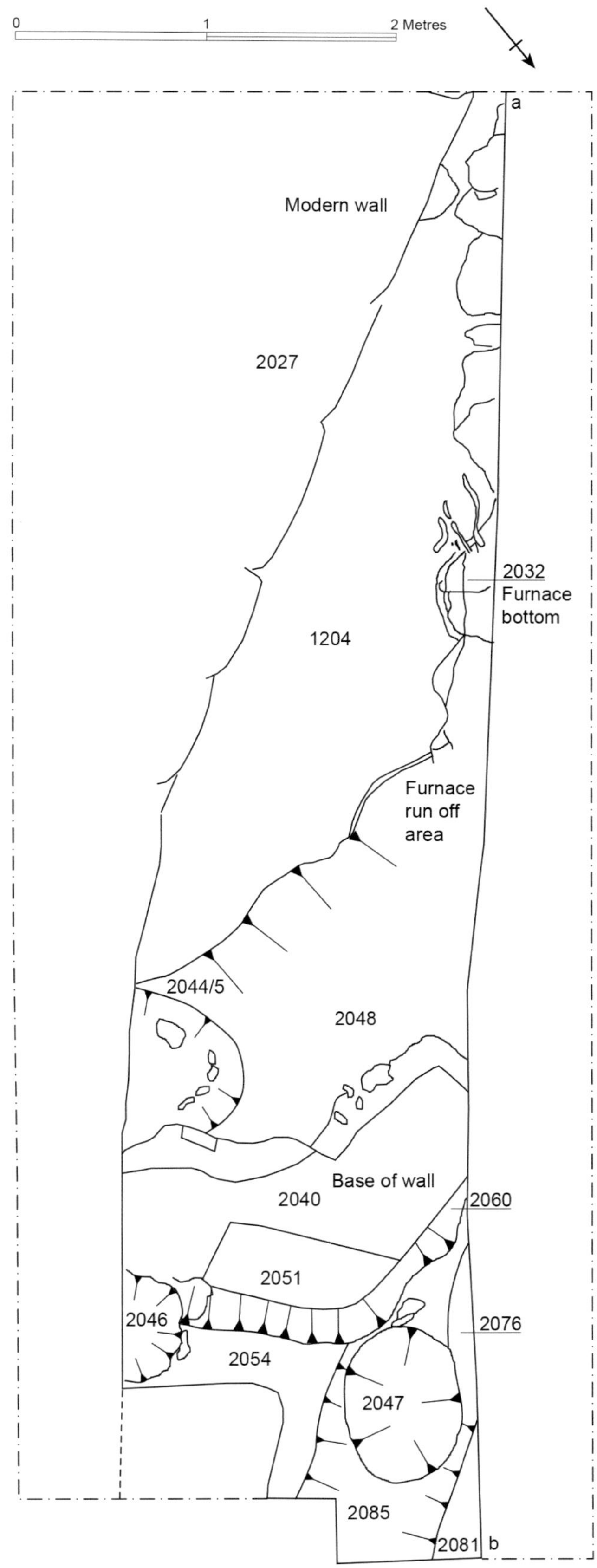

Figure 23 The Bonded Store: area B, trench 2, lower level showing the hearth and associated features.

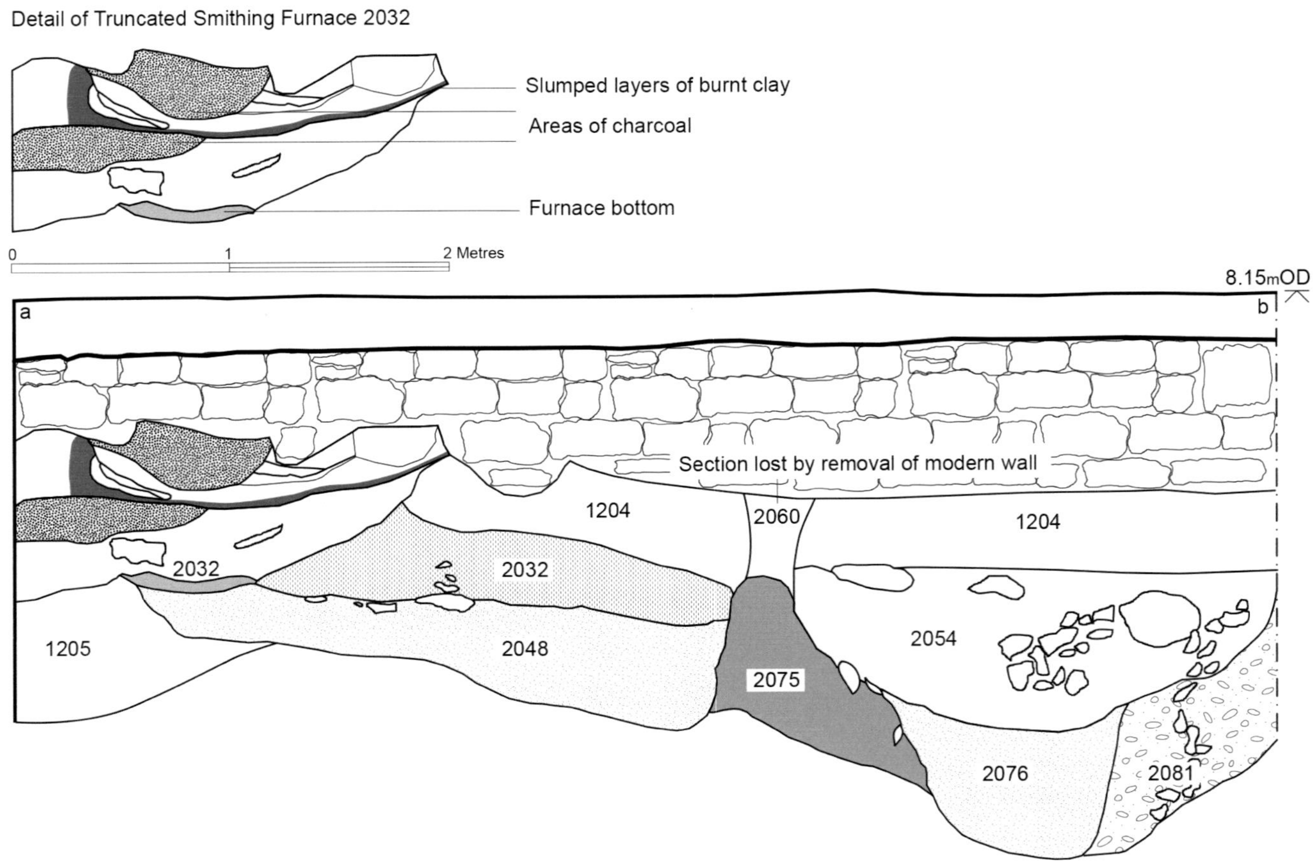

Figure 24 The Bonded Store: area B, trench 2, south-facing section through hearth and associated features.

ditch, 0.69m wide and 0.42m deep. The fill, a light orange clayey soil with angular stones at the base, contained Iron Age pottery, including vesicular wares similar to those found at King's Road. The base was reddened by natural iron-pan. The relationship of the ditch B2085 to the later Roman features was difficult to establish as it had been compromised by the modern wall B2040.

At the interface between the top of this feature and an area of stones containing slag and burnt bone (B2054) above it, there was an Iron Age copper alloy stater, attributed to the Baiocasses (small-find 53, see p. 99). B2054 had been truncated by a 19th-century wall (B2040) and the aggregate foundations of the Bonded Store, but it survived to 1.90m by 0.68m, and 0.54m in depth. Its fill consisted of a very dark, burnt and gritty clay-like soil, containing angular stones and fragments from the base of a smithing hearth. In addition to slag and burnt bone, other finds included charcoal and late Iron Age pottery.

Area B2054 was associated with the remains of a hearth, perhaps from a smithing furnace (B2032), *c*. 1.23m in width, with the base 0.64m below its truncated upper surface (at 7.32m OD). The floor of the furnace was formed of a dark brown, burnt clay pad, approximately 0.42m by 0.08m, with a rim of burnt orange clay about 0.06m thick around its edge. Examination of the slag and vitrified material found in the hearth matrix does not conclusively prove that this feature functioned as a smithing furnace, but it may have been one component in a larger zone of smithing activity in this area (see the metal-working report, Chapter 5). There was evidence of nails concreted within some of the burnt clay and thus they may have been produced here. Horizontal lenses of burnt clay and charcoal, which had sagged after use, could be seen in the section through the hearth (Fig. 24).

To the east of the hearth was an area of black clay and charcoal (B2048), forming an extension to the main structure B2032. This appeared to have functioned as a run-off or sump area, and survived as a shallow scoop, some 1.23m by 0.47m and 0.67m deep (see Fig. 23). It was filled with a very sticky, dark, gritty clay-like soil, containing substantial amounts of charcoal, flecks of daub, slag and abraded pottery with metal products adhering (at 6.88m OD). There was also a very substantial quantity of burnt and decayed bone, which may have been used in the furnace to generate heat. Other finds included a samian lid and black-burnished wares of the mid- to late 1st century AD.

Other features associated with the hearth included a small oval-shaped pit (B2044), measuring 0.41m by 0.2m and surviving to a depth of 0.35m. This had a fill of loose, crumbly orangey soil with flecks of mortar and slag, and it may have been a run-off area for molten slag. Nearby was a small shallow scoop (B2045), measuring 0.23m by 0.12m, with a depth of 0.56m (at 7.15m OD). This too contained

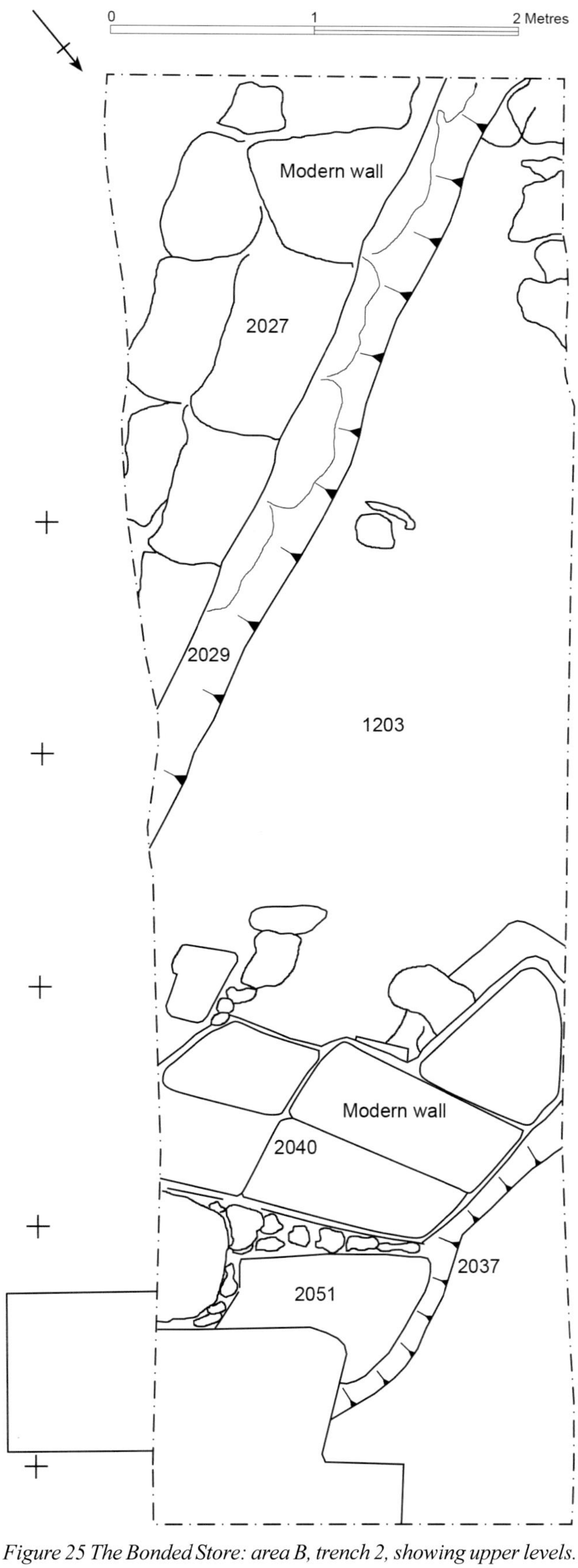

Figure 25 The Bonded Store: area B, trench 2, showing upper levels.

slag deposits, along with pottery and tile, in a fill of gingery gravel with medium-sized angular stones.

Further Roman deposits in this area were revealed following the removal of the 19th-century wall B2040 (Fig. 25). These included a very hard, densely packed, gritty orange soil (B2060), which formed part of the hearth structure. B2040 had been built on top of a deposit of gravel and soft grey clay (B2061), which had Roman finds – including samian pottery and slag – within it. Below this was a ridge of soil (B2075), left behind when excavation removed the 19th-century wall. It consisted of a light brown, clayey soil, containing traces of briquetage. It was cut by a small area of blackened soil (B2076) which appeared circular in plan but as a ditch-like feature in section (see Fig. 24). Another ditch-like feature, context B2081, was traced for 0.53m by 0.48m, and contained a light brown clayey soil, flecked with briquetage, and several stones apparently set vertically (see Fig. 24).

The major Roman structures and deposits in this trench were sealed by B1204, a dark, gritty soil with clusters of angular stones, particularly in the south-east of the trench. Finds were not prolific but included black-burnished wares, glass fragments, and part of a shale bracelet (small-find 127). Fragments of the smithing furnace bottom were also found at this level. This in turn was sealed by the re-deposited rubble layer, B1203, with the usual mixture of finds of all periods.

BT3 was the third trench in Area B, opened in a very restricted area in the south of the Bonded Store (see Fig. 19), where it was initially thought that nothing would survive due to the nature of the foundations between the brick pillars. Several archaeological contexts were uncovered, however, the lowest (B3102) consisting of an orange-brown, gritty and stony soil (Fig. 26). Excavation of this context had to be aborted because of the height of the water table. Above this there was a deposit of grey, silty soil, with some gritty inclusions (B3101), about 0.2m in thickness and containing charcoal, briquetage and very degraded bone.

This in turn was sealed by mid-grey silt (B3100), half-filled with small beach pebbles, typically 10–40mm in size, to a depth of 0.09m. This lay below a wall (B3096a) on the southern edge of the trench. One other feature – interpreted as a beam slot (B3099) measuring 0.12m by 0.08m and running for 1.54m across the trench – was identified below the modern rubble layers. This lay at a height of 6.38m OD and contained very dark, sticky clay.

Area C

Area C was in the south-east part of the Bonded Store building. It was characterised by large areas of burning and hearth-like features, and also by a substantial ditch (C2094), traced for 4.25m across the southern part of CT2, which appeared to form some sort of boundary. The first trench to be excavated in this area, designated CT1, was rich in Roman finds and in particular a substantial amount of roof tile, lodged vertically in the deposits.

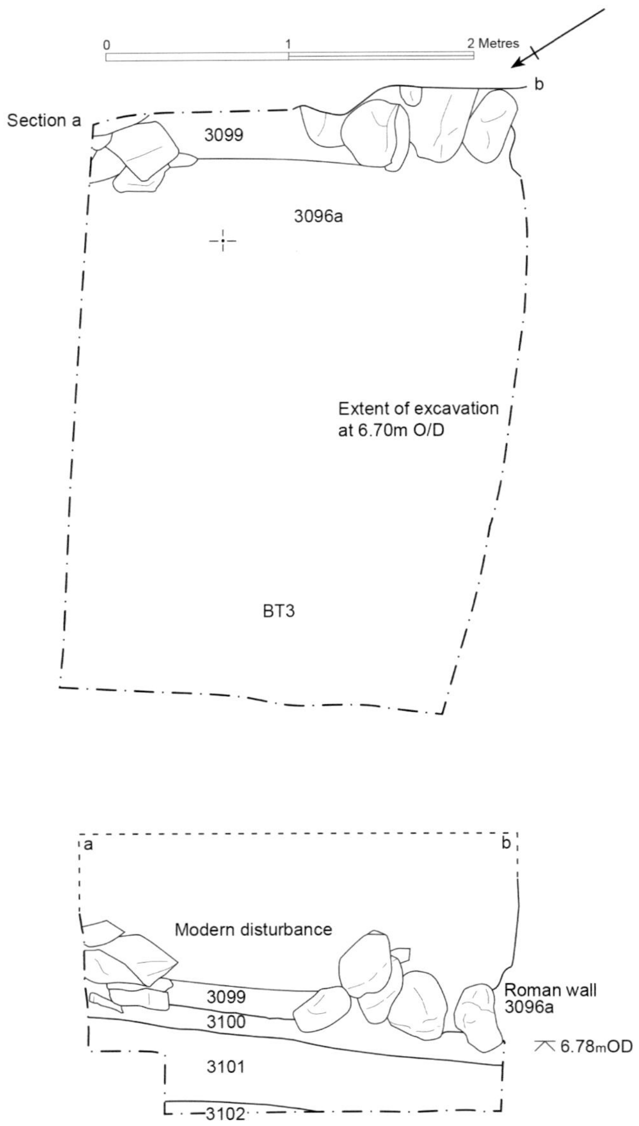

Figure 26 The Bonded Store: area B, trench 3, showing lower level and section.

CT1

The earliest archaeological context in trench CT1 was a dark brown to orange layer of fine gravel (C1007), containing daub, charcoal and briquetage. A gully (C1008) ran across the lowest part of the trench, possibly representing a water channel running in a northerly direction towards the bottom of the valley (Fig. 27). It contained Iron Age pottery.

These deposits were sealed by C1006, a dark brown gravel in which several stone settings and postholes were revealed. Context C1083a was a small, truncated posthole, with a diameter of between 0.18 and 0.22m and a depth of 0.07m, at 6.42m OD. C1084a was a sub-circular pit or posthole, measuring between 0.12 and 0.16m in diameter and with a depth of 0.17m, containing a fill of ash and very dark, sooty soil in three lenses, with a lighter clay lining below. A nearby beam slot (C1086) contained a dark brown, gritty soil, with pebbles below (at 5.82m OD); this measured about 0.10m by 0.07m, and was traced for a length of 0.64m. Beneath it there was a small, dark patch of soil packed with charcoal, interpreted as a post-setting associated with the hearth C1078 (see below). The beam slot may have been associated with a pad of orangey burnt clay (C1083), 0.10m by 0.11m by 0.18m in depth, which appeared to be part of a collapsed clay-bonded wall. This cut into a shallow pit (C1084) containing ashes and very dark black sooty soil sitting on a lighter clay base. Half of this feature, which survived to *c.* 0.92m in length and 0.54m in breadth, had been truncated by the Bonded Store foundations. The fill was *c.* 0.15–0.20m in thickness and its base was at OD 5.89m.

Layer C1006 was in turn sealed by C1005 (Figs 28 and 29), a layer of orangey gritty soil *c.* 0.09–0.11m in thickness that lay under the hearth C1078, deepening to a thicker layer of up to 0.60m at the eastern end of the trench. The lower levels had a more silty consistency and a browner colour, while the upper lenses were a paler orange, loamy soil, containing samian pottery, black-burnished ware and coarsewares. The presence of tile lodged vertically in this deposit suggested that a structure had burnt down here and collapsed.

The hearth C1078 was located in the south-central part of the trench (Fig. 30). It survived as a pad of burnt clay, 0.54m by 0.43m and 0.04m thick, and was surrounded by patches of charcoal. To the south-east of the hearth, large stones appeared to form some sort of flue structure, disturbed by the foundations of the Bonded Store. On a raised area within the clay pad of the hearth there were distinctive ridges, as if caused by raking of the surface. Beneath the base of the hearth there was a small rectangular area of a lighter brown, clayey soil, with large, angular pebbles. Patches of reddened and fire-blackened soil and charcoal delineated the whole of this area. A small fragment of Roman glass (small-find 114) was recovered from the interface between the hearth and the layer below.

Beneath the hearth was a hard-packed, gritty yellow soil (part of C1005), *c.* 0.43m in diameter and between 0.15m and 0.17m in depth. This was interpreted as a possible floor surface into which C1078 had been cut. A semi-circular deposit of black clay (C1082) which delineated the hearth contained sherds of black-burnished wares and Picardy ware.

Other features in the trench also appeared to be associated with metal-working and/or the hearth area. A deposit of water-borne sandy silt (C1067) followed the contour of the south side of the valley, traced for approximately 3.2m and surviving to a depth of 0.67m. There were no significant finds within it other than four small sherds of prehistoric pottery, and it appears as though it may have formed a pond, perhaps used as a quenching area for metal-working. It might, however, have been caused by natural water flow through the area since the Roman period.

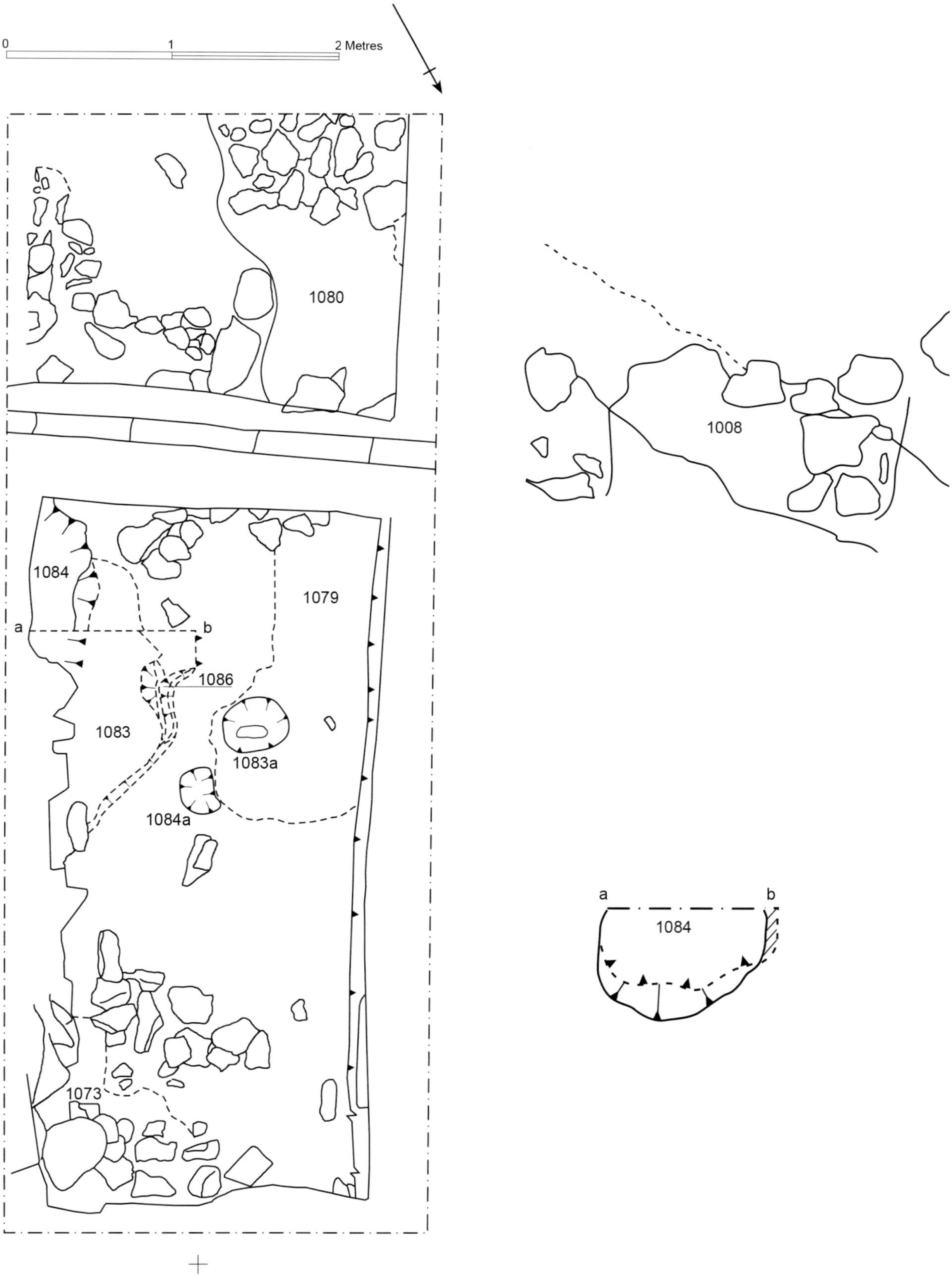

Figure 27 The Bonded Store: area C, trench 1, lower level phase 2.

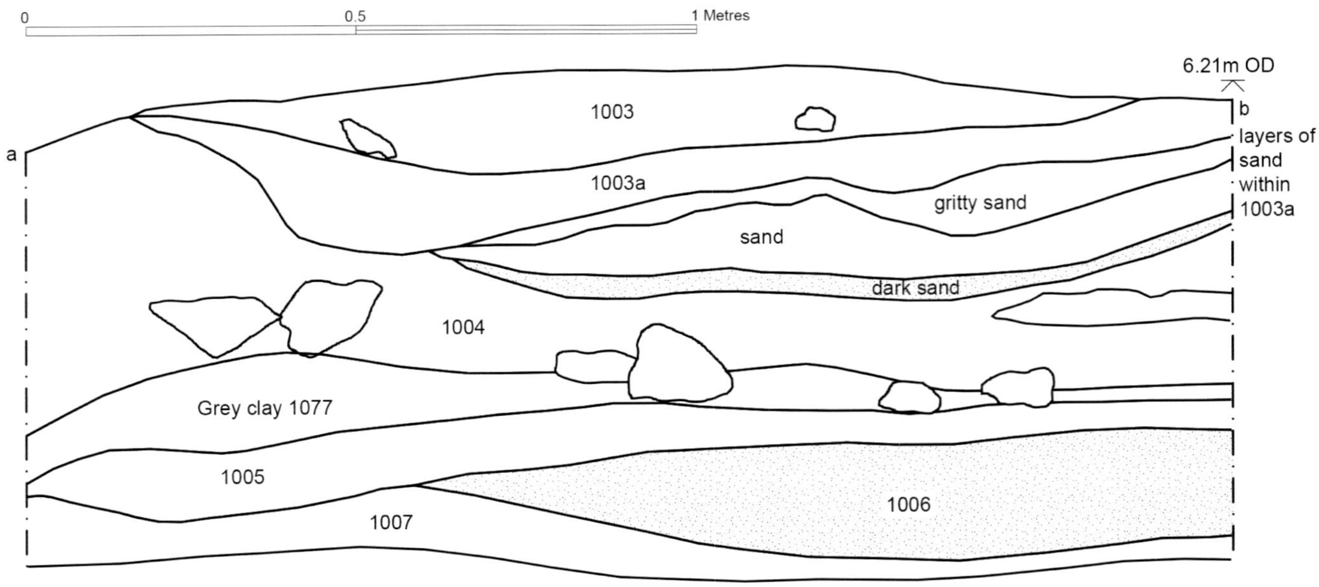

Figure 28 The Bonded Store: area C, trench 1, east-facing section showing levels after removal of chalk.

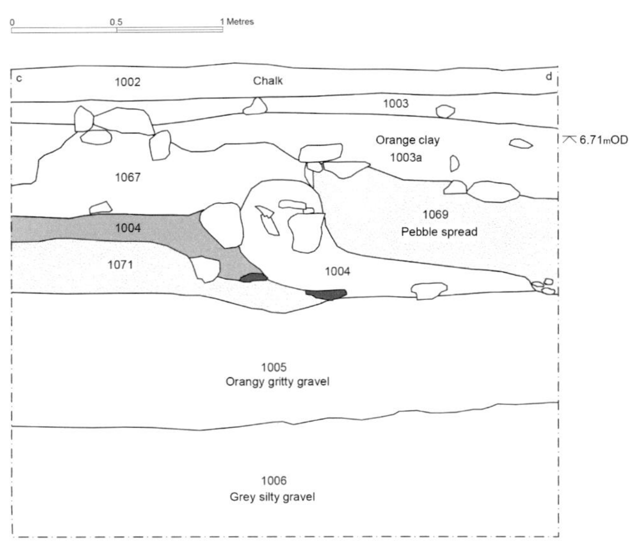

Figure 29 The Bonded Store: area C, trench 1, east-facing section through pebble and gravel spreads.

A hard-packed orangey-brown clay containing several fairly large stones and pebbles was interpreted as another floor surface (C1069). In one area was a dark charcoal-filled patch, measuring 0.81m by 0.69m by 0.09m deep, which contained tile, bone and a few sherds of pottery, including a Dressel 20 amphora handle. A shallow depression (C1070) measuring 1.8m by 1.6m by 0.2m deep (at 6.95m OD), had a fill of black, gritty soil, and contained charcoal, slag, furnace lining and pottery, including samian, black-burnished wares and sherds of fine Rhenish cups. A similar pit-like depression (C1071) was traced for 1.82m to a depth between 0.2m and 0.3m in the south-east of the trench. Finds included degraded bone, tile, glass, and slag. Context C1004, lying between the pebble spread C1069 and C1071 (see Fig. 29), consisted of a blackened silty soil with patches of gingery gritty gravel and contained Roman finds. There was a considerable amount of roof tile lodged vertically within it.

Context C1072 was interpreted as a working area: a small patch of very dark, gritty soil, 0.32m by 0.29m by 0.06m deep, with angular stones set within it, and a large, flat stone which appeared to have been trigged up on the smaller stones. A great deal of vitrified material was recovered from here, including furnace lining. A floor surface (C1003a) was identified to the east of this working area (see Fig. 30), made up of layers of compacted sand and cut on its south edge by C1073, a scoop measuring 0.24m by 1.08m by 0.12m deep, filled with blackened earth and containing pottery, tile fragments, glass, bone, slag and tubular deposits of metallic concretion. This feature had been cut on its eastern edge by a medieval pit (C1068).

At the west end of the trench, the remains of a watercourse or channel (C1077) with a silty, gravelly fill were identified, lying alongside a spread of fine gravel (C1080: Figs 29–30). The latter was traced for approximately 0.98m by 1.31m and was prolific in finds, including some 137 sherds of pottery. It lay above a thin (30–70mm), very stony layer. The channel C1077 was identified for 1.22m by 1.03m by 0.10m deep; it sealed a blackened deposit (C1079) which included black-burnished wares, *terra sigillata* and a tripod beaker lid. Many of the sherds were water-worn.

The Roman layers in this trench were sealed by the disturbed post-medieval deposits C1003 and the chalk floor surface C1002.

CT2

Trench CT2 was located in the south-east corner of the Bonded Store, in the part of the site nearest to the Town Church (see Fig. 19). Archaeological deposits in this area

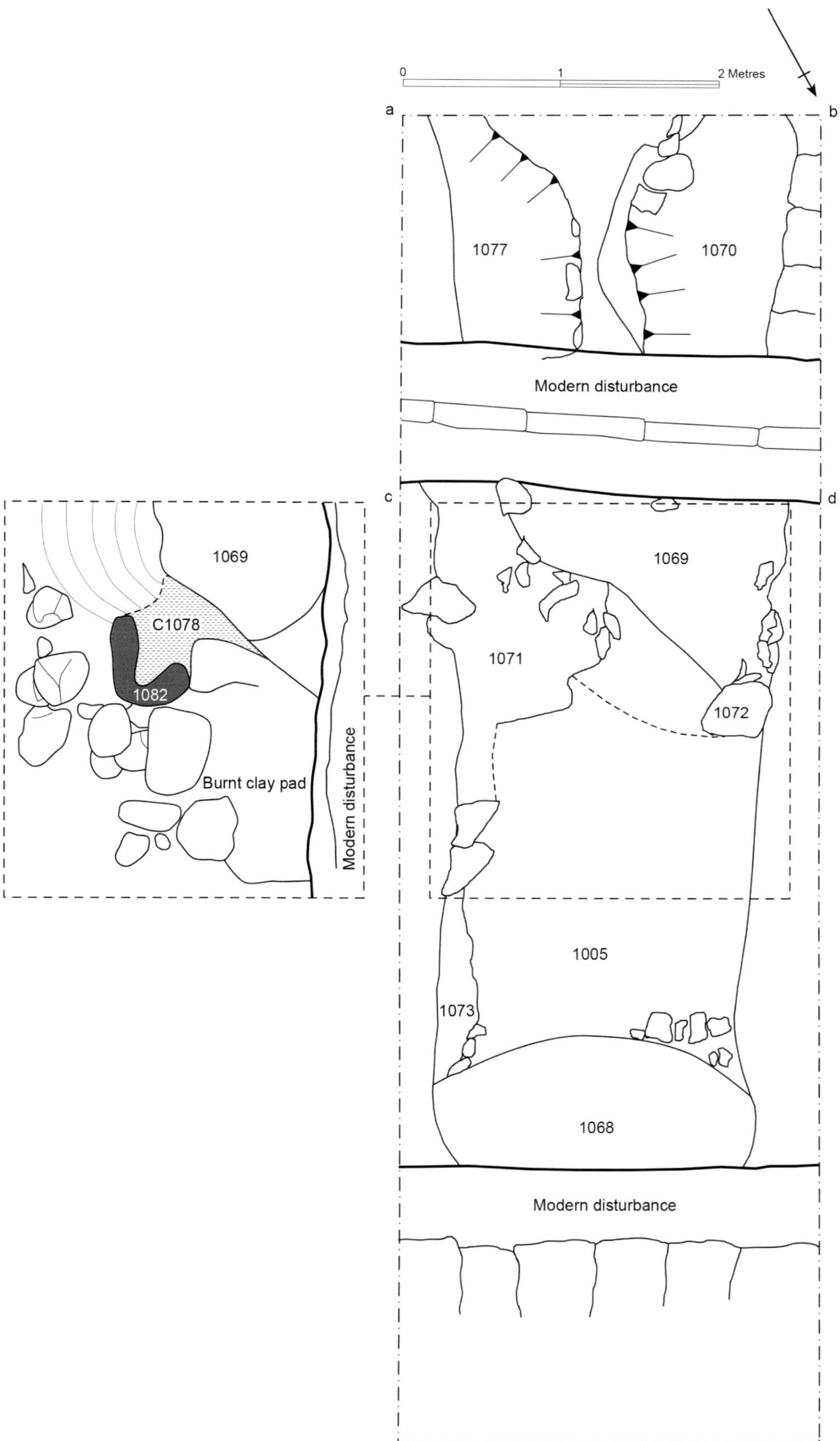

Figure 30 The Bonded Store: area C, trench 1, lower level with detail of the Roman phase 1 hearth area (left) and later phase 2 features.

were shallower and closer to the floor surface of the Bonded Store, because the underlying land rose up to form the southern side of the valley leading to the shore. The layer just above natural was a light, orange/brown gritty soil (C2005); in the south of the trench was an area of shattered, weathered granite forming the bedrock.

The earliest features in this trench consisted of various elements apparently associated with a structure. These included a rectangular pad of orange-red 'fired' clay (C2097), measuring about 1.43m by 1.26m and up to 0.27m in depth. This possible floor surface had been laid on the bedrock, which had been cut to make a platform. Associated with it was a layer of burnt clay (C2098) and burnt daub, which lay over a deposit of ash and small pebbles set in a bright orange matrix (C2100) (Fig. 31). These may have represented successive hearth areas within a building.

Further features related to this structure included a sub-rectangular stake-hole measuring 0.21m by 0.11m, by 0.1m deep (C2101), with a fill of black soil stained with charcoal. This was cut through a rectangular slot of orangey clay (C2102). A clearly defined posthole (C2103) had stone packing, a soft grey clay infill and a decayed timber still *in situ*. This measured 0.61m by 0.42m by 0.25m deep.

An area of burning at the north-west end of the trench (C2104), measuring 1.8m by 0.58m by approximately 0.23m deep, was associated with further postholes (Fig. 32). Posthole C2105 was truncated by ditch C2094 but survived as 0.42m by 0.38m by 0.12m deep. Oval stake-hole C2106 measured about 0.18m by 0.2m, by 0.15m deep, and was filled with a black, clayey soil. Two further stakeholes (C2107 and C2108) were each 0.15m in depth and measured 0.21m by 0.18m and 0.18m by 0.08m respectively.

At the other (eastern) end of the trench there was a pit-like deposit of a very sticky, dark black, clayey soil (C2109), measuring 1.62m by 0.23m by 0.54m deep. It contained a considerable amount of charcoal. It was cut by another small pit (C2110), lined with a band of orange clay, running into the foundations of the Bonded Store (Fig. 32).

Many of the features interpreted as part of a structure in this trench were cut by a ditch (C2094; Fig. 31), which was traced for approximately 4.25m across the western part of the trench. It measured 1.25m in width and 0.75m in depth, rising towards the west. The fill consisted of a dark black, humic soil, with occasional large beach pebbles (particularly in the west) and fine gravel at the base. Finds were very prolific, including very small pottery sherds and flints recovered by wet-sieving. There were also substantial amounts of metal concretion and slag, possibly from the furnace located a few metres to the south-west (Area BT2).

Ditch C2094 appeared to be rising to a terminal at its eastern end but was cut by a large, circular, stone-lined feature (C2091; Fig. 33). The stones ranged in size from approximately 0.07m by 0.12m, to 0.16m by 0.36m, and the diameter of the feature was approximately 0.72m. It was excavated to a depth of 0.45m. The fill was an orange-brown gritty soil, with finds of pottery, bone, slag and charcoal, particularly in the upper levels; Roman pottery was embedded within the structure, suggesting that it may have been a Roman well, re-used in the medieval or post-medieval period. Part of the southern side had collapsed, probably when the foundations for the Bonded Store were inserted. Associated with this collapse was an area of very black soil and rubbly material (C2093), some 0.44m in diameter and 0.25m in depth. Finds from this area included fragments of nails (small-finds 88, 90, 92 and 94), possibly from a barrel, and a fragment of glass (small-find 93).

The Roman features in trench CT2 were sealed by a dark black organic layer (C2004) that contained a range of re-deposited Roman material. The uppermost layer C2003 contained a re-deposited spindle-whorl (small-find 86).

CT3

The principal feature in trench CT3 was a section of Roman wall (3017a). It was built of clay-bonded granite boulders and was traced for 4.40m. It was also identified in trench CT4, to the west.

The lowest archaeological layers in this trench (Fig. 34) consisted of several fairly compact lenses of variable appearance, lying immediately above the natural. These included C3043, a grey/blue silty deposit with some sand and grit, and occasional charcoal; C3045 and C3046, two gingery, silty deposits, the latter with more charcoal; C3042, a layer including tumbled granite blocks, between 0.30m and 0.40m in size; C3039, a grey silt layer with small, rounded pebbles and finds including pottery, charcoal and burnt bone; and C3044, similar to C3039 but containing angular granite stones and some Iron Age pottery.

A layer of orange hoggin (C3037) was devoid of finds. Contexts C3038 and C3041 were probably part of the same deposit as C3037. A silty grey layer (C3034) containing very abraded pottery, charcoal, and small amounts of decomposed bone was probably the same deposit as C3033 directly above it. C3035 was similar, containing burnt bone, charcoal and some glass fragments (small-find 300). C3036 consisted of gritty brown silt, with some sand and grit and occasional small pebbles.

These various layers and deposits were mostly sealed by context C3033, a sticky, dark grey silt that contained considerable quantities of charcoal and pottery, including an almost complete vessel of north Gaulish greyware. The feature was observed over an area of 2.37m by 1.46m, and varied in thickness between 0.20m and 0.80m. This in turn was sealed by C3032, a compacted layer of decayed granite, set in a grey/brown silt, 0.75m deep in the south-west but decreasing to just 0.10m in the north-east. This represented the lowest element of a 'structure' of small, deliberately placed granite stones (C3031), red or grey in colour, measuring 0.48m by 1.56m, at 5.69m OD (Fig. 35). The layer immediately above (C3027), consisting of small pebbles and occasional larger granite

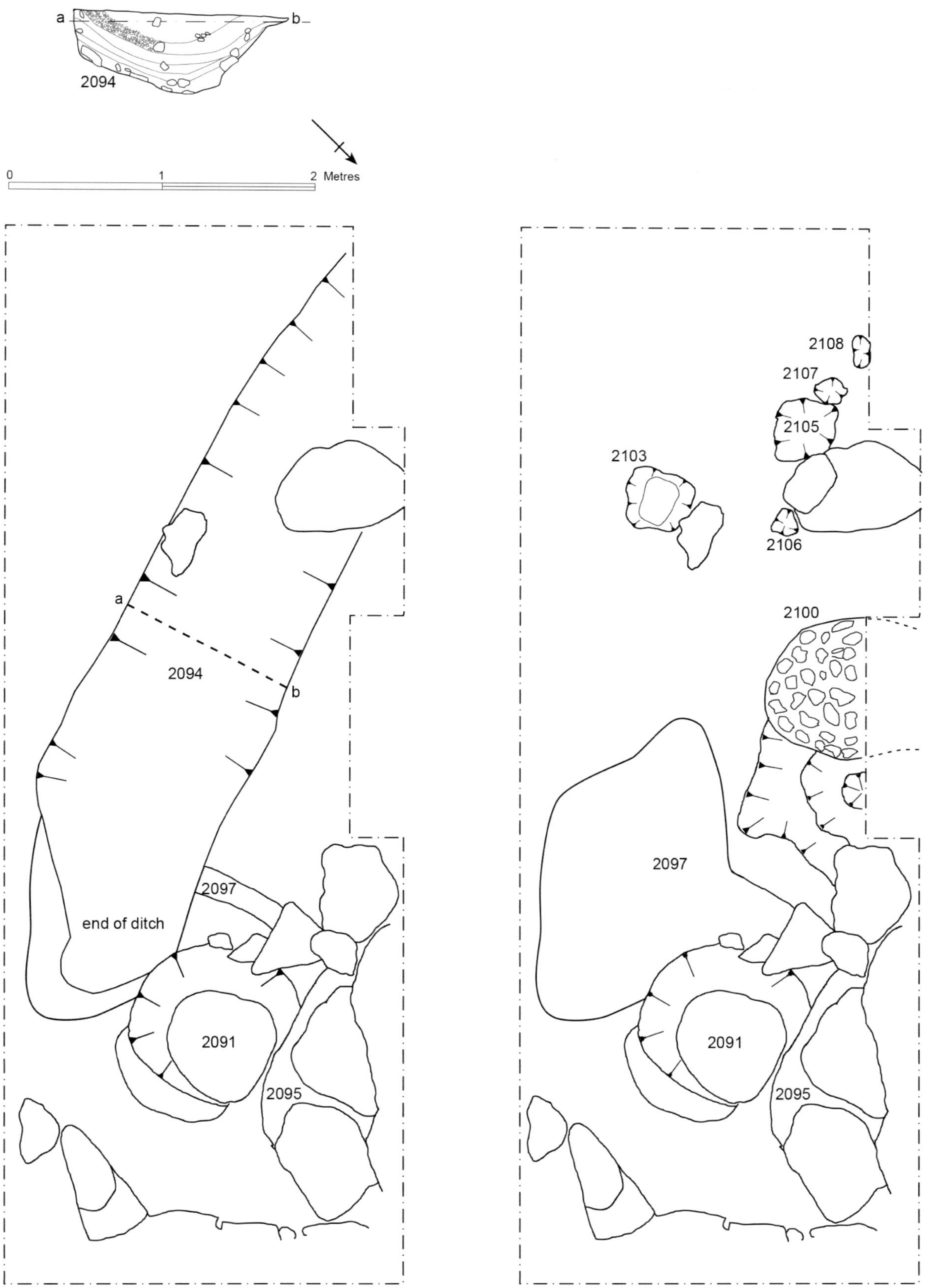

Figure 31 The Bonded Store: area C, trench 2, lower level phase 1, areas of burnt gravel and postholes (right) and phase 2 (left), showing ditch terminal.

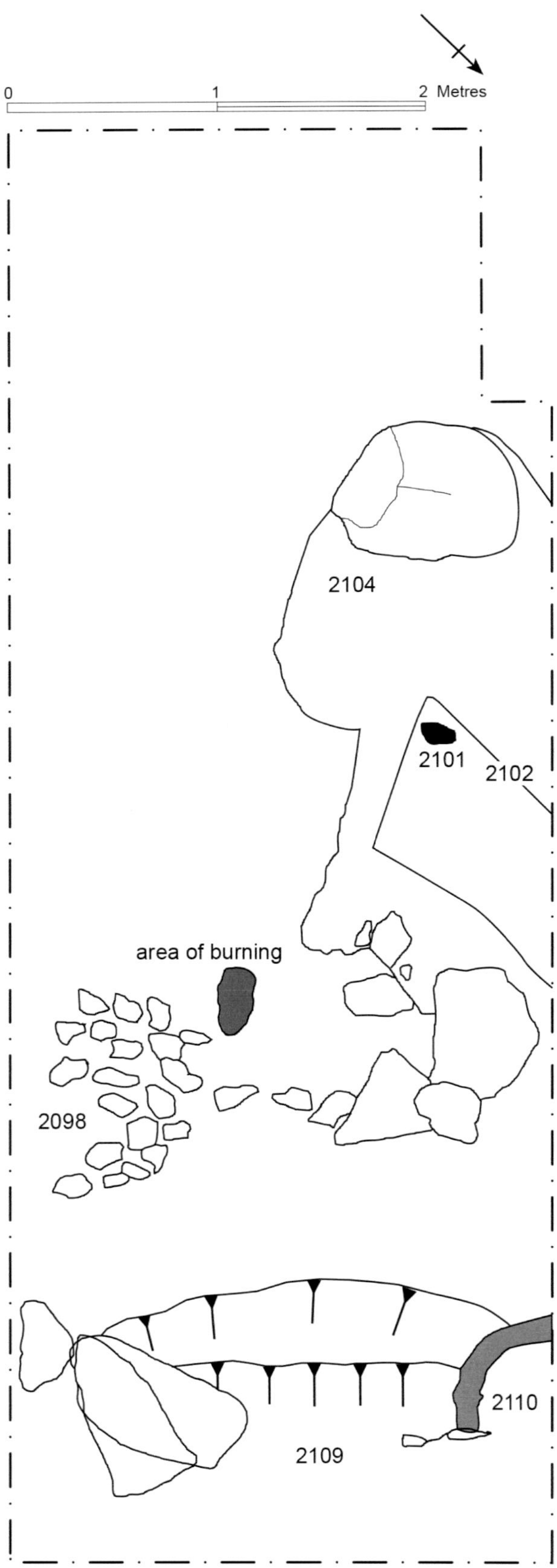

Figure 32 The Bonded Store: area C, trench 2, phase 1, early Roman features.

Figure 33 The Bonded Store: area C, trench 2, upper level showing stone structure C2091.

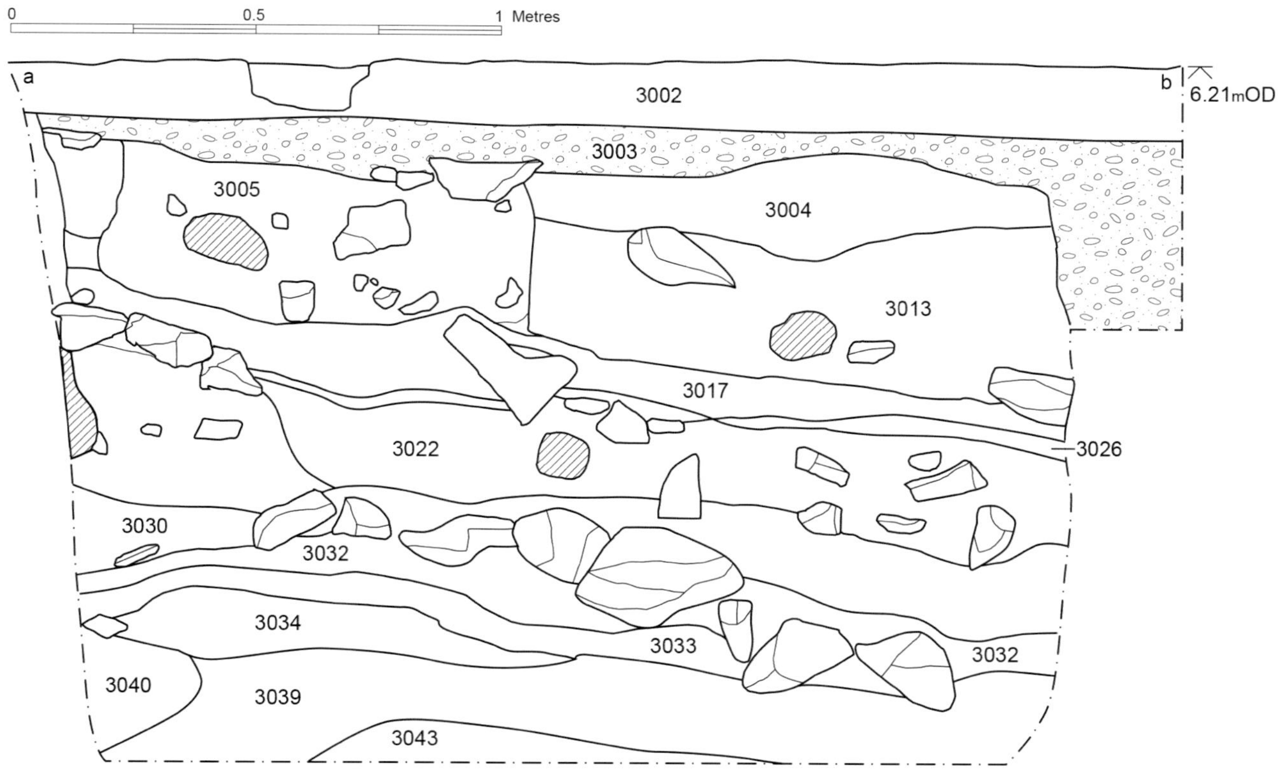

Figure 34 The Bonded Store: area C, trench 3, east-facing section.

blocks in a grey/brown matrix, was probably part of the same structure. The stone structure C3031 was surrounded by a deposit containing much evidence of burning and charcoal (C3030).

Layer C3027 was most likely associated with a linear structure of angular granite stones (C3028), measuring 1.40m by 0.33m at 5.79m OD, running north/south across the trench. This linear feature may in turn have been related to a substantial granite wall (C3017a) and an area of large granite boulders (C3029) tumbled from this wall.

The wall C3017a was traced for 4.4m in trench CT3, running in an east/west direction (Fig. 36). It was 0.86m wide, formed of clay-bonded granite blocks surviving to a maximum of two courses. In the north-eastern part of the trench it divided two possible floor levels: on the south side a mid-brown clayey soil (C3020) containing frequent, compacted pebbles, truncated by the wall at 5.76m OD and measuring 0.38m by 1.22m, by 0.06m in depth; and on the north side C3021, a dark grey clayey soil with small stones, charcoal burning and Roman tile, traced for 0.58m by 0.86m, by 0.06m in depth.

Another possible floor level was identified as context C3022, a dark grey gritty layer containing pebbles and some larger pieces of granite (0.11–0.21m), along with charcoal, Iron Age and Roman pottery, and metal fragments. This context was traced across 2.35m by 1.90m, to a depth of 0.13m. It sealed context C3030. Above this possible floor level was a dark grey silt (C3017) which also sealed the granite wall; it contained pebbles and mid-sized pieces of granite, and was particularly rich in finds, including part of a Venus figurine (small-find 304) and an intaglio (small-find 284). It survived to a depth of approximately 0.17m.

At the west end of the wall was an area of tumble (C3023), formed of angular pieces of granite set in grey silt in a cut (C3025), measuring approximately 0.6m by 2.0m by 0.1m in depth (Fig. 36). Another area of granite tumble (C3024) was identified in the north-west corner of the trench (Fig. 37), set in a dark grey silt and also containing considerable quantities of decomposed bone, charcoal, and Roman tile and pottery. It sealed a deposit (C3026) of a similar colour and consistency measuring 1.90m by 1.02m by 0.27m in depth, again containing substantial quantities of bone, charcoal and pottery.

The cut for the lower remnants of the substantial Roman wall was identified as context C3016, with fill C3015 – a homogenous brown clay, 2.64m by 0.78m by 0.06m in depth, containing very few finds. Lying directly above the wall was a firm and compacted layer of silver-grey sandy loam (C3018), with flecks of iron pan, measuring about 1.27m by 0.38m by 0.1m in depth. It lay adjacent to contexts C3015/16. Also present on top of the wall was a lens of grey clay (C3019) measuring a maximum of 0.06m in depth by 0.30m by 0.12m.

Several contexts were identified above the wall, in essence representing the interface between the wall and the grey silt layer (C3013) above, which covered most of the trench (Fig. 38). These included C3008, C3010, C3011, C3012, C3014, C3018 and C3019. C3010, a dark grey silt

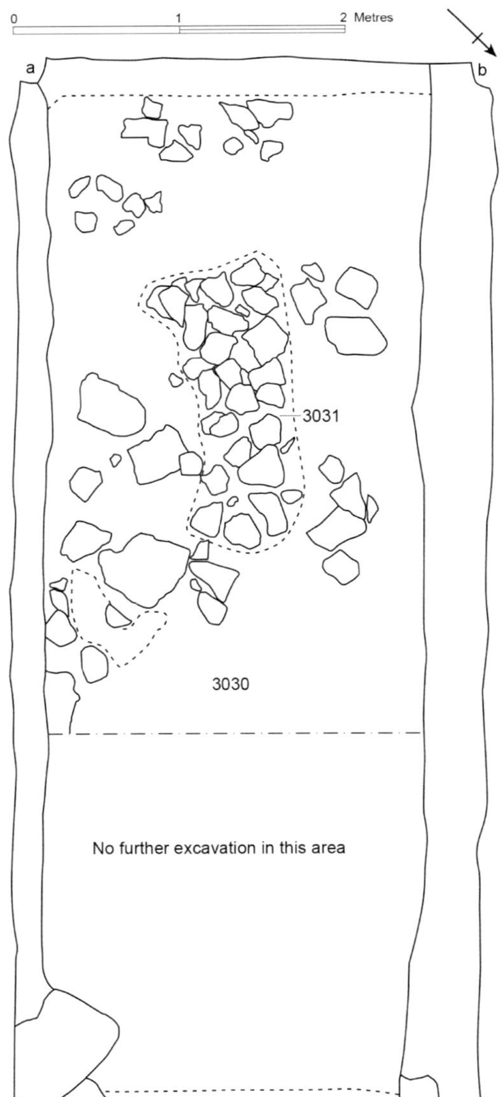

Figure 35 The Bonded Store: area C, trench 3, showing stone feature C3031.

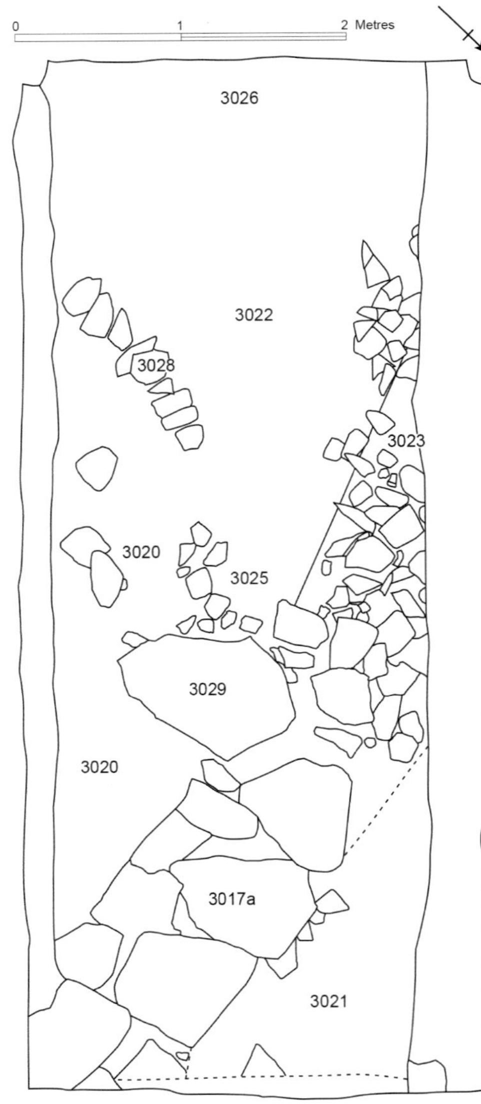

Figure 36 The Bonded Store: area C, trench 3, showing Roman wall C3017a and other features.

with gritty inclusions and much stone tumble measuring 0.83m by 1.03m, was found particularly in the north-east corner of CT3. It was similar to C3017, discussed above: a tumble of granite stones at the same depth, both formed in part from the wall structure below. A layer of rounded pebbles (C3012) in dark silty clay was probably part of the same deposit as C3004 (see below), and associated with C3011. Context C3013, immediately beneath C3004 and sealing C3017, contained small granite stones and pebble-sized granite fragments, along with Roman pottery, and measured 0.59m by 1.02m by 0.38m in depth. A slot filled with a lighter grey silty loam (C3014) was probably part of the same deposit as C3013, measuring 0.36m by 0.60m by 0.38m in depth, and was stained by the proximity of the boulders which had been dislodged from the underlying Roman wall.

A brown clay deposit (C3011) was found in a V-shaped cut between C3008 and C3012, measuring 0.37m by 0.13m at 5.97m OD. The finds here included a re-deposited spindle whorl (small-find 289).

Above C3013, context C3004 represented the uppermost layer of *in situ* Roman material, a mid-brown/grey soil with frequent charcoal flecks, clay, and considerable quantities of tile, samian ware and pottery. This layer was truncated by a modern brick wall, itself cut by a modern path (C3006), which also cut C3004 and sealed a medieval pit (C3005). C3004 was also cut by a linear feature of granite stones (C3007), approximately 0.53m by 0.40m to 0.22m by 0.38m, perhaps representing tumble from a more substantial structure. Another medieval pit (C3009) with many residual Roman finds lay in the north-west part of the trench. Above these features lay the same modern construction layer

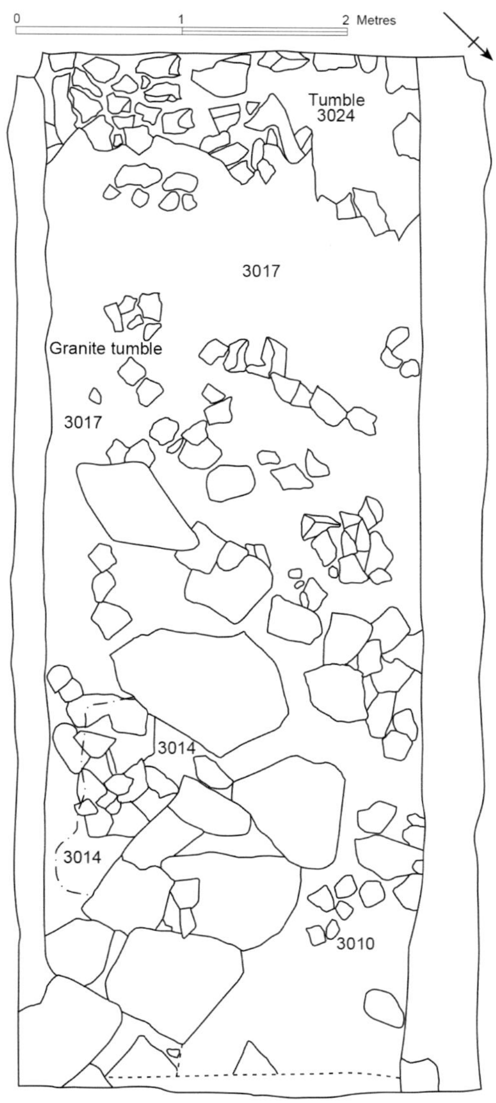

Figure 37 The Bonded Store: area C, trench 3, upper levels of Roman wall.

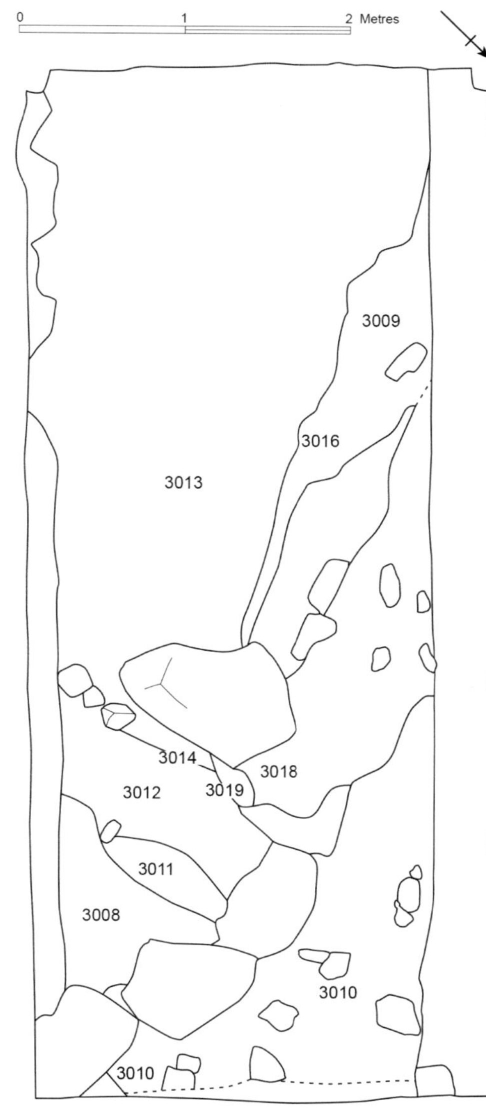

Figure 38 The Bonded Store: area C, trench 3, upper levels.

(C3003) and chalk layer (C3002) found in the other trenches, the former containing the usual array of multi-period finds.

CT4

Trench CT4 was placed in line with the entrance to the Bonded Store (see Fig. 19). It was hoped that this would provide a section through the upper and lower parts of the building, but this expectation was thwarted by the particularly massive foundations for the façade of the Upper Market buildings. It was possible, however, to get a section along most of the trench (Fig. 39).

The lowest (prehistoric) archaeological levels in this trench were contexts C4055 and C4056. C4055 consisted of a grey-blue oxidised loam containing organic material and non-local stone, extending for 1.94m at the eastern end of the trench and surviving to a depth of 0.24m. C4056 was a brown loam, containing briquetage and surviving to a maximum depth of 0.26m.

These deposits were sealed by a silty grey layer of a compact loam (C4054) with some iron panning and charcoal in the matrix. It measured 0.12m in thickness and covered the entire trench. It was partially sealed by a thin (20mm) layer of yellowish gravel (C4053) which extended for some 1.45m across the trench.

Loam C4054 was partially sealed by context C4048 (equivalent to C4049 and C4042), a thin deposit of light grey silt, which contained briquetage and some flint. It was traced for 1.46m across the trench and survived to a depth of 70mm. A straight-sided, rather irregular feature (C4052) was cut into C4054 (Fig. 40); its fill (C4050; Fig. 41) consisted of a mid-grey silty loam and large granite stones. It also contained briquetage, including a whole hand-brick. The

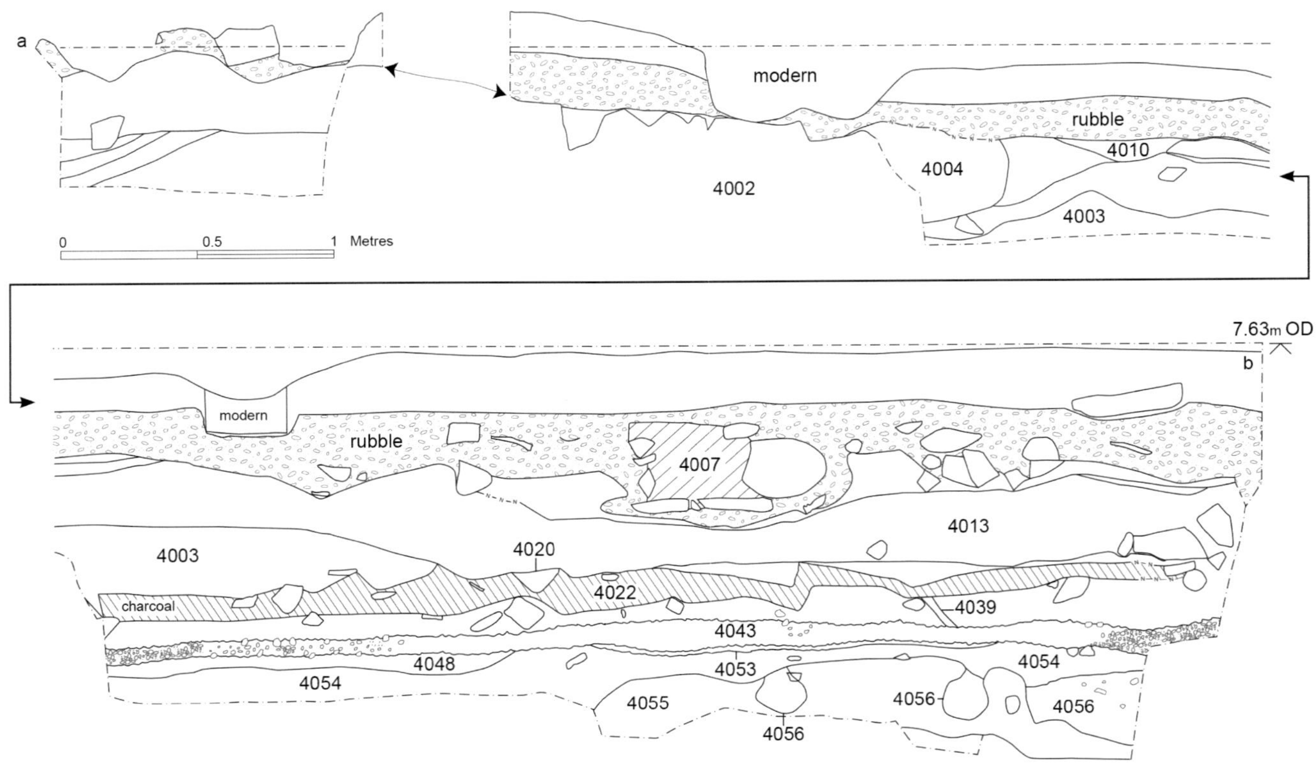

Figure 39 The Bonded Store: area C, trench 4, south-east facing section of the whole trench.

feature measured 2.08m by 0.62m and was excavated to a depth of 0.71m.

These contexts were sealed by a layer of compacted gravel (C4043) extending across the trench to a depth of 0.13m (Fig. 39). The gravel also contained burnt daub, pieces of vitrified furnace lining, and briquetage. It was sealed by an occupation deposit of mid-grey silty loam (C4042), containing considerable quantities of briquetage, small fragments of soft, coarse pottery, and flecks of charcoal. Associated with these deposits was a posthole with its packing *in situ* (C4044/5; Fig. 42) which survived as a circular group of granite stones set in a grey silty loam. It measured approximately 0.37m by 0.44m, with a depth of 0.16m. Another similar feature (C4046/7) was delineated by large stones set in the silty loam; it measured 0.44m by 0.34m, by a depth of 0.18m. Neither of these features contained any finds.

Several features were uncovered in this area that suggested the presence of a building: postholes C4026, C4028, C4030, C4032 and C4041, plus beam slot C4020/1. The latter, represented by a shallow, straight-edged cut, ran across the trench (Fig. 43) at 5.66m OD, with an average width of 0.20m, to a depth of 0.07m. The fill of dark grey silty clay was devoid of finds.

Three of the postholes (C4028, C4030 and C4032) appeared to be placed in line across the trench (Fig. 44). All were filled with a dark, charcoal-stained silty loam. C4028 was a small, circular posthole, approximately 0.14m in diameter, with a flat base and slightly sloping sides. It survived to a depth of 0.1m and the fill (C4027) contained one piece of burnt bone. C4030 was smaller, with a diameter of 0.1m and just 0.05m in depth, the fill (C4029) containing a possible worked stone. C4032 was a sub-rectangular posthole, measuring 0.2m by 0.14m, with a post-pad in the base. It survived to a depth of 0.07m; there were no finds in the fill (C4031).

Immediately to the west of these postholes was a straight-sided slot (C4036) traced for 1.24m across the trench. It had a fill (C4035) of a mid-grey/brown loam. It may have been associated with the beam slot C4020 and more generally with the suggested structure in this area.

Further to the west (Fig. 44) were several more features. C4026 was a large, sub-rectangular posthole, measuring 0.4m by 0.5m and surviving to a depth of 90mm. It contained a charcoal-stained silty loam (C4025), with a pad of light yellow clay in the middle, possibly for a timber post, and one sherd of pottery. There was evidence of later repair and within its southern edge a smaller, straight-sided posthole (C4024) measuring approximately 0.14m by 0.16m and just 0.04m deep. This too had light yellow clay in the middle of the fill, and a single potsherd. Another posthole (C4041) was truncated by the Bonded Store foundations and survived as a sub-rectangular feature of approximately 0.2m by 0.2m, with a depth of 0.15m. The fill (C4040) was once again a charcoal-stained silty loam.

On the other (eastern) side of the line of postholes was a shallow-sided pit (C4039) measuring 1.22m by 1.56m

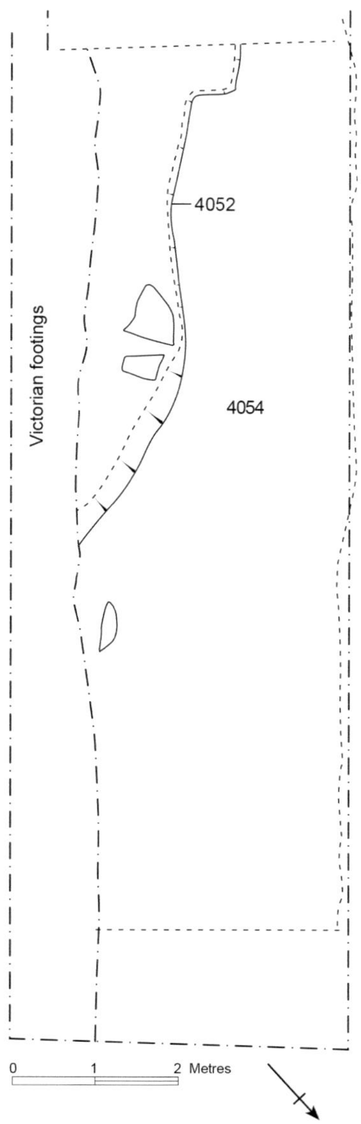

Figure 40 The Bonded Store: area C, trench 4, lower level 2 showing cut C4052.

and surviving to a depth of 90mm. It contained a mid-grey silty loam (C4038), which included some angular pieces of granite, pottery and briquetage. This fill (C4038) was partially sealed by an uneven spread of ashy material (C4037), traced for 0.85m across the trench, 0.82m at its widest point and 0.12m in depth.

A layer of very dark grey silty loam (C4022) sealed these various structural features, which in turn was sealed by two deposits abutting each other (C4015 and C4016). Both consisted of dark grey silt, the former containing occasional granite stones and charcoal, the latter including some decayed granite. Both were sealed by another dark grey silty layer (C4014), with frequent charcoal inclusions, some granite stones, and pieces of tile. It survived to a depth of 0.28m.

The layers above this point mostly included post-medieval or modern material. C4013 was a thin (10–20mm) deposit of a dark, silty loam, measuring 0.8m by 0.7m. It lay beneath

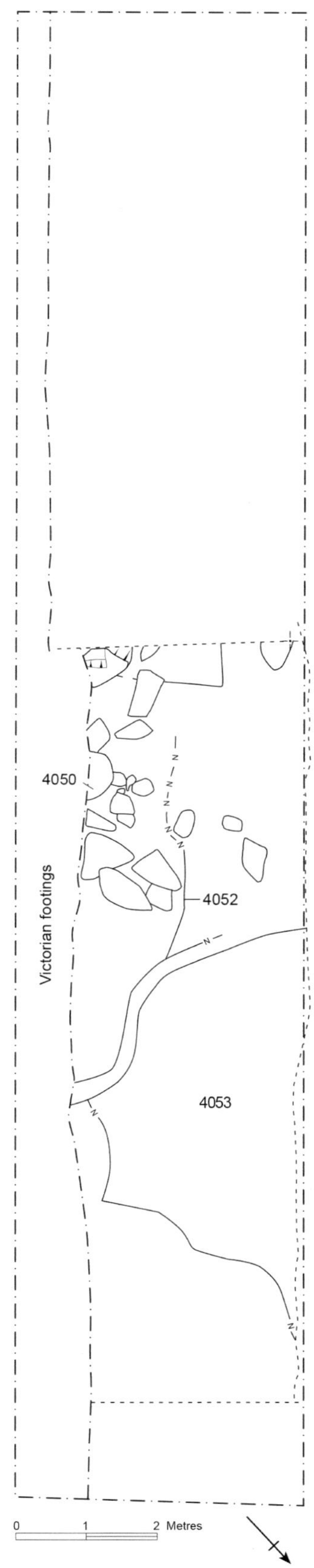

Figure 41 The Bonded Store: area C, trench 4, showing C4052 and stone arrangements.

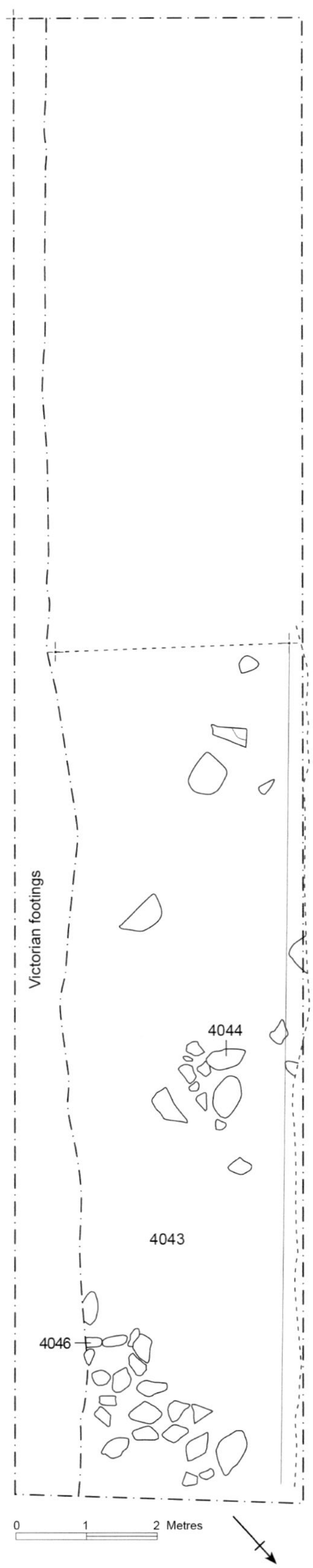

Figure 42 The Bonded Store: area C, trench 4, showing gravel and stone arrangements.

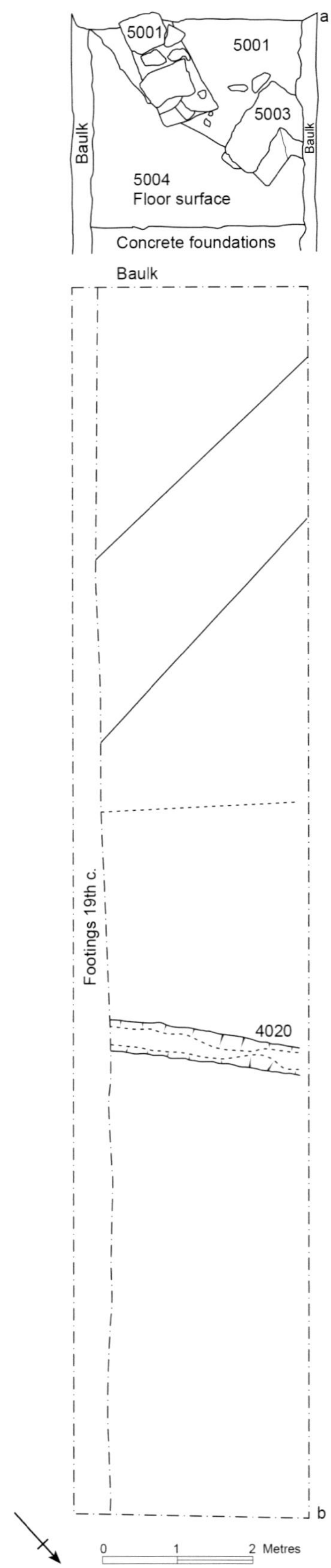

Figure 43 The Bonded Store: area C, trench 4, lower level 1, showing detail of C4020.

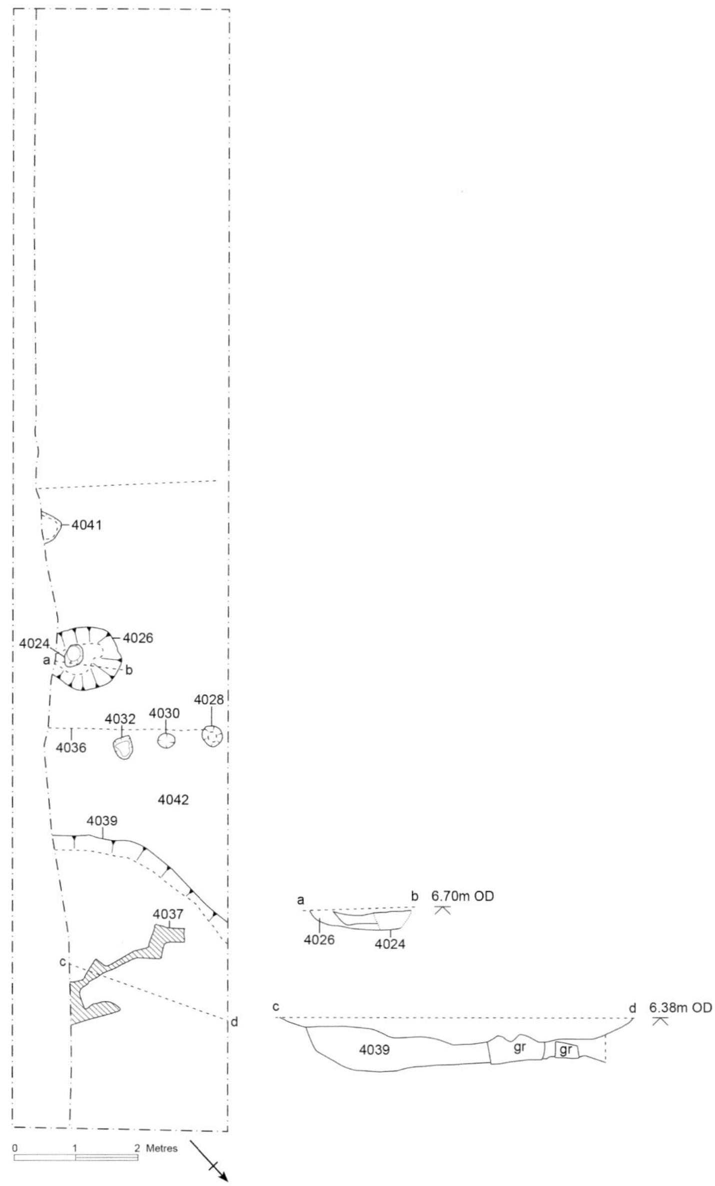

Figure 44 The Bonded Store: area C, trench 4, lower level 2, showing posthole sequence and section through C4039 and C4024.

a Victorian drain (C4007). The drain was traced for just over 1.0m across the trench (Fig. 45), and measured 1.35m at its widest point, with a depth of approximately 0.35m.

The Roman wall C3017a previously identified in CT3 was observed again in CT4 (recorded as C4002). It extended for 2.1m across the trench, with a width of 0.8m (Fig. 45). The wall sat on a mid-grey silty layer (C4003a) about 0.36m thick, which contained charcoal, metal fragments and pottery, including several large sherds of samian ware. To the north-east of the wall, context C4004 represented a linear construction trench for the wall, 0.28m in width and 0.33m in depth, containing rubble and Roman tile. It may have been associated with C4010, a patch of yellow sand with a ring of reddish burning, measuring approximately 0.52m by 0.09m by 0.1m in depth.

In the north-west of the trench a dark grey silty layer (C4003) was located abutting the wall, filled with patches of decayed granite (see Fig. 45). It was 80mm in depth and contained Roman pot and tile. All these features were sealed by the typical overburden (C4001) and modern floor levels.

CT5

Trench CT5 was opened in an attempt to achieve a section running the whole length of the Bonded Store area. This proved not to be possible, however, as an unexpected section of modern foundations was encountered, and the trench yielded only modern finds apart from traces of a medieval midden (C5005).

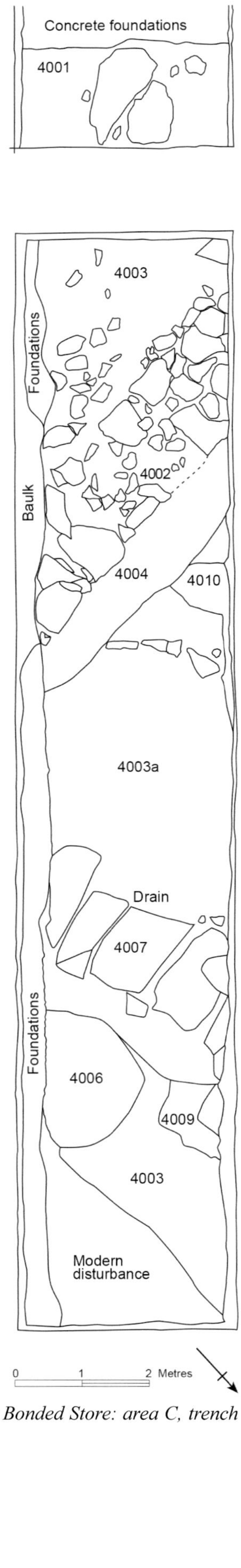

Figure 45 The Bonded Store: area C, trench 4, upper levels.

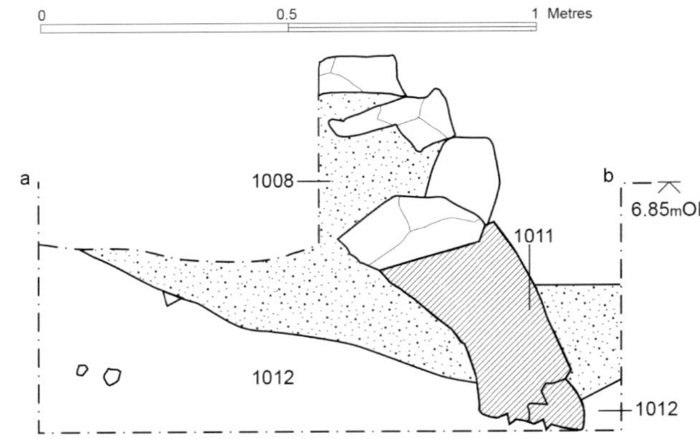

Figure 46 The Bonded Store: area D, trench 1, section through prehistoric wall D1011.

Area D

The four trenches in Area D were located in the north-west part of the site (see Fig. 19), opposite Area B. The foundations of the Bonded Store were rather deeper here than elsewhere, and as in all the other areas they had severely disturbed the earlier archaeological deposits.

DT1

The earliest deposits in trench DT1 consisted of two alluvial layers (D1009 and D1010). The latter was a natural deposit of sterile, blue-grey clay encountered at 5.19m OD. It was observed for 0.38m by 1.88m across the trench. D1009 consisted of soft grey clay, containing flecks of charcoal and Iron Age pottery, traced for 1.10m by 2.18m across the trench, with a thickness of 0.22m.

Another deposit of grey clay (D1012) extended across the trench, 0.36m thick, containing daub, flecks of charcoal, and traces of prehistoric pottery. On top of it was a prehistoric wall (D1011; Fig. 46), which survived to a height of 0.72m (Fig. 47). It was formed of large angular stones, ranging between 0.12m by 0.18m to 0.18m by 0.48m in size, with no bonding. It was traced for approximately 2.15m in a south-west/north-east direction and may have served as a boundary wall. There was no evidence for a foundation.

At the eastern end of the trench, a deposit of compacted red-brown soil (D1008) had formed at the interface between the blue/grey alluvial clays D1009/10 below it, and a brown, gritty soil layer (D1005) which lay above. Soil D1008 was traced across the width of the trench for approximately 2.5m, and measured 0.12m to 0.48m in thickness. At the west end of the trench, a grey/brown silty soil (D1007) contained small stones and finds including a Venus figurine (small-find 201, at 7.55m OD), and very degraded bone deposits. The context was traced for approximately 0.57m by 2.85m across the trench, to a depth of 0.35m. It was sealed by soil D1005, already mentioned, which included Iron Age pottery. Above this was a layer of dark grey silt (D1004), varying in thickness between

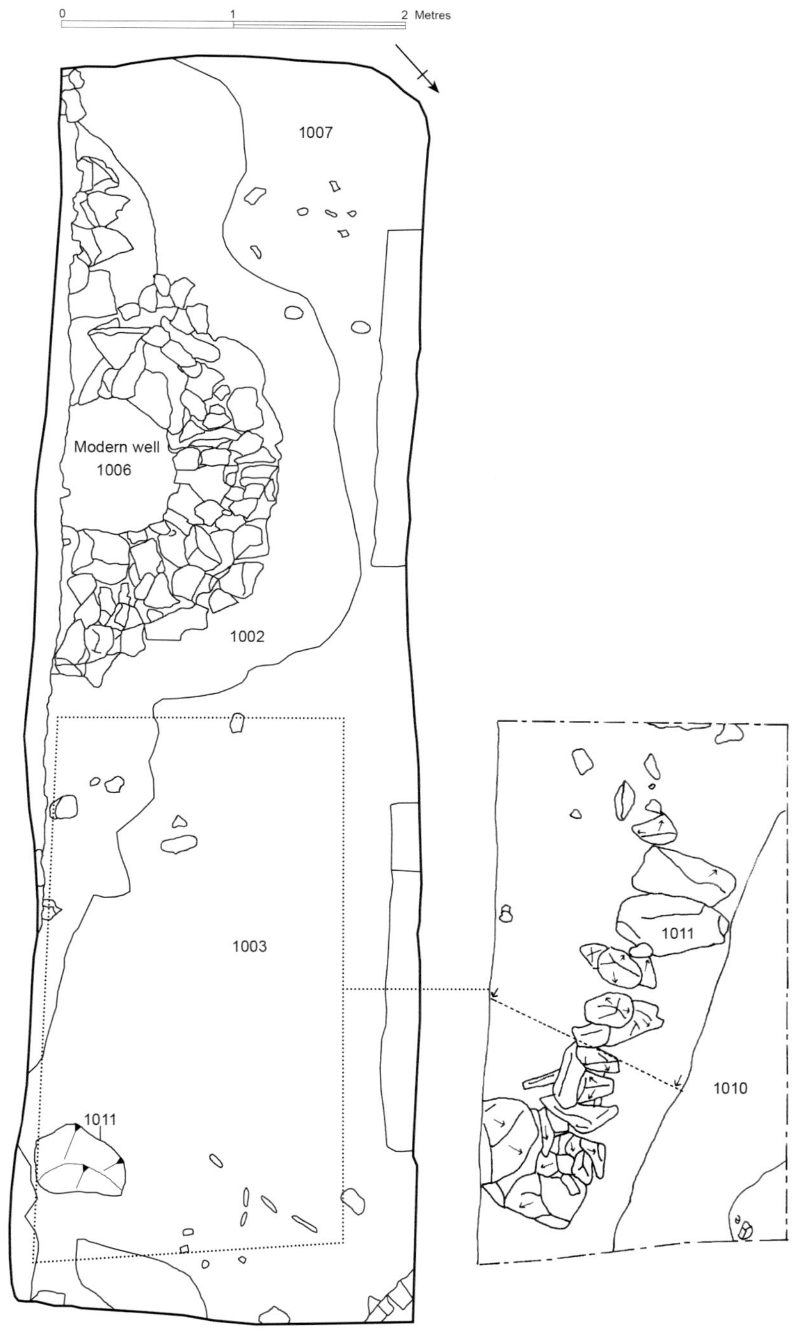

Figure 47 The Bonded Store: area D, trench 1, upper levels showing modern well in relation to the prehistoric wall.

0.1m and 0.5m, which contained a few angular stones and Roman material.

The construction of a post-medieval well (D1001) cut through D1007, D1005 and D1004. About two-thirds of this substantial stone structure (Fig. 47) survived, the walls of which were approximately 0.65m wide and the overall diameter estimated at 1.94m. The top of the well was located at 7.38m OD. The interior (fill D1006) was excavated to a depth of 1.5m, until the water table was reached at *c.* 5.0m OD; it contained post-medieval material. Frogged bricks found in the upper courses suggest that the upper section at least may have been rebuilt comparatively recently.

The well was sealed by a deposit of homogenous silty clay (D1002), which contained pottery, charcoal and flint. This was traced for about 3m around the well structure, and down to about 5.8m OD.

DT2

The lowest archaeological levels in this trench consisted of dark grey clays including D2014 (Fig. 48), 0.32m in

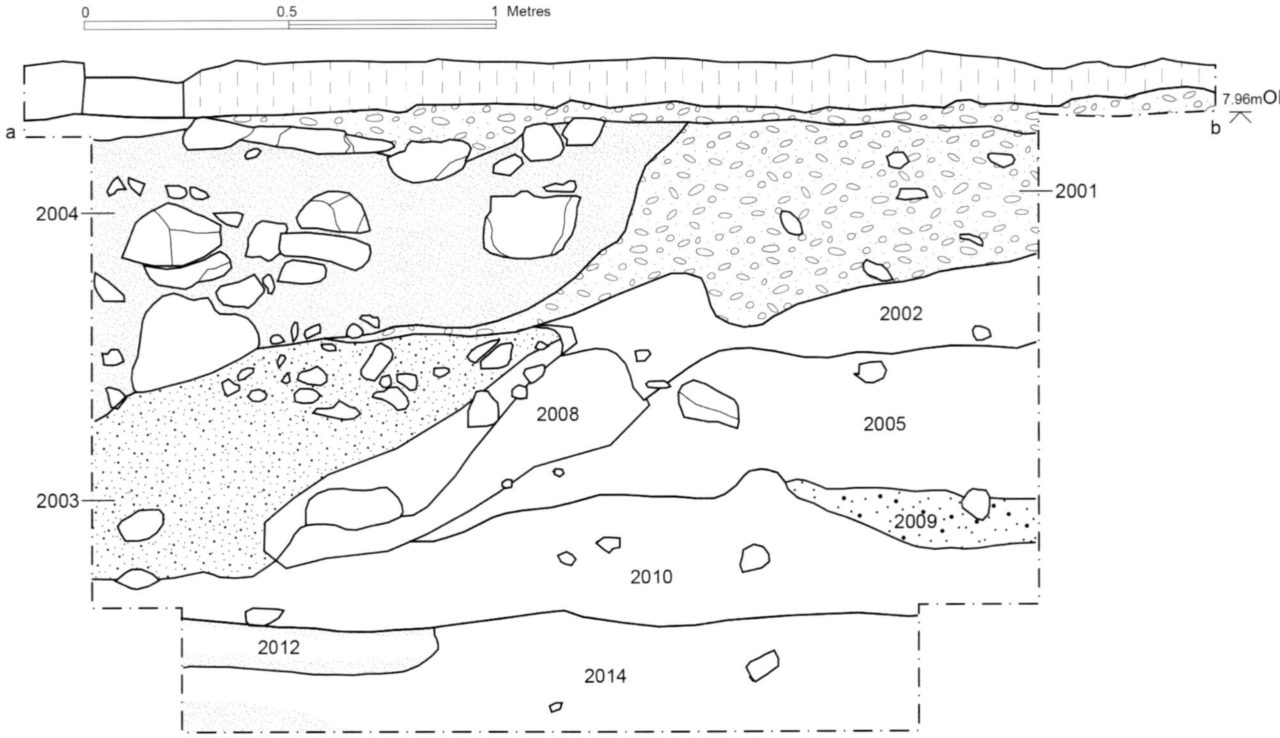

Figure 48 The Bonded Store: area D, trench 2, south-west facing section.

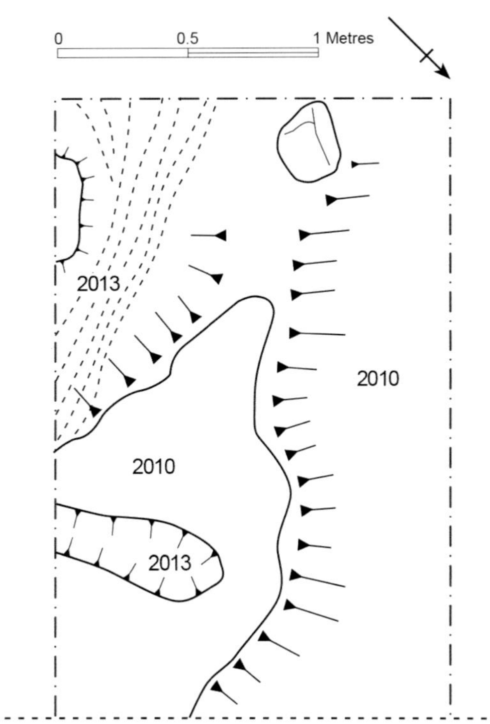

Figure 49 The Bonded Store: area D, trench 2, late Iron Age/early Roman features.

thickness, and D2013 (Fig. 49); both deposits contained considerable quantities of charcoal, some sherds of late Iron Age and early Roman pottery, and calcined bone. A pit (D2012) approximately 0.40m by 0.30m by 0.08m in depth, was cut into D2014.

These contexts were sealed by a similar dark grey clay (D2010), containing a few small pebbles and some charcoal spreads, and surviving to a depth of 1.1m. This deposit was only partially excavated because of difficulties with the water table. Within it there was a lens of black, anaerobic soil (D2008), measuring 0.33m by 0.75m with a depth of 0.22m. Cut into D2010 was a linear arrangement of stones (D2015), a single course (0.32m) in height and apparently clay-bonded. This structure measured 0.76m by 0.38m at its widest point. There were no finds associated with it, and it may have been a boundary wall similar to D1011 in trench DT1.

Above these deposits there was a layer (D2011) of dark grey, soft clay in the north-east end of the trench (Fig. 50); this contained very few finds other than large amounts of charcoal, and daub. It was traced for approximately 1.28m by 0.40m, surviving to a depth of 0.38m. It was sealed by a grey/brown gritty layer (D2009) containing a wide range of finds, including Roman coarsewares, amphorae, samian ware, glass, and flint. It was observed across the trench and extended to 0.9m in depth.

D2009 was sealed by layer D2005, a mixed clay between 0.3m and 0.4m in depth, which was encountered across the trench. It included lenses of light grey clay and a grey silt, and may perhaps have been re-deposited during the Roman period. Finds from this context included a samian sherd stamped *Magio* (*c.* AD 160–90) and a red jasper intaglio of a *gryllos* (small-find 212, see p. 107). The same layer D2005 sealed an irregular, pit-like feature (D2006), measuring 0.91m by 1.30m, by 0.25m deep. Its fill, a gritty brown soil

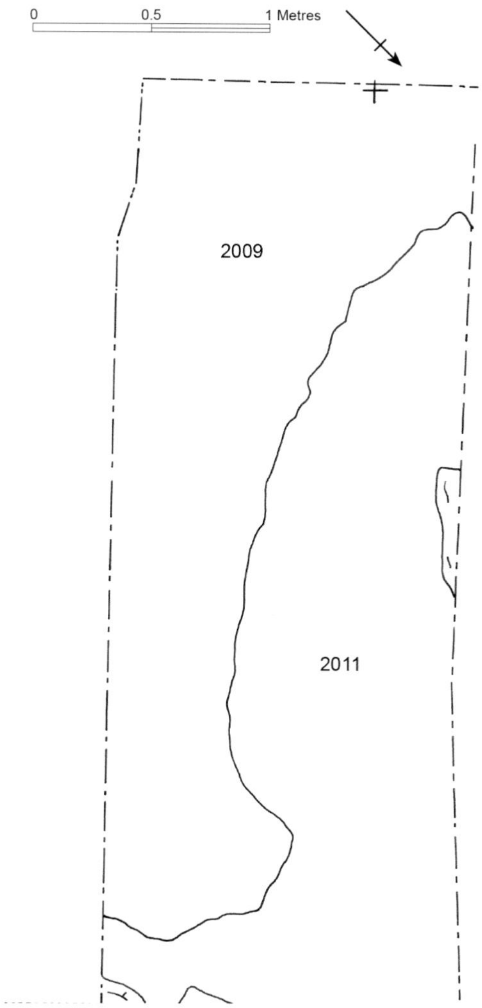

Figure 50 The Bonded Store: area D, trench 2, lower levels.

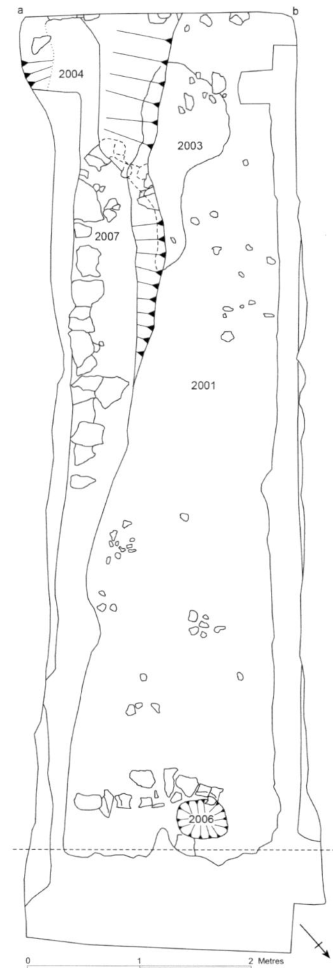

Figure 51 The Bonded Store: area D, trench 2, upper levels.

with angular stones, also included part of a granite quern, pottery and charcoal.

The upper levels of this trench (Fig. 51) consisted of a section of medieval wall (D2004), which survived more fully in trench DT3, and a series of layers (D2001, D2002 and D2003) which were disturbed and contained modern material. The wall was traced for 0.58m by 0.28m wide in the south-western part of the trench, with a depth of 0.76m.

DT3

The lowest archaeological context in this trench consisted of a thin (40mm) grey clay (D3012) containing pottery, burnt bone charcoal and a spindle whorl (small-find 233) (Fig. 52). It was traced across an area 1.22m by 1.38m. Above this was a deposit (D3006) of blue-grey clay, containing a few angular stones within it, which was traced across the trench to a maximum depth of 0.42m. It held few finds other than some pottery, charcoal and burnt bone. It was cut by D3007, a small ditch with a fill of brown, gritty soil. This feature measured approximately 0.42m in width and survived to a depth of 0.34m.

Other early contexts included a yellow/brown soil (D3009) containing prehistoric pottery, and a yellow gritty layer (D3011), at the south-west end of the trench below D3009, containing a small amount of pottery and tile.

A stone structure (D3013) of Roman date lay on the surface of the blue/grey clay D3006 (Fig. 53). It was clay-bonded, with a finished face on its west side. It ran parallel to D3014, which may have been part of the same structure, as it was also clay-bonded with a finished face on the west. Alongside it was a deposit of a red/brown, gritty soil (D3015), with a lens of grey ash within it. This contained fragments of pottery, bone, charcoal, daub and furnace lining, and was traced across an area of 0.94m by 0.06m, to a depth of 0.40m.

Another wall structure (D3010), consisting of a single course of stones, was traced for 1.51m in length by 0.22m in width, surviving to a depth of 0.38m. It was located at approximately 6.7m OD.

The upper levels of the trench were dominated by a medieval wall (D3002) sitting on a brown gritty layer with traces of iron pan (D3005), above the blue-grey clay D3006 (Fig. 54). This was a continuation of the wall D2004 that

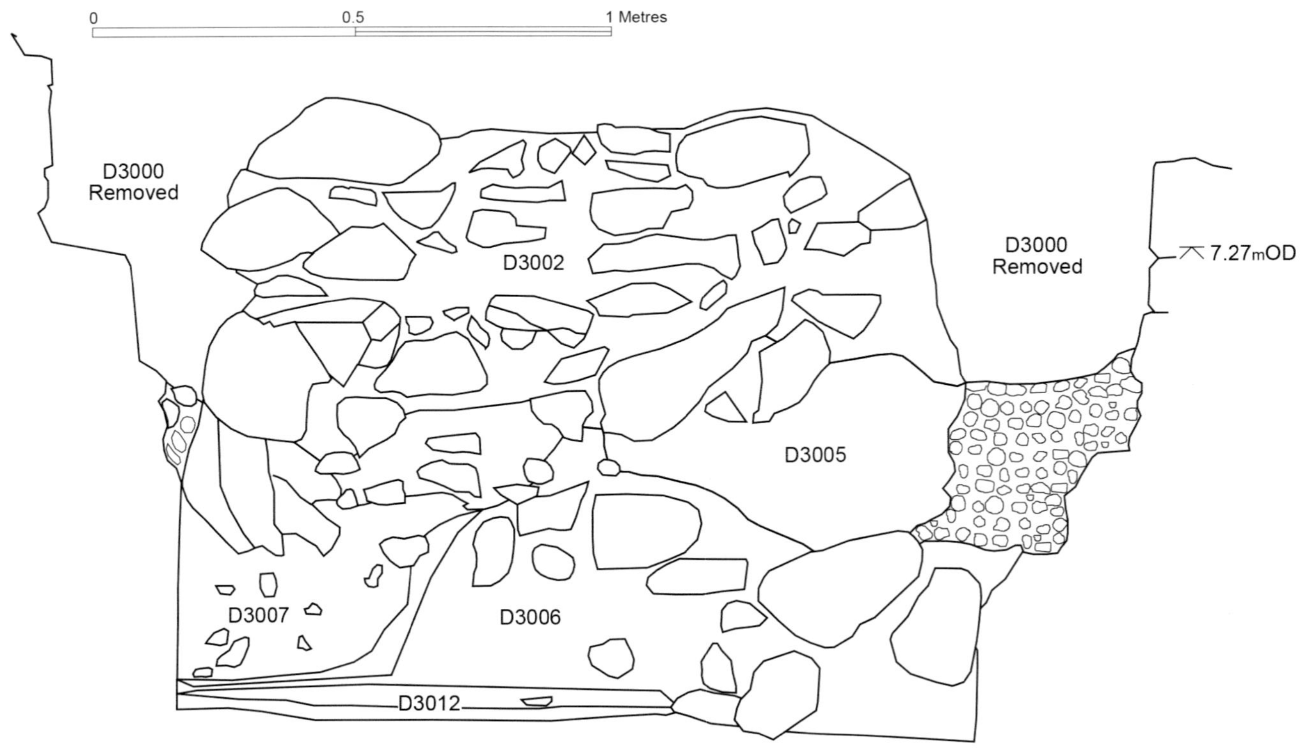

Figure 52 The Bonded Store: area D, trench 3, north-west facing section.

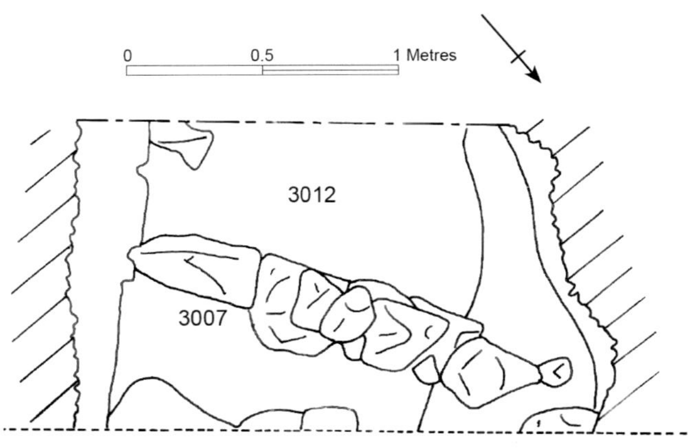

Figure 53 The Bonded Store: area D, trench 3, detail of wall structure D3013.

had been observed in DT2 (see Fig. 51). The base of the wall contained substantial stone grounders, between 0.4m by 0.6m and 0.6m by 0.8m in size. The wall was not particularly well made, but may have been faced on its north-western side. It was traced for a length of 7.45m across the trench, and was 1.45m at its widest point.

The contexts above the medieval wall included a dark grey/brown clay layer (D3004), 0.25m in thickness. Above that was a layer with a similar matrix (D3003), also 0.25m in thickness, containing re-deposited Roman and medieval material, post-medieval pottery and clay pipe. The deposits at the south-western end of the trench were partially sealed by a post-medieval brick building.

DT4

The lowest levels excavated in trench DT4 included a deposit of light grey silt (D4118a) which was present on either side of an alignment of granite stones (D4119). The stones measured 0.48m by 0.26m wide, with a depth of 0.70m. The grey silt was 0.60m deep on both sides of the stones. Above this were various mixed gravelly and silty layers, with much evidence of burning. An orange/brown silt with burnt clay (D4117), containing Roman firebricks, was traced over an area 0.38m by 0.95m, with a depth of 0.15m. A grey silt deposit with pebbles (D4116), 0.32m thick, was observed in an area of 2.04m by 0.28m; it contained a fragment of Roman glass (small-find 320). D4114 was a red/brown gritty deposit, 0.58m by 0.8m and 0.14m deep, which filled cuts D4112 and D4113 (Fig. 55). It contained pottery, bone and building material. A grey/brown silt deposit (D4110/4111) was identified for 1.11m across the south-west corner of the trench, with a depth of approximately 0.34m.

Above these silty layers was a deposit of a brown, silty loam (D4109) traced for approximately 1.40m by 1.66m, to a depth of 0.11m. Finds from this context included metal fragments (small-find 317). This in turn was sealed by a layer of similar consistency (D4105), lying between a wall structure (D4106/7) and the south-west corner of the trench (Fig. 56). D4105 was traced for 0.95m by 1.42m, to a depth of 0.28m. The wall D4106/7 ran north-west to south-east across the trench for approximately 1.65m, measuring 0.48m at its widest point and 0.28m in depth, with more than one course surviving. Within the wall was a large portion of a

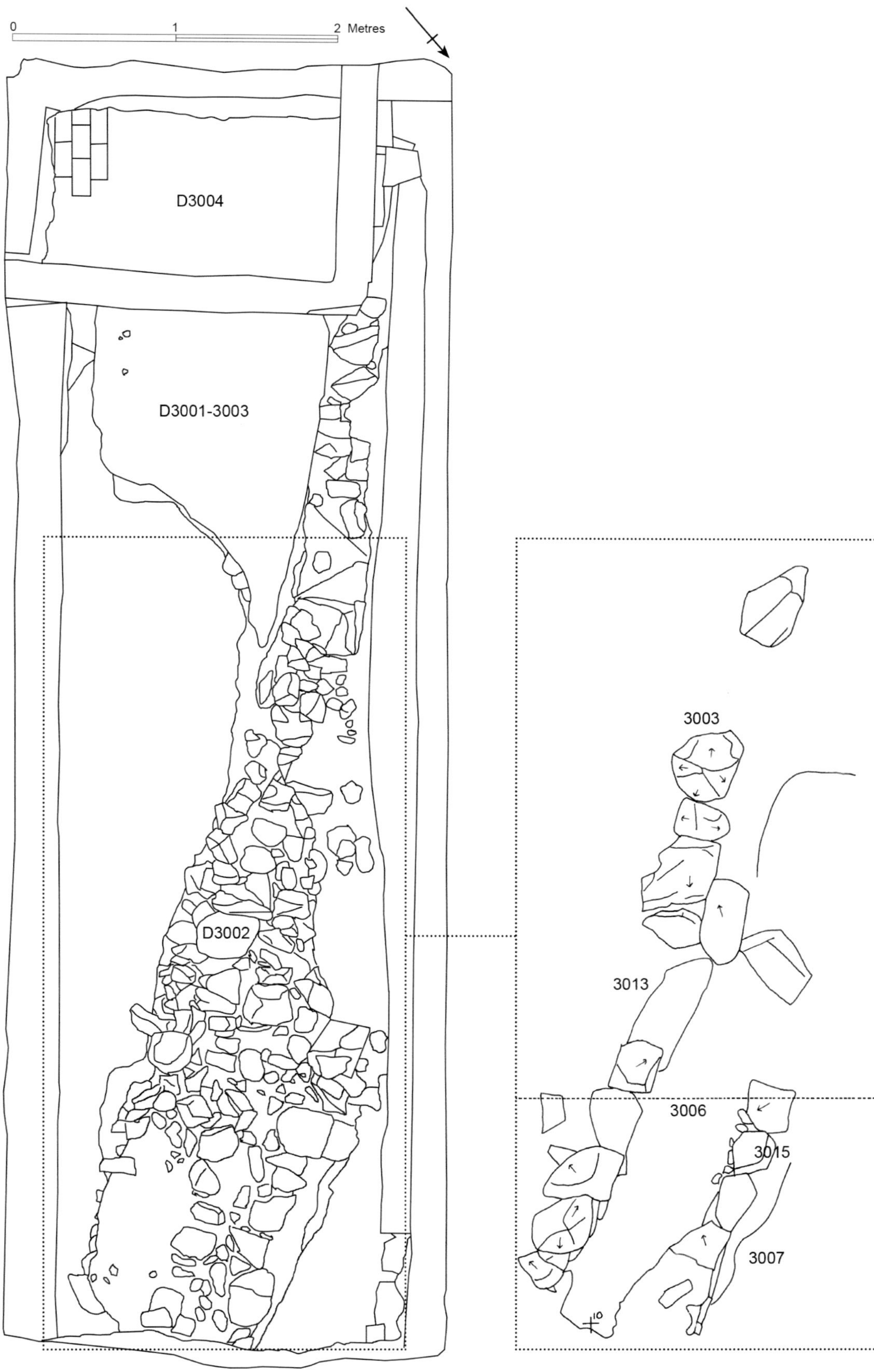

Figure 54 The Bonded Store: area D, trench 3, upper levels and position of earlier wall feature D3013.

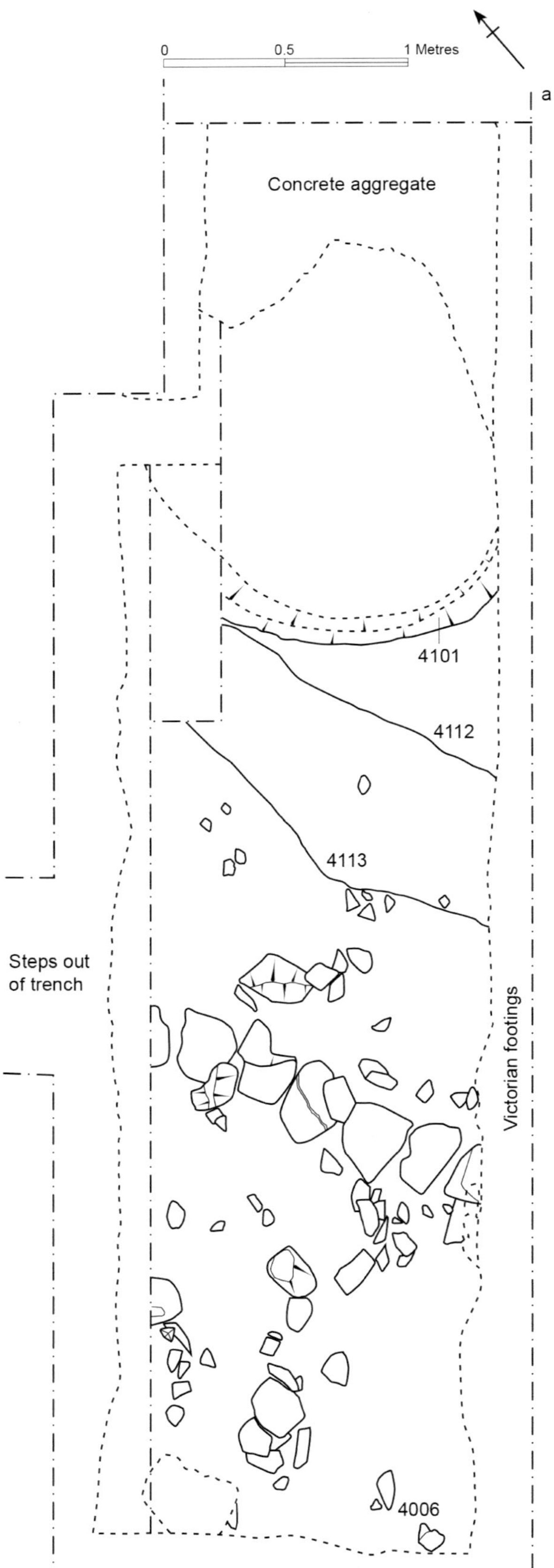

Figure 55 The Bonded Store: area D, trench 4, lower level phase 2.

rotary quern (small-find 313), and one of the large lower stones was burnt. The wall may have been associated with the industrial working indicated by the firebricks and other features on the site. A further structure of large stones (D4108) lay perpendicular to D4106/7, measuring 0.92m by between 0.30m and 0.40m wide, with a height of 0.82m.

A layer of blue/grey silt (D4103), 0.30m thick at its deepest point, extended across the central part of the trench for approximately 0.78m (Fig. 57). It included quantities of briquetage and a fragment of carved stone masonry (small-find 310).

The highest Roman deposits were encountered in this trench at 6.81m OD. D4005 was traced for 0.96m to a depth of 0.10m to 0.15m and it was 0.74m at its widest point. D4006 was a light grey clay lens with charcoal staining, measuring 0.46m by 1.02m by 0.31m in depth. It contained no finds. There were also no finds from a burnt black deposit (D4100 and D4100a) that lay within an irregular cut (D4101) measuring 0.45m by 1.54m and 0.54m deep.

The uppermost layers in this trench (Figs 58–59) consisted of a grey, gritty disturbed deposit (D4004) in the north-east end of the trench, and a mid-grey clay (D4003) mostly at the south-west end, which contained a spindle-whorl (small-find 232). D4004 measured 1.43m by 0.92m, to a depth of 0.40m, and included medieval and post-medieval pottery in its fill. D4003, which spread across 3.22m, contained large angular stones and post-medieval finds. These deposits were sealed by the modern construction layers.

Summary of Bonded Store phasing and discussion

Due to the nature of the site and the method in which it had to be excavated between the pillars of the 19th-century building, the stratigraphic relationships were often compromised, and much of the artefactual material recovered came from the disturbed layers created by the building of the Bonded Store. However, some dating sequences could be constructed, and the main phases of activity on the site identified.

Mesolithic

Traces of Mesolithic material survived in re-deposited contexts, suggesting that there may have been peoples in the area exploiting the natural resources of the valley and the proximity of the sea, albeit as a transitory or perhaps seasonal presence. In context A1204 a Mesolithic flint blade (small-find 18) was recovered from a later disturbed layer.

Neolithic

No diagnostic Neolithic material was found within secure contexts on the site, although debitage and several worked flints were recorded in re-deposited contexts; the flint report is in the Museum archive. Excavations in the 1980s for a lift-shaft at the Guilles-Allès library, just to the south-west of the Bonded Store, produced early Neolithic pottery of

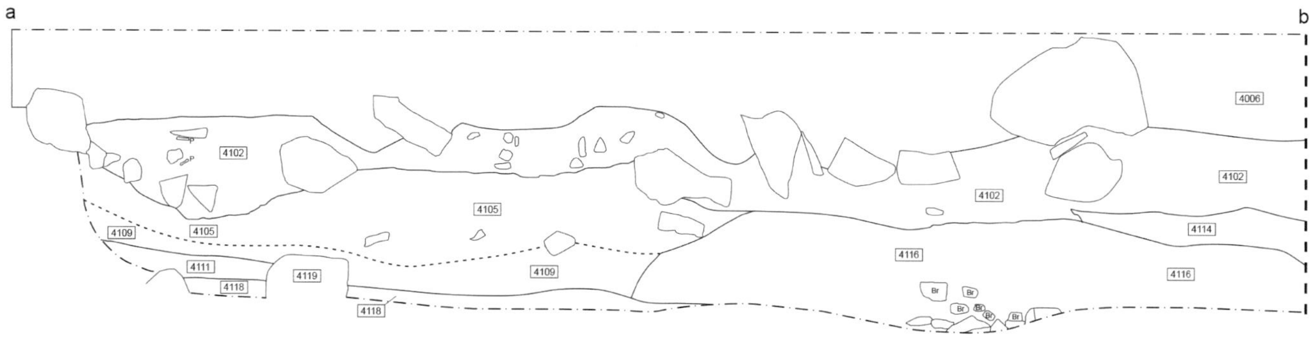

Figure 56 The Bonded Store: area D, trench 4, south-east facing section.

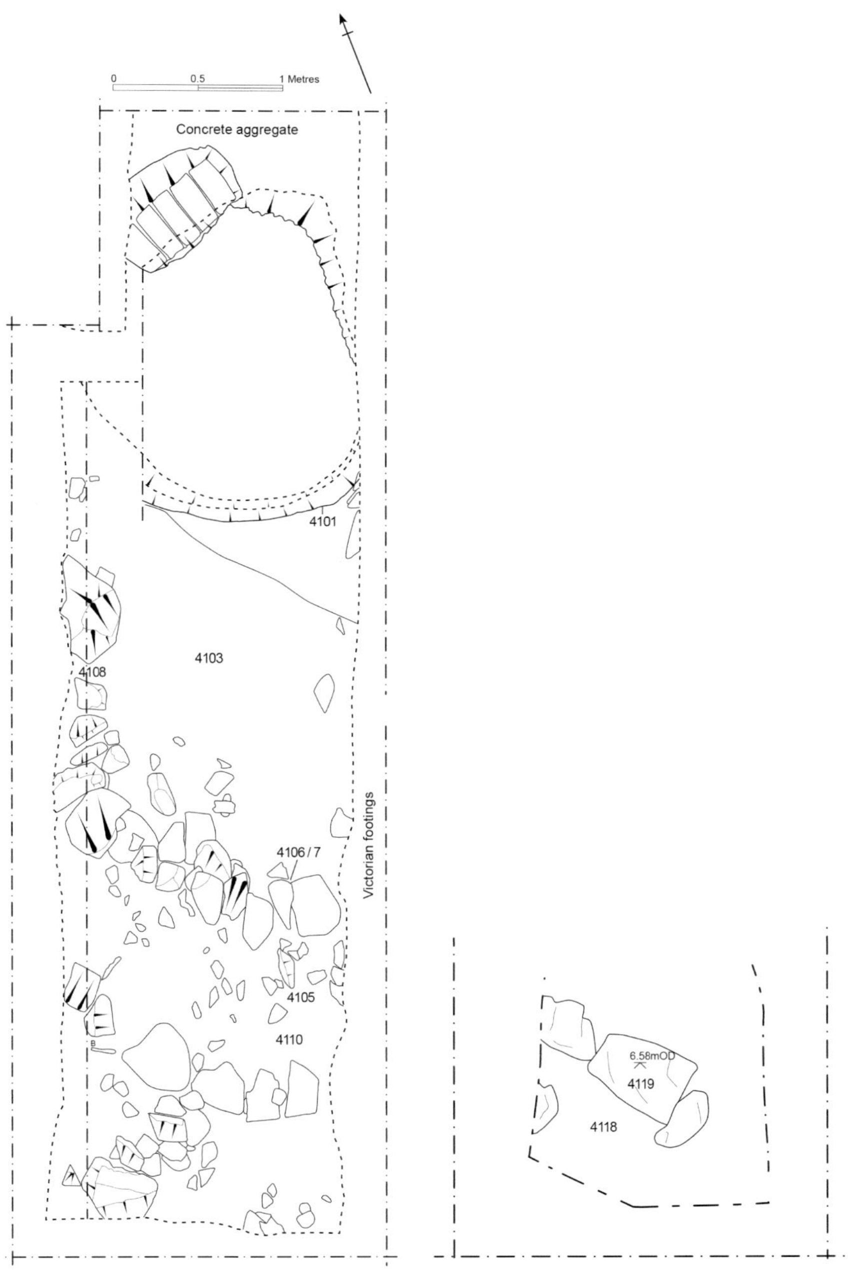

Figure 57 The Bonded Store: area D, trench 4, lower level phase 1.

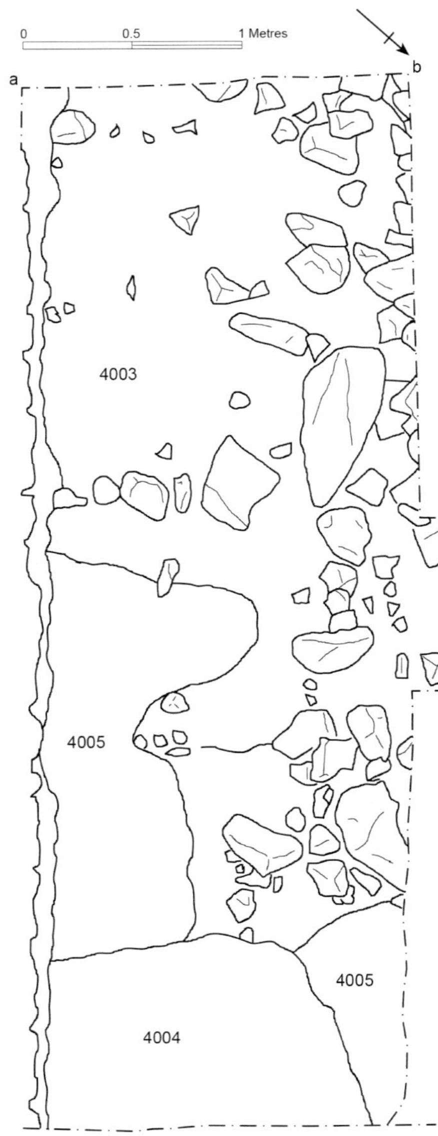

Figure 58 The Bonded Store: area D, trench 4, upper levels.

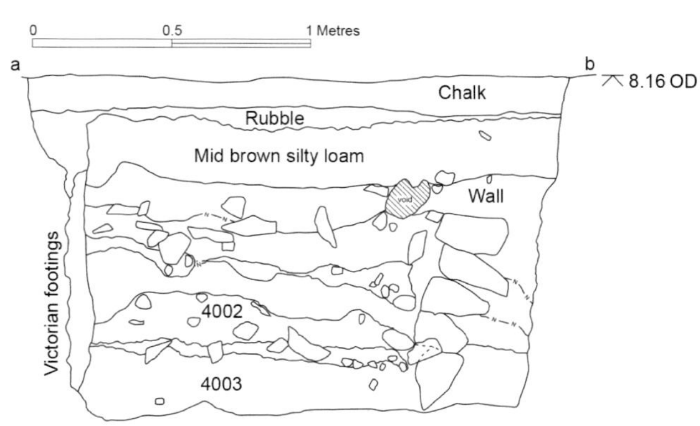

Figure 59 The Bonded Store: area D, trench 4, north-east facing section through the upper levels.

Cerney type (I. Kinnes, pers. comm.), so there is other evidence for early activity in the area.

Bronze Age

The earliest phase of occupation of any substance dated from the Bronze Age. Some evidence of occupation of the valley side was found beneath the Roman levels. Small pits or 'scoops' cut into the natural bank of the valley contained traces of very degraded prehistoric pottery and some flint and stones which could have been used as pot-boilers (contexts A1055 and A1056). In Area D, below the Roman features, a linear stone feature (D1011) which may have served as a boundary wall was traced across the trench in a north-west/south-east direction for approximately 2.15m. It was associated with layers containing only prehistoric pottery. The environmental report for this area (Chapter 5) does not suggest any concentrated activity at this time, however, so any settlement may have been some distance away. Sherds of Beaker pottery were recovered from the general disturbed layer B1203, and several pieces of worked flint of probable Bronze Age date were recovered from re-deposited contexts, including a honey-coloured secondary flake (from context A2034, small-find 9) with a good match to the matrix of the Breton barbed and tanged arrowheads from Les Fouaillages, in the north of the island.

Iron Age

In almost all of the trenches there were remains of Iron Age features, which had mostly been cut by later Roman features, or truncated by the foundations of the Bonded Store building. The features were characterised as ditches, pits and gullies, some containing briquetage or salt-working material.

The ceramics and other artefacts indicate that people were living in the area, taking advantage of the strip of land at the bottom of the valley in close proximity to the sea, particularly in the last century before the arrival of the Romans.

The majority of the Iron Age finds came from Areas C (in the south-east) and D (in the north-west) of the site. Approximately 20% of the ceramic finds were pre-conquest, with notable similarities to material recovered from other Iron Age sites on the island (see pottery report, Chapter 4). Substantial quantities of briquetage material were discovered, indicating salt-working in the vicinity. The finds included both hand-bricks and earthenware vessel sherds for the evaporation process, similar to material from the same period from other areas of the island (Cunliffe and de Jersey 2000). A bronze stater of the Baiocasses (small-find 53), dating to *c*.60 BC, was found in Area B.

Spindle-whorls were found, providing evidence for the use of wool for weaving and cloth production. Further evidence of agricultural activities is provided by the presence of fragments of quern and environmental evidence, which indicates that barley was being grown nearby.

Roman

The principal finds from the Bonded Store excavation fall into the Roman period, ranging from the conquest to the end of Roman rule in the region. The occupation identified on the site is split broadly into three phases: (1) late Iron Age/early Roman, (2) mid-2nd century AD, and (3) later Roman.

1. The early Roman features were characterised by features similar to the Iron Age remains, but also included arrangements of postholes (such as in CT2) which had sherds of Pascual amphorae associated with them. Also in trench CT2, context C1082 contained a group of early 1st-century AD pots, including north Gaulish greywares, *céramique fumigée* and oxidised flagon fabrics. The presence of sherds of Dressel 1A and B amphorae suggests significant activity on the site between 120 BC and 10 BC.The layers A1205, B1204 and C1070 produced Pompeian red ware, and late Iron Age black cordoned and rilled micaeous wares were found in layers C1006 and C1007. Other wares within the early Roman sealed deposits include *mica dorée* imported from Gaul, and decorated early Roman Durotrigan sherds which may show trade returning from Roman Britain to France via Guernsey. The presence of three *vases bobines* from Aquitaine in context C1005 also gives credence to this idea of trade along the Atlantic coast. A small amount of samian, particularly from southern Gaul, was coming in at this early period alongside amphorae of the Camolodunum185a/Haltern70 type, which was found in contexts C1005 and B2054 associated with the smithing activities.
2. The main phase of occupation on the site is dated, principally by the ceramics, to the mid-2nd century AD; this includes the metal-smithing activities, which were identified particularly in trench B2 where the bulk of the features were associated with a smithing furnace (2032/48) but also in trenches C1 and D4.The pottery included the rim of a tripod bowl, sherds of a Gauloise 12 amphora and flagon handle. Context B2054 in this trench, associated with the hearth and industrial activities, also contained amphorae. There was also oxidised flagon and creamy buffware, a *vase tronconique* from Picardy and residual earlier material, such as Dressel 1A amphorae in a black sand fabric, dated to the pre-Caesarian period, and 1st-century *terra nigra*. Other mid-2nd-century AD material was located in trench CT1 (context C1005) and also in trench CT2 (context C2097). Elsewhere in Area C, features from the same period included C3012, C3026 and C3033 (in CT3), and C4035 and C4038 (in CT4). In Area D, contexts D1007, D2005 and D2009 also contained material from the mid- to late 2nd-century, as did D3005, 3006 and D4102. The bulk of the mortaria on the site also date from this period, as does most of the samian ware from Lezoux.
3. The site continued to be used from the late 2nd century into the 3rd century AD. The ditch feature in Area C (C2094) contained material from the mid-2nd century to the late 3rd century, including New Forest wares and *céramique à l'éponge*. In A2007, Rhenish ware from Trier was present, indicating activity into the early 3rd century AD. In A2004, the presence of *Eifelkeramik* suggests a date from the late 3rd century and into the early 4th. In context C1004, a flanged BB1 dish was found alongside an early 4th-century BB1 cooking pot, and *céramique à l'éponge*. Elsewhere in Area C, BB1 and New Forest wares were found in C3013, and a tripod bowls in C3017. In D2005, the finds also suggested a mid-2nd- to early 3rd-century date, including BB1 alongside quartz-tempered wares and tripod bowls.

   There may perhaps have been local manufacture of the tripod bowl in the mid- or late 2nd century AD (see p. 64). Later 3rd-century wares were present in D3004.There is less 3rd- and 4th-century material at the Bonded Store than at La Plaiderie (see p. 65). There are, however, some large tripod bowls, and hollow foot amphorae, which may date from the late 4th to early 5th century AD.

Early medieval

Two roller-stamped greyware sherds were found, indicating some presence on the site in the very late Roman or early medieval period. One possible Merovingian sherd was found in a disturbed context (A1203).

Medieval

The construction of the Bonded Store in 1879 necessitated a massive clearance of land, unfortunately removing any traces of the previous buildings and the surface on which they stood. Many sherds of French green-glazed wares and Normandy gritty wares were recovered in re-deposited contexts, particularly in the rubble layers above the Bonded Store foundations.

Post-medieval and modern

A wide range of post-medieval material was recovered from the rubble layers above the foundations. Further details of these finds will be published elsewhere.

Conclusions: the nature of the Roman settlement

The position of the Bonded Store site, in close proximity to the sea, must have been a major factor in the development of the area. The good natural harbour with adjacent area of land at sea-level would have provided an ideal location for both industrial and domestic buildings. The assemblage of material recovered from the Bonded Store provides an indication of the nature of this settlement, although somewhat curtailed by the amount of disturbance caused by the later medieval and Victorian buildings on the site.

The scanty evidence of buildings, from beam slots and other structural features, gives an indication of the various activities which took place on the site, some of which were likely to have been industrial. The site may have begun as a quayside area providing iron-working for ship repairs, as the evidence for industrial activity includes smithing and suggests that smelting may have taken place nearby. The section of walling that survives represents the lower section or foundation of a building wall but gives little clarity as to its use, due to damage from the Bonded Store foundations, other than its proximity to the industrial features.

Some evidence of more high-status buildings survived, in the form of floor and roof tile, small amounts of *opus signinum*, a little window glass and a fragment of carved stone. The high ratio of samian pottery also suggests that residential buildings were close by, perhaps higher up the valley above the lower level of the strand that ran along the shoreline. This might suggest that the nature of the settlement may have changed to residential or other civic buildings associated with a Roman town.

II

The finds

4

The Roman pottery

by Mark Wood and Jason Monaghan

The late Mark Wood examined the pottery from La Plaiderie, and at a later stage the pottery from the Bonded Store and some other sites. Based on this work he wrote an extended essay on Roman pottery in Guernsey and maritime trade. The current report is based on extracts from that essay, edited by Jason Monaghan, with additional analysis of the quantified assemblages. Mark also left a provisional drawing list, from which the Catalogue has been developed. The original essay is held in the Museum archive, together with samian and mortaria lists, and it is intended to publish Mark's thoughts on maritime trade separately.

Introduction

The excavations at La Plaiderie and the Bonded Store each produced about 60kg of Roman pottery. Although this is small in comparison to major UK or French sites, there is a remarkable array of imported pottery present. Taken together, the two pottery assemblages date from pre-Roman to early post-Roman times. The sources of origin of the wares demonstrate both the regional and long-distance connections of Guernsey during the period, indicating that ancient St Peter Port was a well-known port-of-call from the late Iron Age onwards.

Trade in Roman wine along the Atlantic seaboard during the late Iron Age bears witness to the connections Guernsey had with Armorican Gaul and Hengistbury Head in Britain (Cunliffe 1987). Guernsey's links with these areas can now be seen to be far more significant than was thought previously. There is also now, for the first time, evidence linking Guernsey with northern Gaul, Germany and south-eastern Britain from early Roman times, via the Channel. In the light of the discoveries at La Plaiderie and the Bonded Store, it is clear that that not only were there movements across the Channel (the focus of which changed over time during the Roman period), but also along the Channel; these appear to feed into the Atlantic system from a very early date. Guernsey was a link in that overall system, but its significance is hard to assess.

The broad range of mid- to late Roman imported pottery dumped in the Roman Quay site at St Magnus House in London (Dyson 1986) bears a striking resemblance to that which is present and was used on the town sites in Guernsey. While the character of the deposits and the quantities or presence of certain wares may differ, both the site in London and St Peter Port itself clearly represent important ports along Roman maritime routes at either end of the Channel. These distant areas were undoubtedly connected via a series of principal ports-of-call along the Channel coasts.

Previous work

Significant finds of Roman pottery in Guernsey were first made only when La Plaiderie was excavated in the 1980s (Wood 1991; 1994). Further articles on specific Roman wares included reference to material from La Plaiderie (Wood 1993a; Williams and Wood 1995). Selected material from maritime sites was also studied during the same period (Monaghan 1988; Monaghan 1990; Rule and Monaghan 1993). An initial appraisal was also made of material from the Bonded Store (Monaghan 1998). Examination of museum collections and unpublished pottery from Alderney revealed material dating from the late Iron Age through to the late 4th century AD (Wood 1990). Overall quantities of pottery from Alderney are not large, but it clearly also had a significant Roman presence and may have been a port-of-call from the late Iron Age. Curiously, only a handful of Roman sherds were found in excavations around the Roman fort at the Nunnery between 2009 and 2012 (Monaghan 2011–12). Some 500 sherds examined from an as yet unidentified site on Longis Common, thought to have been excavated in the 1950s, included 'legionary' type pottery and other wares of the late 1st to 2nd century (Monaghan and de Jersey 2014–15).

The Bonded Store and La Plaiderie assemblages

Methods and condition

The La Plaiderie assemblage was used to establish a series of codes for fabric, form and decoration (see Appendix). These were applied a decade later to the Bonded Store.

Brenda Dickinson and Kay Hartley have commented on the samian and mortaria respectively. Certain diagnostic amphorae sherds from La Plaiderie were also identified by David Williams. The Roman pottery from both sites is particularly fragmentary, indicating the heavy disturbance these sites have undergone. The acidic nature of the soils in Guernsey has also affected the condition. Rounded water-worn sherds are frequent among the assemblages from both sites, as well as badly abraded and soil-stained ones. There is a fresh water stream with a fluctuating water table at the Bonded Store and both sites lay close to the ancient shoreline, and thus were particularly exposed to weathering. Although the majority of the Roman sherds appear to be residual in later levels, both assemblages have been studied in as much detail as possible due to their significance for Roman studies both within and beyond Guernsey. Coarse pottery was quantified by sherd count (Table 4), with samian quantified separately. Coarse pottery and amphorae were also weighed at the Bonded Store, as were some groups at La Plaiderie. It was decided not to use estimated vessel equivalents (EVEs) due to the small size of deposits and the scrappy nature of much of the pottery. Guernsey has not yet yielded stratified deposits of sufficient size to produce a firm ceramic phasing.

Dating of the sites

The Bonded Store offers the best evidence for the late Iron Age to Roman transition, and has a stronger 1st-century component. The combined evidence of the coins, samian and mortaria attest to activity at La Plaiderie mainly from the later 1st through to the mid-/late 3rd century AD, while the samian and mortaria alone suggest there was a broadly contemporary period of activity at the Bonded Store. La Plaiderie has significantly more east Gaulish samian in the 3rd century, and more activity in the later Roman period. From the 1st century AD through to the end of the Roman period, both assemblages share essentially the same range of fabrics.

The late Iron Age and late Iron Age/Roman transition

During the late Iron Age, the imported pottery consists of Italian wine amphorae and Armorican wares alongside locally made copies of the latter.

i) La Plaiderie

Activity at La Plaiderie cannot certainly be said to have taken place on the site itself until sometime around the second half of the 1st century BC/early 1st century AD. A few scraps of coarse pottery were found in poor condition and were indistinguishable on the basis of fabric alone either from pottery dating to the Roman period (fabrics

Table 4 The Bonded Store and La Plaiderie: summary of coarsewares.

	Bonded Store				*La Plaiderie*	
	sherds	*%*	*weight/g*	*%*	*sherds*	*%*
Iron Age or late Iron Age	264	5.6	3094	7.1	4	<0.1
Gallo-Belgic wares	204	4.3	1174	2.7	65	1.2
all finewares	149	3.2	861	2	374	6.6
céramique fumigée	284	6	2710	6.2	254	4.5
all BB and Durotrigan wares	154	3.3	1341	3.1	722	12.8
all North Gaulish grey fabrics	841	17.9	6733	15.5	838	14.9
tripod bowl fabric	558	11.9	10,768	24.7	523	9.3
all other grey and sandy wares	552	11.8	5103	11.7	550	9.7
oxidised wares	1588	33.7	10,440	24	2175	38.6
white wares	67	1.4	436	1	50	0.9
others	40	0.8	919	2.1	85	1.5
Total	4706	100	43,579	100	5640	100

TBF1 and AQR) or indeed the prehistoric (Bronze Age) material also found on the site. However, a solitary body sherd from a corrugated bowl, in a different and distinctive vesicular fabric, definitely does date to the late Iron Age. Such suspected local products have been found associated with a few Dressel 1 amphorae (Williams 1996, 51) and pottery types imported from Armorica (along with copies of these in local fabrics other than vesicular ware) on the site at King's Road on the western edge of St Peter Port (Burns *et al.* 1996).

Although no late Iron Age Armorican imports are present in the assemblage from La Plaiderie, the Dressel 1B amphora and the sherd of distinctive vesicular ware represent intriguing evidence for activity (the precise nature of which is unclear) dating to the late Iron Age. Allowing for the fact that the earlier Dressel 1A type may be present among the other four Italian amphorae from the assemblage, this late Iron Age activity can only be dated loosely to the period *c.*120–10 BC. A few scraps of vessels of Aquitainian origin in *céramique fumigée* (fabric SCFR) were also present. The third type of Armorican import also usually found associated with Italian Dressel 1 species amphorae is graphite-coated ware. This ware is probably also present but not immediately recognisable due to the graphite-coating having been worn away during deposition. Late Iron Age La Plaiderie therefore remains enigmatic, and it is likely that intensive Roman use of the site has destroyed much evidence of what went before, and is responsible for the poor state of the pottery.

ii) The Bonded Store

The late Iron Age presence at the Bonded Store is markedly more emphatic than that at La Plaiderie. Pottery from trenches excavated in Areas C and D in particular shows that activity began on the site during the late Iron Age. The range in date of the Roman wares in the site assemblage and evidence for their use suggest that the site was then occupied without any discernible break through to the end of the Roman period.

Associated with Italian Dressel 1 amphorae are numerous examples of pottery imports from Armorica, particularly black-cordoned and rilled micaceous wares. Added to the presence of locally made copies of these Armorican imports, a picture emerges of activity on the site that was directly linked with other sites on the island and beyond. The one sherd of vesicular ware at La Plaiderie, along with the Italian amphorae from that site, assumes greater significance in view of the substantial material of late Iron Age date from the nearby site at the Bonded Store.

Occupation on the site at King's Road, where Italian amphorae, Armorican imports and local copies of these wares are all present (Burns *et al.* 1996), was clearly contemporary with that at the Bonded Store during the late Iron Age. Both of these sites have significant quantities of local wares (including vesicular ware) but the imported Italian amphorae and Armorican wares are present in greater numbers at the Bonded Store. Over 16kg of briquetage, including some briquetage 'furniture', is present at the Bonded Store and this appears to be mostly associated with the late Iron Age activity on the site although some undoubtedly belongs with the subsequent early Roman activity.

The apparent absence of other early Roman amphorae types and other early Roman imported wares from the site at King's Road is intriguing. The briquetage at the Bonded Store could indicate that initial activity on or near the site was seasonal. Assuming that there was more than just a redistribution/exchange of goods connection between these two sites during the late Iron Age, it is possible that the focus of activity moved from King's Road to St Peter Port (illustrated by the Bonded Store) in the early Roman period. There is then some evidence suggested by the pottery for activity recurring at King's Road from around the mid-1st century AD and continuing during the 2nd century AD (Wood 1996, 52–5).

As at La Plaiderie, potentially the earliest of the early Roman period amphora types present at the Bonded Store are 16 body sherds of Camulodunum 185A/Haltern 70 (dated mid-1st century BC to the mid-1st century AD), followed by at least eight Pascual 1 amphorae of probable Augustan date. The remaining early Roman amphorae from the Bonded Store are not numerous and mostly date between the later 1st century BC and the early 2nd century AD. Apart from the Dressel 20 and Gauloise 4 amphorae, these other types include nine sherds of Dressel 7–11, three sherds of Camulodunum 189 ('carrot amphora'), and a handful of sherds that represent further types, the most important of which are a possible (Spanish) Dressel 2–4, Dressel 28, Beltran IIB and Richborough 527.

The material associated with the earliest of these amphora types is much the same as at La Plaiderie, except for the fact that there is both a greater variety of forms and quantity of semi-fine table wares, as well as the presence of two particular coarsewares not found at La Plaiderie. One of the latter was imported from Gaul (fabric MDER) and the other (fabric DUR) is the earliest import from pre-Roman Britain. Aquitainian *céramique fumigée* (fabric SCFR) is more noticeable than at La Plaiderie; this includes at least three *vases bobines* (dating between 20 BC and AD 40), a jar (Santrot and Santrot 1979, form 221, dating to the last decade of the 1st century BC), and a bowl dating from the latter decade of the 1st century BC through to around AD 70. Pompeian Red ware dishes are also present at the Bonded Store but only one is probably Augustan in date. A greater range of largely 1st-century AD Gallo-Belgic wares (fabrics GB and GB/TR) are present at the Bonded Store with sherds from at least nine vessels, including beakers (mainly), cups and plates. Central Gaulish terra nigra and Armorican *céramique fumigée* (fabrics MCF and SCFO) are also well-represented with three further *vases bobines*, four plates, several cups, bowls (some from Rennes) and jars dating to the 1st century AD. A particularly aesthetically pleasing form is a cordoned bowl (fabric SCFO), imitating a late Iron Age form, that would appear to have been produced in Armorica where the form originated. As at La Plaiderie, further terra nigras (fabrics EGGS, SCFO, STN, STNR, MCF and GCF) from various Gallo-Roman sources appear to be more common at the Bonded Store from the early/mid-1st century AD onwards.

The distinctive jars with an internally-grooved rim (fabric MDER; Cam. 262) are typically very late 1st century BC/early 1st century AD. Around seven of these vessels are present at the Bonded Store, most of which came from central Gaul, but one is in a different fabric and may be Armorican in origin. Central Gaul also supplied many of the flagons of early Roman date at the Bonded Store, represented largely by body sherds and ribbed handles with a cream slip. Other sherds from flagons in a distinctive orange/red fabric and an off-white slip identical to flagon sherds found at the native site of the Tranquesous (see below) appear to be Gallo-Roman (Mougon) products of around the mid-1st century AD. The direct link with the Tranquesous is further strengthened by the five non-spill bowls (fabric DUR) from the Bonded Store as well as the terra nigras present on both sites. One example of the same DUR bowl form is present at the Tranquesous (Wood 1990, 57). These bowls from the Bonded Store and the Tranquesous are significant as they represent the only pottery imports from pre-Roman Britain. They are indicative of 'return loads' as well as continuing contact with central-southern Britain seemingly post-dating the late Iron Age links epitomised by the Armorican wares and Italian wine.

In summary, it would appear that La Plaiderie was probably founded slightly later in date than the site at the Bonded Store, but otherwise both sites were occupied continuously through to the end of the Roman period, while only La Plaiderie seems to have had a slim early medieval (or 'Dark Age') component.

The early Roman period

By the early Roman period, virtually all of the pottery was imported and, with the exception of the wine amphorae from the Catalan coastal region of north-eastern Spain, all but two of the other pottery imports were semi-fine table wares. The latter are mainly *céramique fumigée* and related terra nigra and terra rubra, imported initially from south-west Gaul then central and northern Gaul (*i.e.* Gallia Belgica) as well as Armorica. Coarsewares represent the two further imported wares: one is also from central Gaul (jars with moulded rims) while the other is the only known import from pre-Roman Britain (Dorset; fabric DUR non-spill bowls). There are also a few Pompeian Red ware plates/dishes of Mediterranean origin.

Semi-fine table wares from the areas described above continued to be imported during the course of the 1st century AD. Camulodunum 185A amphorae, Spanish olive oil amphorae and southern Gallic wine (Gauloise 4 amphorae) are present and while most were imported from the early 1st century AD onwards, some types could have been imported earlier. Fine wares from south Gaul also appear at around the same time with samian from Montans and La Graufesenque, but no Arretine wares have been identified. Flagons from Mougon were presumably imported along with other central Gaulish wares including further flagons and terra nigra. Accompanying the later Gallo-Belgic wares from northern Gaul are coarse greywares, terra nigra-type wares and the first imported mortaria from Picardy.

A handful of sherds represent the remaining early Roman amphora types present at La Plaiderie, and while their periods of production collectively span some 200 years, the majority of them were probably imported during the second half of the 1st century BC and the remainder during the 1st century AD. These include Camulodunum 185A/Haltern 70, Pascual 1, Camulodunum 186A, Gauloise 5 and Dressel 28. Potentially the earliest of these are the few sherds of Camulodunum 185A/Haltern 70 amphorae (mid-1st century BC to mid-1st century AD) followed by two Pascual 1 amphorae of probable Augustan date.

La Plaiderie was also receiving small quantities of semi-fine table wares during the earlier Roman period. Initially, these were imported from south-west and then western and northern Gaul, and to a lesser extent central Gaul. A few cups and bowls of Aquitainian origin in *céramique fumigée* (fabric SCFR) were imported from Augustan times. At least three of the four Pompeian Red ware dishes from the site, fabric PRW2, could belong to this period. Probably slightly later in date are the body sherds from four or five Gallo-Belgic drinking vessels (fabric GB) and some featureless sherds of central Gaulish terra nigra (fabrics CF and MCF). Armorican *céramique fumigée* and allied terra nigras in a variety of other fabrics (EGGS, SCFO, STN, STNR, MCF and GCF) from a number of Gallo-Roman sources appear to be more common from the early/mid-1st century AD, around the time that the earliest (Tiberio-Claudian) samian was being imported from south Gaul. There are undoubtedly flagons dating to this period (body sherds in white, pink and red fabrics) but particular types cannot be determined due to the complete absence of diagnostic sherds and the largely indistinct range of fabrics. Signs of use of these imported wares (see below), along with other evidence, suggests that occupation occurred at La Plaiderie during the early Roman period.

Around the mid-1st century AD, possibly from the early Claudian period, jars and other vessels in a terra nigra-type ware were being imported from northern Gaul. These grey/black jars (fabric GCF), with crudely burnished horizontal bands on the short neck of the vessels, are the forerunners of the *gobelet à col tronconique* form that is particularly common at La Plaiderie and the Bonded Store during the 2nd and 3rd centuries AD (fabrics NGGW 1–2). An identical earlier jar in the same fabric (GCF) is present at King's Road along with a sherd from the later, developed greyware type (Wood 1996, 52, nos 228 and 245 respectively). From the mid-/late 1st century AD the growing diversity and quantity of imported wares is more marked, suggesting that occupation at La Plaiderie was by then well-established. The supply of south Gaulish samian and terra nigra continued, amphorae continued to be imported (Dressel 20, Gauloise 4, Gauloise 5 and Dressel 28) and the first mortaria from northern Gaul appeared.

The earliest pottery of potentially local origin in the early Roman assemblage consists of just three vessels: a bowl, a reeded-rim jar and a cheese press (fabric AR). It is not even certain that these were local products, and all the other early Roman pottery found at La Plaiderie appears to have been imported. Excavation on the native site at the Tranquesous in St Saviour's parish produced a number of vessels including reeded-rim jars in a fabric (identical to fabric AR from La Plaiderie) which the excavator thought might be local, but was more probably imported (Burns 1978, 202, fabric type IV). The Tranquesous vessels appear to derive from the latest phase of activity on that site which is contemporary with the early Roman phase of activity at La Plaiderie. Pottery of 1st-century date which was indisputedly imported at the Tranquesous (mostly dating to the latter part of the century) included samian, terra nigras and greywares, demonstrating a clear link between these two sites.

A small amount of early Lezoux samian imported from central Gaul in the later 1st century AD was found at La Plaiderie. Other colour-coated fine wares from central Gaul began to appear from the later 1st century/early second century AD in the form of 'hairpin' beakers. These, like the 2nd- and early 3rd-century AD colour-coated drinking vessels from Gaul (fabrics CC and CGCC) and Germany (fabrics KOLN, RHT and RC) were presumably imported along with the samian of the period from these areas. Dating to around the same time as the 'hairpin' beakers are the two Dressel 20 amphorae mentioned above and the first import from Roman Britain (a stamp-decorated bowl from the potteries in the Little and Much Hadham region; fabric LEST). North Gaulish greywares (NGGW 1–2 series of fabrics) also started to appear on the site during the later 1st century AD; principally jars decorated with distinctive horizontal lustrous bands, although the majority of vessels from this source are later (see below).

The early Roman activity at the Bonded Store would appear to have continued on from the preceding late Iron Age activity. The imported wares of early Roman date testify to further significant activity on the site that was contemporary with that at La Plaiderie. Gallo-Belgic wares make up much of the fineware, with south Gaulish samian contributing only some 1% of the pottery. Greywares, *ceramique fumigée* and oxidised flagons make up much of the rest.

High Empire

During the High Empire period the differences between the Bonded Store and La Plaiderie assemblages are chiefly in the respective quantities of a given fabric.

The bulk of the samian at both sites is 2nd century AD in date and principally from Lezoux. Both sites (especially La Plaiderie) were also receiving samian from sources in east Gaul during the 2nd century AD, as well as a few vessels during the first half of the 3rd century AD. At the Bonded Store, central Gaulish samian makes up over 6% of the total assemblage of all periods (excluding amphorae), indicating how important the ware was.

From the later 1st century up to the early 3rd century AD, fine wares from central Gaul (Lezoux) predominate, including 'hairpin' beakers, samian and black colour-coated wares. East Gaulish samian of Antonine and early 3rd-century AD date, mainly from the Argonne and Rheinzabern, is present in remarkable quantities. Other colour-coated wares from the Argonne, Trier and Cologne are also present and were accompanied by coarsewares from Urmitz and the Rhineland/Tavernay mortaria.

A significant range of mainly 2nd- and 3rd-century AD semi-fine wares and coarsewares were imported from a number of production centres in the Nord/Pas-de-Calais/Somme Valley area of Gallia Belgica. These include *vases tronconiques*, pentice beakers, pinch-neck flagons and hooked-rim jars along with other greywares. The neighbouring area of the Seine Valley supplied both Gauloise 12 amphorae and a range of flagons including 'pulley-wheel' types.

Jars, pentice beakers and flagons were imported from northern Gaul in the 2nd and 3rd centuries (fabrics NGGW and NGWO). These later imports from north Gaul constitute around one quarter of the entire assemblage from La Plaiderie, and are associated with further wares of the period from the same general area of northern Gaul and Germany (samian, mortaria, plus fabrics NGGW 3–4, EIFL, MARB and see below). Various other greywares, coarse and semi-fine wares also appear to have been imported from the general area of northern Gaul from at least the late 1st century AD and throughout the remainder of the Roman period, although the quantities diminish significantly during the later 3rd and 4th centuries AD. Similarities between their fabrics and the NGGW series of fabrics, as well as the presence of types of distinctive form known to have been produced in this area, leave no room for doubt that the majority of kitchen/table wares (excluding samian) found on the site prior to the later Roman period came from sources in northern Gaul.

It is not possible to date vessels in some of these fabrics (e.g. CCB) more closely than 2nd to 4th century AD. Vessels in fabrics NGSG and MG certainly began to appear during the 1st century AD and continued to be imported up to the 3rd century, but the number of vessels concerned is no more than thirty or so in all. First- and 2nd-century vessels in these fabrics and certain varieties of the QT series of fabrics (particularly QTG) were also found at both the Tranquesous and King's Road sites. Prior to the detailed study of the La Plaiderie and Bonded Store assemblages it was considered that some greywares from King's Road could have been produced locally (Wood 1996, 54), but this now seems very unlikely as far greater quantities and a wider range of forms would be present on all the sites concerned; Gaul is the more likely source for most of the greywares.

The pottery from both La Plaiderie and the Bonded Store establishes the fact that there were some surprisingly strong links with the general area of northern Gaul. An interesting aspect of both assemblages is the lack of hard evidence for High Empire period pottery from sources in Brittany (Armorica) and western Normandy, in contrast to the late Iron Age and late Roman periods. While there are a number of unsourced Roman fabrics (GG, MR, FOXO, and QTW), some of which may originate from these areas, on present evidence only fabric GOW would seem to be a (western) Normandy product and even then the solitary small two-handled flask from La Plaiderie in this fabric is mid-/late 3rd century AD in date. Also, the Normandy amphorae (and flagons) are more characteristic of the area of Haute-Normandie around the Seine estuary, further to the east. Even if products of these areas are present among the unassigned fabrics (and Kay Hartley believes some unsourced mortaria may be Breton in origin), the number of vessels concerned is quite small.

Weak links with eastern Roman Britain are suggested at La Plaiderie by the presence of the solitary stamp-decorated bowl (fabric LEST) and at least three black-burnished ware 2 (fabric BB2) vessels; one of these is probably 2nd century AD in date while the rest are 3rd century. BB2 also occurs at the Bonded Store and in finds from the harbour, but is clearly unimportant compared to its prominence in eastern Britain in the 2nd and 3rd centuries. Pottery does not seem to be shipped in any great quantity from the Thames estuary sites (see Monaghan 1987) to Guernsey, indicating this material probably arrived on the back of other trade or the movement of people. Intriguingly, a significant amount of BB2 and 2nd-century Thames estuary products have in contrast been found in Alderney (Monaghan and de Jersey 2014–15).

In the 2nd century AD, black-burnished ware 1 (fabric BB1) from Dorset also began to be imported to the site. Initially, it appears only in very small numbers as the vast majority of vessels (83 out of a total of around 90) are later than AD 270 in date. BB1 appears to have been imported throughout the late 3rd and 4th century AD. The presence of these and other Romano-British wares is significant as they testify to a change in the character of the La Plaiderie assemblage that became more marked from around the later 3rd century AD and continued through to the end of the Roman period. This is also the case in the Bonded Store assemblage, and BB1 is prominent amongst the few sherds found in Alderney.

Both sites were receiving some mortaria during the later 1st century AD, but Kay Hartley dates the majority to the 2nd/mid-3rd century AD with sources of supply principally within the area of northern Gaul/Germany.

Late Roman (after AD 270)

While pottery from Gallo-Roman sources continued to be imported, both the quantities and number of sources concerned were far less than previously. Sources in Roman Britain were supplying much of the pottery imported to both sites during the late Roman period (or much of the pottery that can be confidently dated to after *c.* AD 270). Contemporary occupation on both sites, though still significant, may have been less substantial than it was during the High Empire.

Of all the Romano-British wares found at La Plaiderie, BB1 is by far the most common although there are fairly significant but lesser quantities of further Romano-British black-burnished type wares (fabric BBT series). Sherds from some 20 Alice Holt and New Forest greywares (fabric AH/NF) are present that together appear to span the 4th century AD. Late 3rd/4th-century AD colour-coated wares from both the New Forest and Oxfordshire potteries (fabrics NFCC and OXRC) are also represented by at least 12 vessels: beakers, cups and flagons in the main. A solitary sherd from a late Romano-British parchment ware bowl/dish decorated with brown paint is also present. The dating of a New Forest mortarium to probably the second half of the 4th century AD (Monaghan 1990, 68), dredged off the seabed to the north of the harbour, provides external evidence suggesting the continued importation of wares from southern England to Guernsey during the same period.

Imports from Gaul during the later Roman period derive from three areas. Most of the hooked-rim jars and bowls (fabric NGGW 3) from north Gaul, along with the greyware vessels (fabrics NGGW 1–2), are certainly mid- to late Roman in date, but some products could have continued to be imported during the late 3rd/4th century AD. Indeed, one further type from the same area in a distinctive range of forms (fabric NGLTN) belongs to the later occupation on La Plaiderie and suggests that other imports may have continued to come from northern Gaul. These strongly moulded jars and bowls with excised decoration mark a revival of the earlier terra nigra tradition. All told, these imports represent just a handful of vessels, far fewer than was previously imported from the same area during the High Empire period.

In the late Roman period, importation of pottery from western Gaul is more prominent. The 15 *céramique à l'éponge* (fabric EPON) bowls and (mostly) drinking cups found at La Plaiderie derive from an area where wine contained in barrels may also have been imported to Guernsey. The presence of *à l'éponge* bowls on the later 3rd-century Roman wreck recovered from the harbour mouth in St Peter Port (Rule and Monaghan 1993, 129) is significant. It establishes an early date for the importation of this ware, suggests a direct link with the town sites, and means that some of the pottery from them dates to the same period as the wreck. However, the later 4th-century AD date of other wares found at La Plaiderie, as well as the evidence from sites elsewhere both in Britain and in neighbouring Gaul, demonstrate that *céramique à l'éponge* continued to be imported throughout the 4th century AD (Wood 1994, 164).

Fine wares from the New Forest and Oxfordshire are present in roughly equal amounts to those from Gallia Belgica (fabric NGLTN) and western Gaul (fabric EPON) combined. Further fine wares from the Nene Valley (fabric NVCC) may be represented by sherds from a flagon/bottle.

La Plaiderie was also receiving some coarse pottery from the northern Cotentin region of western Normandy during the later Roman period. Although no production site has yet been located, it is believed that a local imitation of black-burnished ware was being made in the area due to the presence on a number of sites in the north of the region of certain forms in a characteristically local micaceous fabric (Blaszkiewicz 1992, 38). Six of the large cooking pots concerned (fabric WNMW) are present at La Plaiderie and presumably date within the same period as the Cotentin finds: from the second half of the 4th century to the early 5th century AD (Blaszkiewicz and Jigan 1994, 135).

An important coarseware (the TBF fabric series), representing around 10% of each of the La Plaiderie and Bonded Store assemblages, merits detailed comment at this point. On the basis of this ware at La Plaiderie, the possibility of significant local pottery production in Guernsey during the Roman period was suggested some years ago (Wood 1990, 53). Adding the caveat at the time that the Cherbourg region was also a possible source gave due consideration to a number of facts: finds of this ware principally occurred in these two areas, no production sites had been located, and given the similar geology of the island and neighbouring Normandy either area was possible as a source for the ware (*ibid*). Naturally, should it be proved that production did not occur in Guernsey, then by definition both the start date and amount of material that may otherwise have been imported from western Normandy assumes far greater significance. Conversely, should the ware indeed be a Guernsey product, it would be significant in both local terms and as a known export in the later Roman period. On present evidence, and in the continuing absence of a known production area, there are strong grounds for believing that the ware is a local Guernsey product.

The principal forms in this ware are tripod bowls, lids and jars which on the basis of fabric variations have been divided into three groups (fabrics TBF1, TBF1 GREY and TBF2). These divisions do not alter the fact that the fabrics are all broadly similar and indeed are indistinguishable from certain suspected local fabrics of late Iron Age date from sites elsewhere in Guernsey (cf. Burns *et al.* 1996, 48–9). Fabric TBF1 is by far the most common but all three fabrics, except for the range of forms involved, otherwise exhibit the same wide variations in colour, coarseness and inclusions of the more common fabrics of their potential local late Iron Age forebears.

Only the tripod bowl form is recorded as being found on sites in the Cotentin, as is also the case with the sparse finds from southern England (Wood 1994, 162); the full range of forms is only known at present on both town sites in Guernsey. All the finds outside Guernsey are late Roman in date (mid-/later 3rd to the end of the 4th century AD, *ibid*) but evidence from the town sites as well as two further sites in Guernsey suggests that production of the ware began during the mid-/late 2nd century AD. A foot sherd from a tripod bowl was found in 2000 at Route de Carteret near the west coast, associated with central Gaulish samian of Antonine date. Part of a lid and other pottery types of 2nd-century AD date are present at King's Road; this piece (Burns *et al.* 1996, 70, no. 244) is drawn as a base but is the handle part of a lid. There is no record in either the Cotentin or southern England of tripod bowls in this fabric being found on sites earlier than the late Roman period. Moreover, not only are examples of this ware found either in England or in the Cotentin limited to the tripod bowl form, all those finds are large-size examples of the form. The high percentage of this ware in the town assemblages, the variations in the size and profiles of the principal forms suggestive of chronological developments, and particularly the presence of the ware on Guernsey sites from the 2nd century AD onwards, point towards the ware being a local product with a period of production spanning some 200 years.

A reconsideration of the assemblage after the death of Mark Wood, when phasing became available, indicates that fabric TBF makes up a significant component of Phase 1 at the Bonded Store. This supports the assertion of an early start in Guernsey; indeed it may have been around in the 1st century AD, or even be the continuation of an Iron Age tradition. Sherds from lids of this fabric (if not over-washed) have traces of sooting on their interior surface, complementing the burning/burnt residue on the interior of the tripod bowl. This suggests the two vessels were used together, with the lid acting as a *couvre-feu*. Finds of tripod bowls outside Guernsey and Alderney (Wood 1990, 55) are not, to date, associated with either the lid or jar forms.

The Bonded Store has less late 3rd- and 4th-century AD imported pottery than La Plaiderie. BB1 is represented by around 25 vessels, one quarter of the amount found at La Plaiderie, while each of the remaining Romano-British wares are present in roughly half the amounts of those present at La Plaiderie. The Gallo-Roman imports are equally less-well represented, with five *céramique à l'éponge* drinking bowls and a flagon, around four vessels in NGLTN and two WNMW large cooking pots.

Late/post-Roman period

There is no apparent break in the occupation at La Plaiderie suggested by the pottery, but the date of the end of occupation is just as uncertain as the start of activity on the site. The same is true of the Bonded Store, but occupation seems to end earlier.

Two vessels from La Plaiderie illustrate the bottom end of the scale of the wide variation in coarseness of the potential local Guernsey fabrics. These vessels (fabric AQR) are either late Roman or sub-Roman in date and their fabric is akin to the local briquetage of late Iron Age/early Roman date found on sites in the Bailiwick (Burns *et al.* 1996, 120). Crude copies of a tripod bowl and a BB1 flanged bowl form are present in this 'briquetage type' fabric. The presence of these late or sub-Roman vessels is intriguing given the final amphora type (see below) found at La Plaiderie and the apparent presence of early medieval pottery as well. Their combined presence, along with the inability to date the majority of the late Roman pottery more closely than the period AD 270–400+, means that determining the end of occupation on the site is somewhat difficult to establish. Also, it is not possible to tell whether the scant early medieval material represents a continuation of occupation from the late Roman period or the nature of the activity it represents.

Together with the late Roman tripod bowls (fabric TBF1), the western Normandy cooking pots (fabric WNMW) represent the clearest dating evidence for occupation continuing on the site during the second half of the 4th century AD and with the latter, perhaps even into the early 5th century AD. The presence of at least two late Roman Palestinian amphorae only adds to the difficulty in determining the end of/a break in/continuation of occupation issue on the site during the late Roman period into the early medieval. Although usually dated 5th/6th century AD (Peacock and Williams 1986, 191), it is believed that this amphora type could have been imported into Britain from the late 4th century AD onwards (Holbrook and Bidwell 1991, 11). These Palestinian amphorae could therefore date anywhere from the late Roman period into the early medieval. Added to this, there is the handful of sherds of post-Roman coarsewares from the site that provide a tantalising glimpse of Guernsey during the 5th/6th century AD (Wood 1994, 163). These sherds (fabrics MG, PR? and a possible E Ware base), though scarce and of unknown significance, nevertheless represent a potential land-based counterpart to the Merovingian jugs of 6th-century AD date found on the seabed of the modern harbour (Monaghan 1988, 455). The La Plaiderie fabrics suggest that most derive from western Normandy, although the potential E Ware vessel is a product of western Gaul; the fact that the fabric of the latter is also similar to earlier Gallo-Roman (Petit-Niort) products from the same general region means that some doubt must remain as to its date in the absence of a more helpful diagnostic sherd. Whether or not this early medieval presence at La Plaiderie represents a continuation of occupation on the site from the late Roman period, it was certainly ephemeral compared with previous Roman occupation on the site.

It would appear that occupation at the Bonded Store continued into the late 4th/early 5th century AD, again best illustrated by the presence of the large-size tripod bowls in fabric TBF1, the WNMW vessels, and a possible sherd of a Kapitan II ('hollow foot') amphora. This type of amphora is not present at La Plaiderie, just as the late Roman Palestinian amphora type is not present in the Bonded Store assemblage. There are two roller-stamped greyware sherds (fabric MER?) from the Bonded Store that are possibly post-Roman in date but given their poor condition it has to be said that this is by no means certain. Evidence for early medieval activity at the Bonded Store is therefore slight.

La Plaiderie and the Bonded Store: comparisons

The pottery present in both assemblages provides clear evidence for domestic occupation on both sites (Table 5). This is evident from the outset at the Bonded Store, where the late Iron Age assemblage compares with that from King's Road, including prestigious imports of Italian wine alongside Armorican imports and local wares. The presence of briquetage 'furniture' suggests that salt-working took place on or near the site at the Bonded Store and the quantity of material present may indicate more than just provision for on-site consumption of salt. The late Iron Age local wares and briquetage signify that the site was initially a 'native' concern and it is tempting to suggest that Armorican Gauls themselves were involved in some way, given the imported wares present on the site from that area.

The purely 'Roman' nature, as opposed to a native undertaking, which has been suggested for the site at La Plaiderie would seem to be confirmed not only by the fine pottery present but also from an early date by the presence of high-status metal objects such as bronze mixing-bowls, one of which is Claudio-Neronian in date (cf. Frere *et al.* 1992, 308). Similarly, fine pottery is present at the Bonded Store from a very early date, as well as high-status glass vessels including some of Claudio-Neronian date. From the

Table 5 The Bonded Store and La Plaiderie: detailed breakdown of coarsewares.

	Bonded Store				*La Plaiderie*	
	sherds	%	*weight/g*	%	*sherds*	%
Iron Age or late Iron Age	264	5.6	3094	7.1	37	0.7
Gallo-Belgic *terra rubra*	43	0.9	160	0.4	–	–
Gallo-Belgic miscellaneous	–	–	–	–	9	0.2
Sandy *terra nigra*	156	3.3	973	2.2	56	1.0
Pompeian Red	5	0.1	41	0.1	–	–
Central Gaulish colour-coated	16	0.3	51	0.1	42	0.7
Rough Cast ware	13	0.3	30	0.1	20	0.4
Cologne colour-coated	8	0.2	33	0.1	8	0.1
Trier	11	0.2	37	0.1	50	0.9
New Forest	16	0.3	300	0.7	31	0.5
Oxford	5	0.1	15	0.0	10	0.2
Marbled ware	4	0.1	10	0.0	15	0.3
Nene Valley colour-coated	–	–	–	–	5	0.1
Early mica-dusted ware	32	0.7	181	0.4	9	0.2
Eggshell ware	2	0.0	3	0.0	–	–
Céramique à l'éponge	14	0.3	77	0.2	108	1.9
Miscellaneous colour-coated	28	0.6	124	0.3	40	0.7
Parchment ware	–	–	–	–	1	0.0
Céramique craquelée bleutée	–	–	–	–	35	0.6
Céramique fumigée	54	1.1	473	1.1	5	0.1
Grogged *céramique fumigée*	113	2.4	1358	3.1	114	2.0
Smooth *céramique fumigée*	33	0.7	150	0.3	85	1.5
Reduced smooth *céramique f.*	84	1.8	729	1.7	21	0.4
Misc. *céramique fumigée*	–	–	–	–	29	0.5
Durotrigan ware	6	0.1	80	0.2	–	–
BB1	105	2.2	935	2.1	604	10.7
BB2	5	0.1	26	0.1	11	0.2
BB2 type	38	0.8	300	0.7	107	1.9
North Gaulish greyware	685	14.6	4681	10.7	731	13.0
North Gaul late *terra nigra*	45	1.0	664	1.5	26	0.5
North Gaul sandy grey	111	2.4	1388	3.2	81	1.4
Tripod bowl fabric	558	11.9	10,768	24.7	523	9.3
Alice Holt/Farnham	15	0.3	182	0.4	13	0.2
Quartz-tempered	292	6.2	2997	6.9	175	3.1
Greywares	64	1.4	536	1.2	–	–
Grey scraps	100	2.1	196	0.4	–	–
Coarse quartz/granite greyware	68	1.4	1029	2.4	53	0.9
Eifelkeramik	3	0.1	34	0.1	19	0.3
Miscellaneous sandy	15	0.3	129	0.3	228	4.0
North Gaul oxidised	655	13.9	4272	9.8	1541	27.3
Oxidised, flagon-type fabric	659	14.0	5569	12.8	633	11.2
Sandy oxidised micaceous	17	0.4	99	0.2	1	0.0
Miscellaneous oxidised	257	5.5	500	1.1	–	–
Quartz-tempered white ware	15	0.3	154	0.4	50	0.9
White wares	52	1.1	282	0.6	–	–
West Normandy micaceous	31	0.7	830	1.9	82	1.5
Vesicular ware	9	0.2	89	0.2	1	0.0
	4706	***100***	***43,579***	***100***	***5609***	***100***

early Roman period onwards on both sites there are Spanish wine (Pascual 1) amphorae, then later wine amphorae from southern Gaul and Normandy, plus olive oil amphorae. These amphorae, or rather their contents, as well as the range of imported kitchen wares and fine table wares present throughout the Roman period, are indicative of a Romanised way of life of some standing. The Roman glass from both sites underlines this theme from the 1st century and into the 3rd/4th century AD.

Food preparation and consumption is also evident from an early date and throughout the Roman period. There are colanders from both sites, a cheese press from La Plaiderie, and a complete range of kitchen and table wares which bear signs of use; the trituration grits on some of the gritted samian and other mortaria have been worn away. All the Pompeian Red ware plates/dishes have traces of sooting on their external surface which is characteristic of use rather than a catastrophic fire, and the various greywares and late Roman BB1 cooking vessels continue that theme right through into the later Roman period. Sooting is also evident on the bases of some of the High Empire pinch-neck flagons (fabric NGWO) which suggests the heating of liquids. The large quantity of oxidised, off-white and 'white' sherds presumed to come from flagons is noticeable on both sites, and indeed is a common feature of sites included in the Gazetteer.

Stirring marks are present on samian vessels from the Bonded Store and a bowl (fabric GCF) from La Plaiderie. While the samian supply during the High Empire period was apparently sufficient for any broken vessels simply to have been replaced, life may not have been quite so simple either during the early Roman period or towards the end of the samian supply to the sites. A pre-Flavian form 27 from La Plaiderie and a late 2nd/1st half of the 3rd-century AD form 31 from the Bonded Store both have drill-holes which indicate the vessels were sufficiently prized for them to be mended with metal rivets.

The tripod bowls (fabric TBF series) are particularly interesting as a characteristic of these vessels is that they all have traces of burning/burnt residue on their interior surface (just as the lids are sooted on their interior surface). This is presumably the result of a cooking process where the tripod bowls could have served as portable stoves with lids acting as a *couvre-feu*. They may also have functioned as a light source in view of the absence of any evidence for lamps (cf. Wood 1993b).

The pottery from both sites also indicates other activities. In addition to late Iron Age and early Roman salt-working, there is evidence in the Bonded Store assemblage for other Roman period activity in the form of fragments of ceramic with a vitrified surface and evidence of smelting. 'Metal-working' appears to have occurred at La Plaiderie given the 3rd-century AD coin-counterfeiting moulds (Burns 1986, 96). Spindle whorls, fashioned from Pascual 1 amphorae and coarseware sherds (particularly fabric TBF1) are fairly numerous at the Bonded Store, although a fragment of a ground-down sherd from a drinking cup (fabric EPON) from La Plaiderie could either be a spindle whorl or a gaming piece. Further gaming counters ground down from a variety of wares are present on both sites.

Fragments of 2nd-century AD ceramic figurines from central Gaul are present including one statuette of Venus on each site showing the popularity of this cult. There is also one 'dea nutrix' figurine from the Bonded Store. While enough of this statuette survives to be able to type the piece (due to the basketry impression of the chair the matron sat in), there is insufficient remaining to know whether one or two infants were being suckled. A further figurine, this time of a household god (*lares*) was found at Fort Le Marchant in the north of the island (Burns 1987, 36, no. 43). This site has also produced 2nd/3rd-century AD samian and most notably north Gaulish greywares.

Only one piece of evidence survives for burial practice in the form of a cremation urn (fabric TBF1) at La Plaiderie of late 3rd-century AD date (cf. Burns 1987, 34, no. 22). It was the general Roman practice to bury adult dead away from habited areas, which raises the question of where the limits of Roman St Peter Port were at that date. Guernsey's Roman burial-grounds are yet to be located.

Other religious connotations are suggested by a *post-cocturam* graffito on a mid-3rd-century AD mortarium from La Plaiderie (*ibid*, 34, no. 25). Further examples of graffiti on pottery are present at the Bonded Store, including simple marks on a samian sherd as well as the remains of lettering on coarseware vessels that could represent names (p. 90).

The presence of a wide variety of fine imported Roman wares, Roman glass and metal vessels as well as commodities contained in amphorae suggest that the town sites were of some standing. It should be remembered, however, that the availability and variety of such material could be due more to the fortuitous location of the island than the sophistication of its citizens. St Peter Port could receive whatever was being transported along the Atlantic and Channel maritime routes, when cargo ships took advantage of Guernsey as a convenient stopping-off place (Monaghan 1990). Some rare items, like the LEST fabric bowl or the late Romano-British parchment ware vessels, were more likely to have been brought by their owners as personal possessions than via bulk trade. One can imagine these being swapped by sailors or travellers for goods or services in ancient St Peter Port. Additional considerations, such as state-controlled supply (whether or not directly in the hands of the military or their agents) set against shipping undertaken by civilian merchants would also have had a bearing (Wood 1990, 58).

With the exception of the late Iron Age local wares and (arguably) the TBF fabric series, all the other wares were imported by sea. This knowledge simplifies our assessment of the meaning of these wares (see Monaghan 1990, 63).

Assuming that the TBF fabric series is indeed a local product and not a further import, the remaining 90% of each assemblage by sherd count was imported: 82% and 85% by weight for the Bonded Store and La Plaiderie respectively. Should it be proven that the TBF fabric series was also imported, then both Roman assemblages would essentially consist of entirely imported material. It is clear from the range in date of all the imported pottery found on the town sites that visiting ships were using the ancient anchorage of St Peter Port not merely as a safe haven in times of dire need, but on a 'regular', purposeful basis from the late Iron Age onwards, throughout the Roman period. The number of suspected shipwreck sites in the approach to the port supports this.

It was suggested by the excavator of La Plaiderie that the site was a 'large trading establishment', a 'way station' (Burns 1986, 96). Analysis of the Roman pottery assemblage suggests that the activity on the site did not seem to have involved major 'warehousing' of large quantities of vessels for later sale, exchange or redistribution. Other, as yet undiscovered, sites in St Peter Port could, however, have fulfilled that function and the port as a whole certainly appeared to fulfil the role of a way station (Monaghan 1990, 68). Samian vessels that usually occur in sets are present at the Bonded Store, but Brenda Dickinson has commented that there is no way of knowing if they were bought in sets. The quantities of wares present at any given time during the centuries the sites were occupied would not seem to suggest anything other than the requirements of domestic occupation. Warehousing of items other than pottery cannot, however, be ruled out.

Overall, a familiar picture emerges of St Peter Port as an entrepôt. The town fulfilled this role during medieval and post-medieval times, and its general character can, without any difficulty, be projected back to the Roman period and into the late Iron Age. The more recent role of the Bonded Store to store alcohol in transit offers an interesting link with its ancient origins.

Amphorae

Amphorae were being traded for what they contained, rather than in their own right. They therefore illustrate Guernsey's trading networks much more directly than coarse and fine pottery, which could have arrived by more indirect routes.

At La Plaiderie, 20% of the amphorae assemblage consisted of a number of identifiable types of amphorae and unassigned sherds of early date (Table 6). While it is not possible to ascribe some of these sherds to a particular type with certainty, there are clearly Spanish, Gallo-Roman and (more significantly) Italian and other fabrics among them; the Italian sherds are mostly rounded and water-worn, suggesting they may have come up from the beach. There are nine body sherds in Italian fabrics, differences in which suggest that there are four different amphorae present that are best described as Dressel 1 species (as their poor condition prevents further distinction being made). Fortunately, there is also a diagnostic basal spike (and a body sherd in the same fabric) from a fifth amphora; the thickness of this spike suggests it is from a Dressel 1B amphora (as opposed to the earlier Dressel 1A type). These two sherds represent the earliest amphora from La Plaiderie that can be ascribed to a particular type with some certainty and date to the period 75–10 BC.

Table 6 La Plaiderie: summary of amphorae.

	Sherds	*% sherds*
Gallic, PW27, PW55 plus PW30, 31	246	58
Italian, PW2, 3, 4, 6	17	4
Spanish PW25 (Dressel 20)	71	16.7
Other Spanish, PW 6B, 15	43	10.1
Tunisian PW34	1	<1
Algerian? PW38	1	<1
Palestinian PW46	11	2.3
Unidentified and miscellaneous	34	8
Total	424	100
amphora/100 coarseware sherds = 7.5		

PW = Peacock and Williams (1986) types.

Some 50% of the amphora assemblage from the Bonded Store is late Iron Age or early Roman in date (Table 7). With the late Iron Age amphorae, diagnostic sherds (i.e. rims *etc*) are just as scarce as at La Plaiderie, but some body sherds are in better condition and the thickness of these can be taken as a reasonable indicator of the presence of a particular form type. Fifty-three sherds in Italian fabrics are present, representing around 14 Dressel 1 species amphorae on the basis of differences in the fabrics present and a few diagnostic sherds. Just over half of these would appear to belong to the earlier Dressel 1A type, with the remainder being the later Dressel 1B. It is clear from the presence of these amphorae types and other associated imported wares, as well as local copies of the latter, that significant activity occurred on the site from around 120 BC (as is indicated by the earliest date for the Dressel 1A type) and continued down to around 10 BC (on the basis of the latest date for the Dressel 1B type).

The remaining 80% of the amphorae from La Plaiderie date from the later 1st through to the mid-/late 3rd century AD. Gauloise 12 amphorae (PW55) produced in eastern Normandy are the most numerous (41%), followed by Spanish Dressel 20 (23%) and Gallo-Roman Gauloise 4 (PW27: 17%). These same amphorae types are also present at the Bonded Store where together they constitute around 50% of the identifiable amphorae from the site. Here, Dressel 20 sherds are more numerous (22%), with Gauloise types 4 and 12 being present in roughly equal but lesser quantities (15% each). Dressel 20 is the classic Spanish

Table 7 The Bonded Store: summary of amphorae.

	Sherds	*% sherds*	*Weight (g)*	*% weight*
'Carrot' type PW 12 (Cam. 189)	4	1	38	>1
Gallic (PW27 and PW55)	124	33.5	3109	19.1
Italian PW3/4 (Dressel 1A/1B)	32	8.6	2209	13.5
Other Italian, PW3 and PW10	33	8.6	1073	6.5
Spanish PW15 (Haltern 70)	17	4.5	658	4.0
Spanish PW16	8	2.1	358	2.2
Spanish PW25 (Dressel 20)	73	19.6	6285	38.6
Spanish PW6A and 6B (Dressel 1)	56	15	1940	11.9
Other Spanish (PW10, 19, 24?)	4	1	208	1.2
Aegean 'Kapitan II'? (PW47)	1	>1	12	>1
Unidentified and miscellaneous	19	5.3	372	2.4
Total	371	100	16,262	100

PW = Peacock and Williams (1986) types. Many sherds are burned or water-rolled. All uncertain identifications have been included with the type they are rated as 'probably' belonging to.

olive oil amphora of the period, whilst the two Gauloise types suggest the importation of wine.

Gauloise 12 amphorae are commonly dated to the mid-2nd/3rd century AD. In view of the highly residual nature of the site assemblages and the broad date-span of production of Gauloise 4 and Dressel 20, many of these amphorae types found could date anywhere between the 1st and the mid-/late 3rd century AD. Moreover, more precise dating of certain amphorae types is also restricted by the fact that the vast majority from both sites are represented by featureless body sherds. However, two rim sherds of Dressel 20 from La Plaiderie are from two different vessels, one dating to the late 1st to early 2nd century AD and the other to the later 1st to the mid-2nd century AD. A Dressel 20 rim from the Bonded Store would appear to be 3rd century AD in date.

Eleven sherds from two Palestinian amphorae from La Plaiderie, and the Kapitan II amphora from the Bonded Store are the only late Roman types present.

Mortaria

Mortaria are numerically unimportant at both land sites, with the best examples being found on the seabed and possibly therefore just being carried past the island. Kay Hartley has produced an archive report on 31 vessels – almost all of those found in Guernsey to date. The emphasis is on north Gaul, especially Taverney (Val-d'Oise) and Noyon (Oise). Taverney was the probable source of a number of vessels of form G255 and G272, whilst Noyon is the probable source of mortaria of forms G238 and G255. Some are of forms (if not always the fabric) made in the Rhineland. A number were unidentified and several are suspected to be from sources in Brittany. Marine finds include mortaria possibly originating in East Anglia, Essex and the New Forest (Hartley 1990, 66; 1993, 85).

Quantification and phasing

An analysis of the pottery assigned to the site phasing demonstrates the high level of residuality in the Bonded Store assemblage (Table 8). Even Roman Phase 1 contains 2nd-century material. An element of seriation can, however, be demonstrated by the tail-off of residual Iron Age material and Gallo-Belgic wares in Phases 2 and 3, and *céramique a l'éponge* appearing by Phase 3. A striking feature is the high preponderance of oxidised fabrics in all periods. Much undoubtedly originates in north Gaul, but oxidised fabrics are clearly more important than the miscellaneous greywares. The tripod bowl fabric is there from Phase 1 and although it increases in importance, the quantity in Phase 1 supports the idea of an early start. While not significant numerically, the supply of BB1 can, however, be seen to increase in the later phases. North Gaulish greyware peaks in Phase 2, reinforcing the evidence that it is Guernsey's signature imported coarseware during the High Empire period.

Conclusions

The Roman pottery from the Bonded Store and La Plaiderie has provided the opportunity to place all the known sites and finds in the island within a broader framework of Guernsey during the Roman period. The inescapable conclusion is that Guernsey was a significant port-of-call within the system that moved goods and people along the maritime routes of the Atlantic seaboard as well as along the length of the Channel.

The evidence also points to significant shifts in the trade routes. In the late Iron Age and early Roman period, the predominance of pottery from western Gaul – Armorica and Aquitaine – indicates that Guernsey is on the known trade route which heads up the Atlantic coast of Gaul, then across the Channel to landing points in south-west England such as Hengistbury Head in Dorset. After the invasion of Britain, the trade routes seem to shift to along the Channel. We see more pottery from north Gaul, Gallia Belgica, central and eastern Gaul plus the Rhineland reaching Guernsey during the High Empire. This is also when Guernsey receives the Gaulois amphorae from Normandy and has an imported

Table 8 The Bonded Store: key Roman pottery phasing.

Fabric group	*Sherd count by phase*				*% sherds by phase*			
	1	*2*	*3*	*all*	*1*	*2*	*3*	*all*
Oxidised wares	149	453	268	1588	27.7	34.6	34.1	33.7
North Gaulish greywares	84	237	128	841	15.6	18.1	16.3	17.9
Other greywares	65	138	118	544	12.1	10.5	15.0	11.6
Iron Age or late Iron Age	59	88	10	264	11.0	6.7	1.3	5.6
Gallo-Belgic wares	54	60	18	204	10.1	4.6	2.3	4.3
Céramique fumigée	48	105	39	284	8.9	8.0	5.0	6.0
Tripod bowl fabric	48	127	120	558	8.9	9.7	15.3	11.9
Finewares (except samian)	11	44	24	149	2.0	3.4	3.1	3.2
BB1	7	24	25	105	1.3	1.8	3.2	2.2
Durotrigan ware	5	1	–	6	0.9	0.1	0.0	0.1
White wares	3	17	9	67	0.6	1.3	1.1	1.4
BB2 type	2	6	21	38	0.4	0.5	2.7	0.8
BB2	1	1	–	5	0.2	0.1	0.0	0.1
Eifelkeramik	–	–	–	3	0.0	0.0	0.0	0.1
Others	1	10	5	40	0.2	0.8	0.6	0.8
Total	537	1311	785	4706				100

The 'all' figure for Iron Age or late Iron Age includes post-Roman and unstratified; 26 sherds were found in the Iron Age phase.

pottery suite similar to London. In the later Roman period, after the mid-3rd century, there seems to be a reversion to cross-Channel trade and for the first time there is a significant amount of Romano-British pottery in Guernsey. This may indicate that the eastern Channel became unsafe in the light of incursions by 'pirates' or 'barbarians'.

The imported pottery found in Guernsey and the connections suggested by the sources of origin should serve as a reminder not to underestimate either the frequency or the extent of the shipping involved. What occurred on Roman Guernsey is of direct significance to the broad scope of Roman studies, particularly regarding trading routes.

Catalogue of illustrated coarse pottery

by Mark Wood and Jason Monaghan

The coarse pottery catalogue has been compiled from an initial selection of pots for drawing by Mark Wood, including his fabric codes and identifications. Dating and descriptive information has been supplemented by Jason Monaghan. Vessels are listed by Area and trench, with the earliest contexts first and residual vessels at the end. The generic form description is followed by the colour, fabric description or code, then origin and dating information. The context number or find spot is given at the end. As this is the first substantial body of Roman pottery to be published from Guernsey we have illustrated a number of vessels which would not otherwise be drawn, either due to being fragmentary or of very familiar form (Figs 60–64). Dating information is provided entirely from external parallels.

The Bonded Store

AREA A, RESIDUAL (FIG. 60.1–3)

1. Stamped sherd, light grey MER, possibly Merovingian, 5th–6th century AD (A1203)
2. Pulley-wheel flagon, oxidised F55 (A2007)
3. Tripod bowl, grey WNMW, possibly Normandy, 3rd or 4th century AD (A2007)

AREA B, TRENCH 2 (FIG. 60.4–6)

4. Jar, dark grey surface on light grey core, NGGW2, 2nd or 3rd century AD (B2061)
5. *Vase tronconique*, lustrous grey exterior on light grey core with burnished lines, NGGW1, Picardy, 2nd or 3rd century AD (B2054)
6. Flagon, oxidised FOX (B1204)

AREA B, RESIDUAL (FIG. 60.7)

7. Jar, coarse grey QTG (B1032)

AREA C, TRENCH 1 (FIG. 60.8–16)

8. Jar with lid-seated rim, oxidised, mica-coated MDER, LIA/1st century AD (C1083)

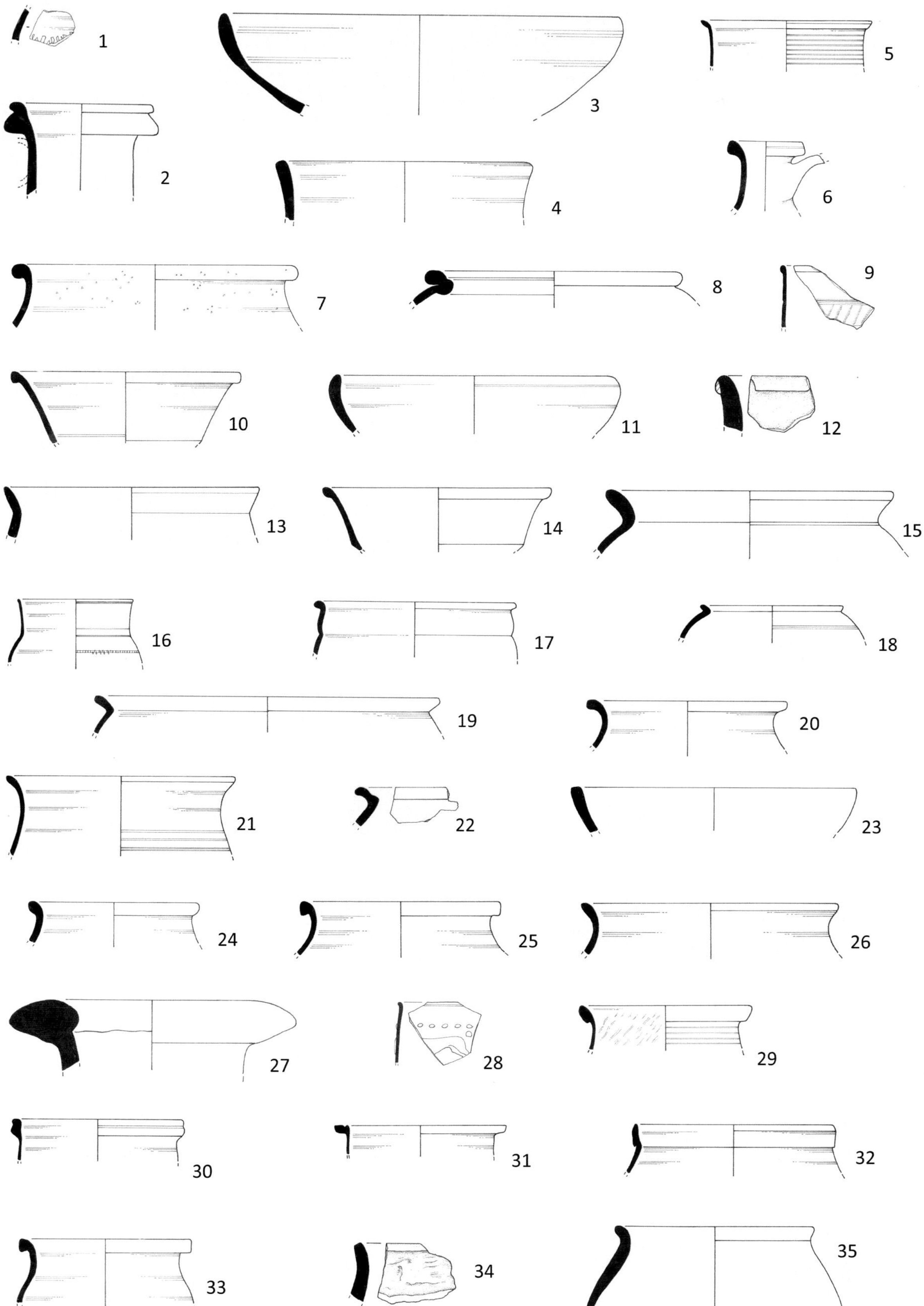

Figure 60 Coarsewares from the Bonded Store, areas A, B and C (trenches 1 and 2). Scale 1:4.

9. Bowl with stamp decoration, light grey sandwiched fabric, *céramique fumigée* SCFR (C1005)
10. Bowl, burnished light grey, *céramique fumigée* SCFR (C1005)
11. Dish, burnished grey on light grey core, NGGW2 (C1005)
12. Bead-rim jar, grey with brownish core, AQR (C1070)
13. Jar, light grey burnished QTG (C1006)
14. Bowl, light grey STN, probably 1st century AD (C1006)
15. Jar, grey with oxidised core QT/GCF (C1006)
16. Beaker, lustrous black-brown on sandwiched fabric, Rhenish (Trier), late 2nd to mid-3rd century AD (C1070)

AREA C, TRENCH 2 (FIG. 60.17–35)

17. Jar or bowl, light grey with near-white core, NGGW1/CF (C2094)
18. Small jar with subtle lid seating, oxidised, mica-coated MDER, 1st century BC to mid-1st century AD (C2080)
19. Jar, dark grey with light grey core, NGGW2 (C2097)
20. Jar, light grey NGGW2/QTW (C2097)
21. Bowl, dark grey surface on light grey fine *céramique fumigée* SCFR (C2097)
22. Bowl, grey fabric QT (C2094)
23. Bowl/dish, dark grey-black and burnished QT (C2094)
24. Jar, grey QT (C2094)
25. Jar, light grey with off-white core, coarse fabric QTG (C2094)
26. Jar, grey with mica at surface, NGGW or Alice Holt/New Forest (C2094)
27. Amphora rim, Spanish form Dressel 20, PW25, 2nd to mid-3rd century AD (C2094)
28. Beaker, 70–80mm rim diameter, hunt-cup design showing hindquarters of an animal, probably a deer; brown slip on white fabric, Cologne AD 120–200 (C2094)
29. Jar, lustrous grey with lighter core and burnished lines, burned and partly discoloured, NGGW (C2094)
30. Jar with bifid rim, light grey but sooted, NGGW3 (C2094)
31. Small bowl with flanged rim, grey NGGW (C2094)
32. Jar with lid-seated rim, grey NGGW3 (C2094)
33. Jar, light grey NGGW2 (C2094)
34. Jar, grey with grey-brown interior, handmade AQG/R (C2094)
35. Jar, grey TBF1 (C2094)

AREA C, TRENCH 3 (FIG. 61.36–46)

36. Cordoned jar, dark grey *céramique fumigée* SCFR, late 1st century BC to 1st century AD (C3034)
37. Jar, dark grey slip on exterior with burnished bands on lighter core, NGGW2/CF (C3030)
38. Jar or bowl, grey with light grey core, NGGW2 (C3030)
39. Small jar, diameter uncertain, dark grey with high silver mica in fabric and surface, possibly AQR (C3030)
40. Jar or bowl rim, light grey with lighter core, NGGW2 (C3021)
41. Jar, grey handmade TBF1, 1st century BC to 1st century AD (C3022)
42. Amphora PW25, Dressel 20, 2nd to mid-3rd century AD (C3036)
43. Bowl or jar, grey with light grey core, NGGW/CF, similar in form to no. 60 (C3023)
44. Small bowl, light grey with off-white core, NGGW1 (C3030)
45. Small bowl, grey lustrous surface on light grey core, NGGW1 (C3026)
46. Bowl with roulette decoration, grey, late TN/NGGW, later 1st century AD (C3033)

AREA C, TRENCH 4 (FIG. 61.47–49)

47. Dish, grey GCF/STNR (C4022)
48. Jar, dark grey with oxidised core, STNR (C4042)
49. Jar, grey with grey-white core, NGGW1 (C4015)

AREA C, RESIDUAL (FIG. 61.50–64)

50. Jar, dark grey burnished surface with light grey core, NGGW1 (C4014)
51. Flanged bowl, grey BB1, form Gillam 231 or similar, late 4th century AD (C4013)
52. Jar, burnt and discoloured grey on exterior else oxidised with golden mica; mica-coated MDER, late 1st century BC to early 1st century AD (C1004)
53. Jar of 'cooking pot' type, grey BB2 type BBTA, form Gillam 143 or 144, later 2nd to 3rd century AD (C2004)
54. Jar, dark grey handmade, LIA, probably 1st century BC to 1st century AD (C2071)
55. Wide-mouthed flagon or jug, rim approx. 120mm diameter, cream NGWO (C4014)
56. Jar or bowl with bifid rim, grey Alice Holt/New Forest (C2080)
57. Bowl, dark grey with light grey core, STN, 1st to early 2nd century AD (C1003)
58. Dish, dark grey with brown-grey core and burnished lines, TBF1 (C1004)
59. Flagon rim, oxidised, FOX (C3017)
60. Bowl/jar, grey with oxidised core (similar to no. 43), NGGW/CF (CT2/L3)
61. Bowl or jar, grey NGGW3 (C4013)
62. Body sherd, soft orange-painted decoration on cream fabric, probably New Forest (coarse) Parchment Ware, mid-3rd to mid-4th century AD (C3017)
63. Dish or bowl, light grey NGGW1/4 (C3017)

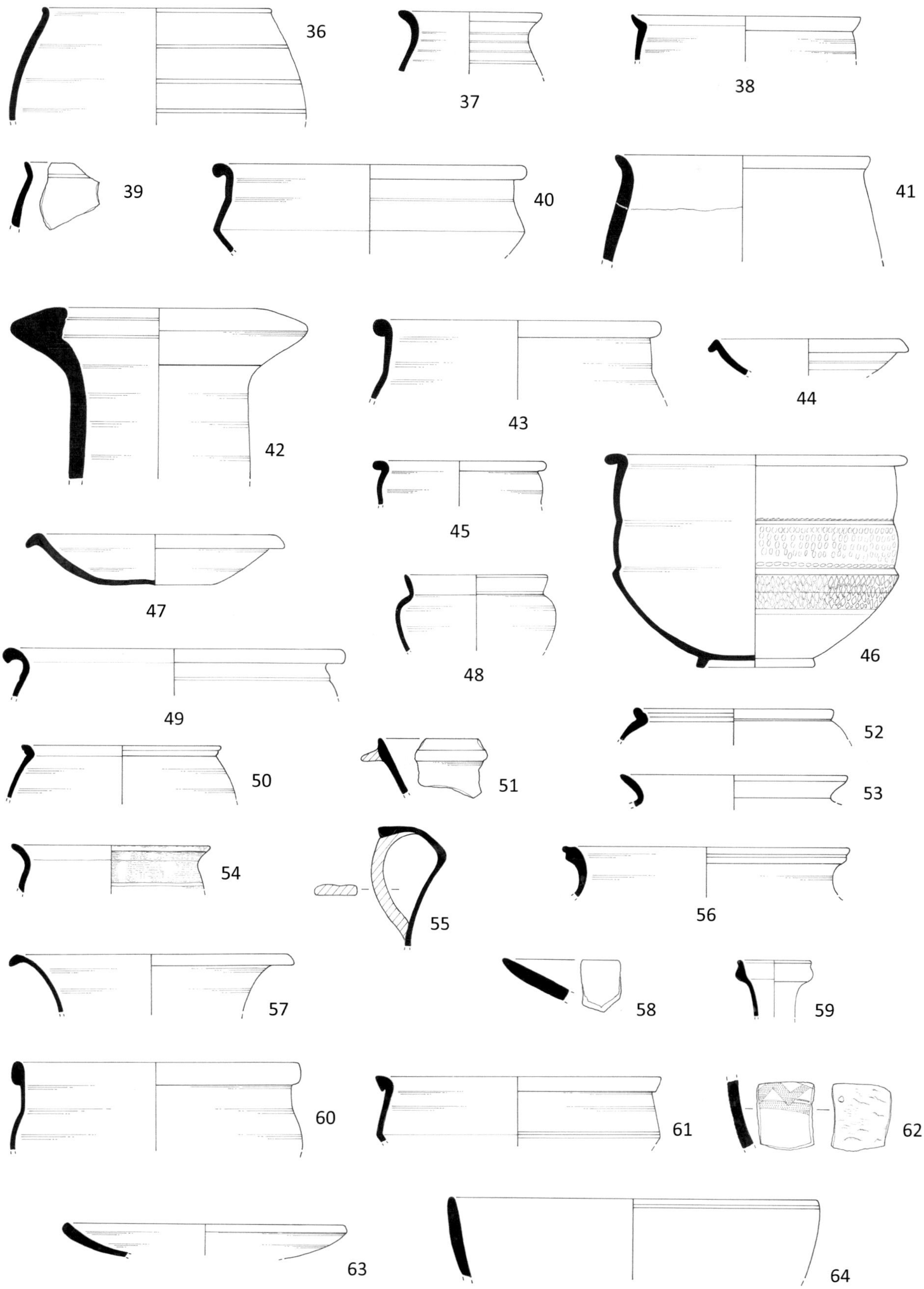

Figure 61 Coarsewares from the Bonded Store, area C (trenches 3, 4 and residual). Scale 1:4.

64. Dish, grey eroded BB1, form Gillam 234, 2nd century AD (C1003)

AREA D, TRENCH 1 (FIG. 62.65)

65. Bead-rim dish, black handmade Durotrigian BB1, 1st century BC to 1st century AD (D1007)

AREA D, TRENCH 2 (FIG. 62.66–69)

66. Jar, grey with sandwiched core, *céramique fumigée* SCFR, Santrot form 221, late 1st century BC to early 1st century AD (D2013)
67. Bead-rim bowl or dish, black handmade Durotrigian BB1, 1st century BC to 1st century AD. Small percentage of rim remaining so wall angle is approximate (D2013)
68. Jar rim and base, abraded dark grey exterior on light grey body, STN, possibly 1st century AD (D2010)
69. Jar, dark grey but surfaces abraded, possibly Durotrigan BB1, 1st century BC to 1st century AD (D2010)

AREA D, TRENCH 3 (FIG. 62.70–71)

70. Bowl, light grey, burnt and discoloured, *céramique fumigée* SCFO, Aquitaine, Menez form 126a, 20 BC – AD 40 (D3007)
71. Jar, light grey SCFR, 1st century BC to 1st century AD (D3006)

AREA D, RESIDUAL (FIG. 62.72–75)

72. Mortarium, cream fabric with flint and quartz grit, Rhineland-Taverney, MORHT, Gillam 255, 2nd century AD (D4103)
73. Jar neck, grey, possibly NGGW (D4103)
74. Dish or bowl, grey coarse QTG (D4007)
75. Small jar, grey with prominent mica, MG (D2009)

La Plaiderie

TRENCH 1 (FIG. 62.76–100)

76. Lid-seated jar, cream EIFL, probably Urmitz, Alzei form 27 (Tyers 174, no. 2), 3rd to 5th century AD (T1/L1)
77. Jar base, pinkish cream NGWO (T1/F29, F20/12, T1/2/Ext)
78. Bowl, grey-brown over oxidised fabric AQR/TBF1 (T1/L2)
79. Jar, dark grey burnished finish on grey NGLTN (T1/L2)
80. Mortarium or bowl, grey surface on coarse cream fabric QTW, appearing to be abraded on interior (T1/L2)
81. Jar, grey with light grey-brown core, STN (T1/L2)
82. Bowl, dark grey with oxidised sandwiched fabric, NGGW3 (T1/L2)
83. Jar, grey-brown with mica at surface, WNMW, 4th to early 5th century AD (T1/L2, T1/F47A)
84. Large jar or bowl rim (T1/L2)
85. Colander or strainer base, grey with grey-brown core (T1/L2)
86. Jar with reeded rim, grey wheel-made harsh fabric AR (T1/L2)
87. Small bowl, light grey metallic slip on grey fabric, NFGW (T1/L2)
88. Leg from tripod bowl, grey fabric with dribbles of white paint, identified as NFGW but would be a curious form from this source, probably 4th century AD (T1/L2)
89. Jar, grey NGGW3 (T1/B2/L3, T1/L3)
90. Jar, grey with grey-white core, possibly *céramique craquelée-bleutée* CCB (T1/L3)
91. Tripod bowl base, handmade, grey discoloured brown in parts, TBF1 (T1/L3)
92. Bowl, with uneven rim, grey NGGW (T1/L3)
93. Lid-seated jar, cream EIFL, possibly Paris Basin, Alzei form 27 (Tyers 174, no. 2), 3rd to 5th century AD (T1/F8)
94. Mortarium base, cream with quartz grits, probably Gallic MORTG (T1/F44)
95. Base with footring from bowl, unusual for this fabric, cream EIFL, 3rd to 5th century AD (T1/F48)
96. Jar or flagon base, cream NGWO (T1/F73)
97. Mortarium, cream, *post-cocturam* graffito DIV I. S and traces of burning, Rhineland-Taverny MORHT, 2nd or 3rd century AD (T1/F69)
98. Two-handled flagon, coarse cream fabric looking like a Roman version of medieval Normandy Gritty ware, GOW (T1/F69)
99. Jar, light grey NGGW (T1/F108)
100. Dish, oxidised micaceous PRW with sooted rim and no slip remaining, 1st century AD (T1/F85)

TRENCH 2 (FIG. 63.101–104)

101. Pulley-wheel flagon, oxidised with remains of white slip, FOXO/F55, probably 2nd or 3rd century AD (T2/L1)
102. Dish, brown surface on grey core, knife-trimmed profile, BBTB, 2nd to 4th century AD (T2/L4)
103. Jar of cooking-pot form, abraded grey-brown coarse fabric BBTB in the BB2 tradition, later 2nd to 3rd century AD (T2/L4)
104. Jar serving for cremation burial, handmade grey fabric sooted on neck and discoloured grey-white on one side, possibly local. Neck forming is quite uneven and there are indications of knife-trimming on lower body (T2/F124)

Other Roman sites (Figs 63.105–121, 64.122–129)

The finds from the St Peter Port harbour seabed have some abrasion, discolouration and marine growths on the surface.

105. Bowl, dark grey with grey core becoming light on interior margin, NGGW (St Peter Port harbour, Gazetteer C7)

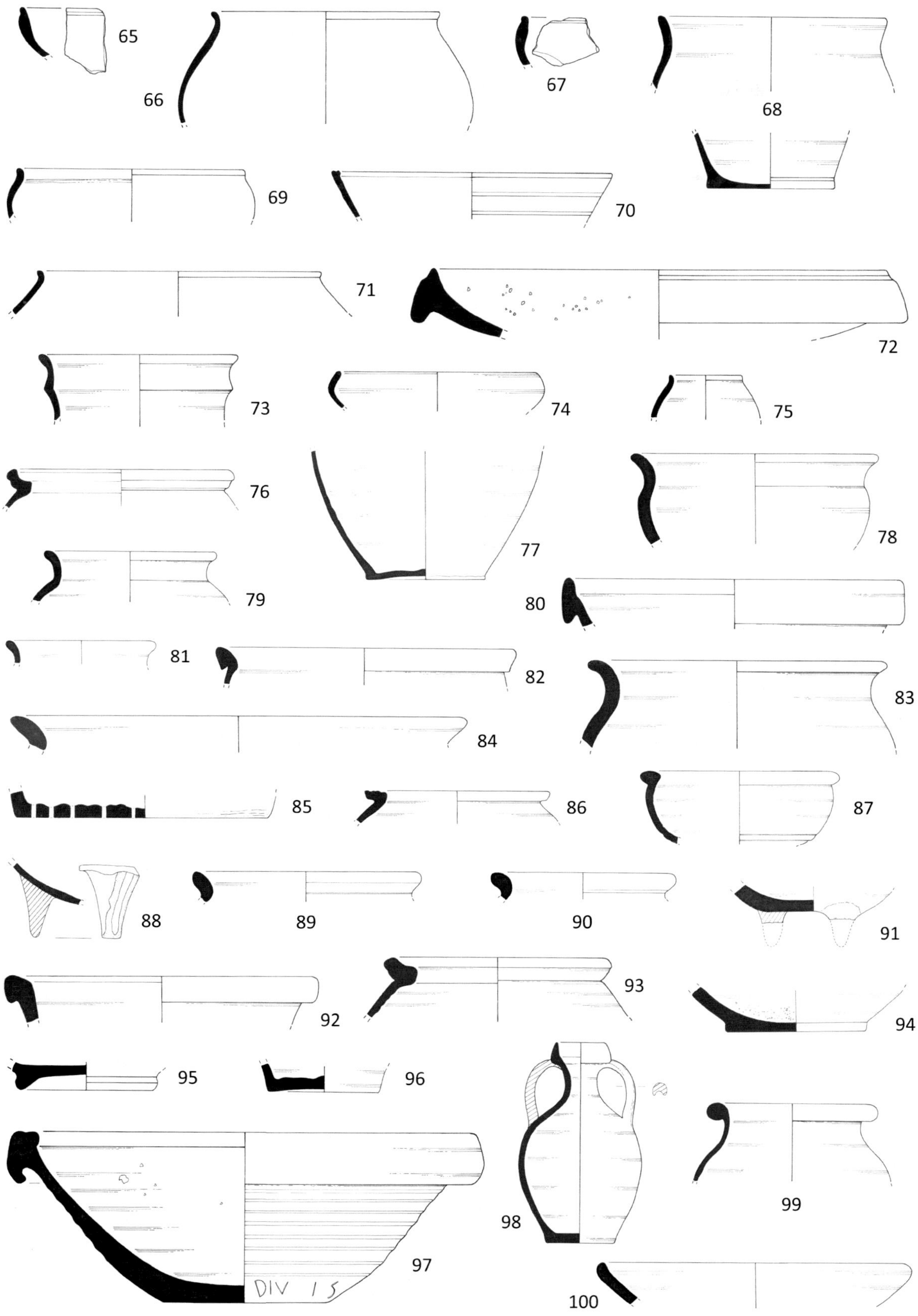

Figure 62 Coarsewares from the Bonded Store (area D) and La Plaiderie (trench 1). Scale 1:4.

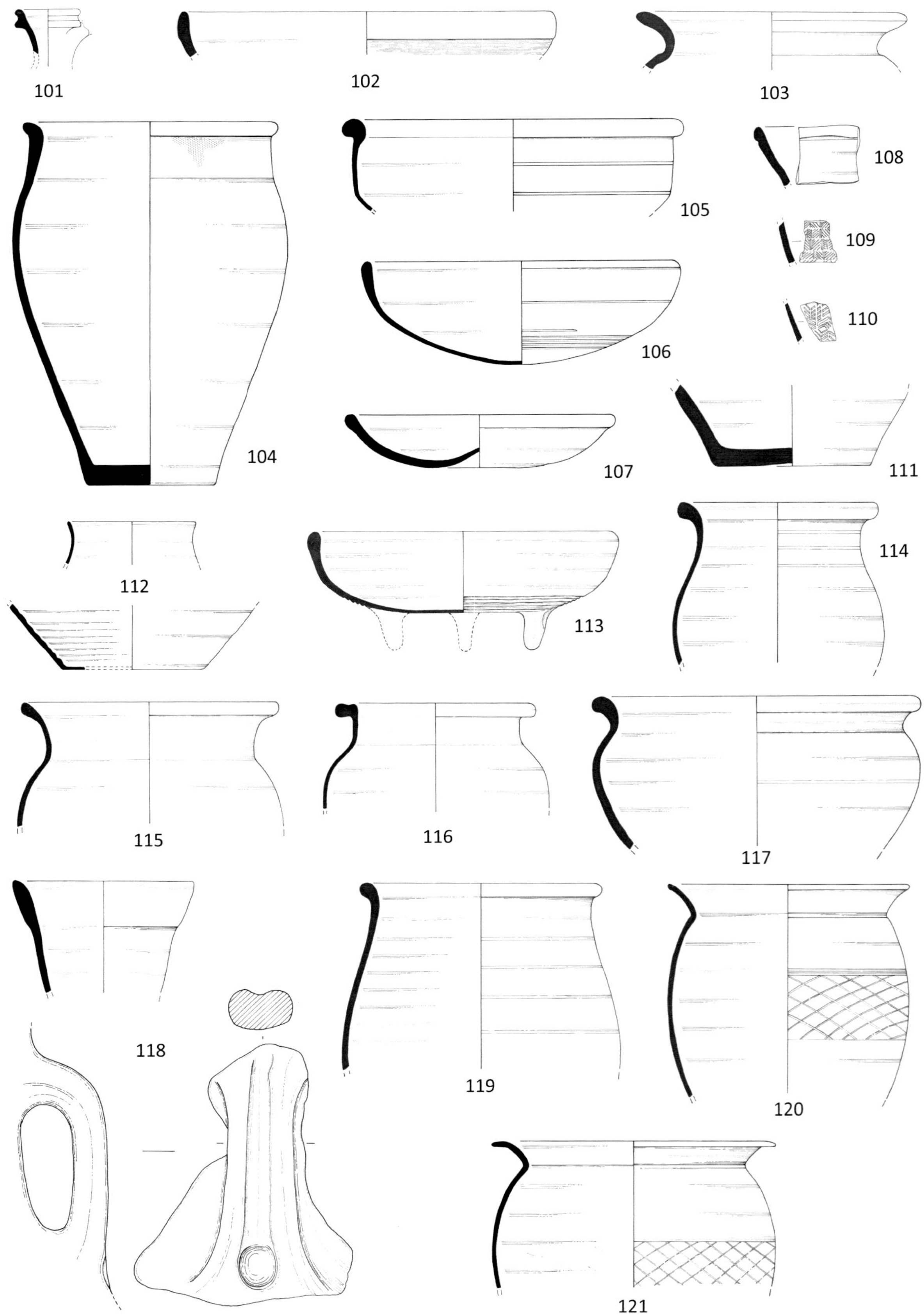

Figure 63 Coarsewares from La Plaiderie (trench 2) and other Roman sites. Scale 1:4.

106. Dish, dark grey surface discoloured white in places, white core, Gallo-Belgic TN, 1st century AD (St Peter Port harbour, Gazetteer C7)
107. Dish, grey to black with white core, Gallo-Belgic TN, 1st century AD (St Peter Port harbour, Gazetteer C7)
108. Dish, discoloured cream-grey surface with sandwiched section, BB2-type BBTA 'dog dish', mid-2nd to mid-3rd century AD (St Peter Port harbour, Gazetteer C7)
109. Body sherd from jar or bowl, discoloured a greenish-grey with grey slightly sandy fabric. Stamping resembles that of Argonne Ware in the 4th century AD (Cow Bay, Gazetteer B21)
110. Body sherd from jar or bowl, cream surface over off-white sandy fabric. Stamping resembles that of Argonne Ware in the 4th century AD (St Peter Port harbour, Gazetteer C7)
111. Bowl base, grey burnished with black bands over wheel-made sandy fabric and brownish core, much like TBF (St Peter Port harbour, Gazetteer C7)
112. Jar, grey with light grey core, STN or NGGW (St Peter Port harbour, Gazetteer C7)
113. Tripod bowl, light grey with traces of sooting, wheel-made fabric (but not TBF), deep incised grooves under base (St Peter Port harbour, Gazetteer C7)
114. Jar, dark grey with light grey core and lustrous burnished bands on neck, NGGW (St Peter Port harbour, Gazetteer C7)
115. Jar, grey handmade coarse sandy fabric. Although abraded the remains of diagonal scoring can be seen (St Peter Port harbour, Gazetteer C7)
116. Lid-seated jar, grey wheel-made quartz-tempered fabric (St Peter Port harbour, Gazetteer C7)
117. Jar or bowl, dark grey but discoloured by brown-black solidified pitch on interior and possibly exterior too. The pitch is very similar to that found on Roman wreck so the sherds making up this vessel may have originated from there (St Peter Port harbour, Gazetteer C7)
118. Amphora, buff fabric with orange core and grey margins, PW Class 15, Haltern 70, mid-1st century BC to mid-1st century AD (found 'one mile north of Tautenay', Gazetteer C2)
119. Jar, dark grey with light grey core and burnished bands, NGGW (St Peter Port harbour, Gazetteer C7)
120. Jar of cooking pot form, black BB1 with narrow band of obtuse burnished lattice typical of 3rd century after *c.* AD 225 (St Peter Port harbour, Gazetteer C7)
121. Jar of cooking pot form, black BB1 with narrow band of obtuse burnished lattice typical of 3rd century after *c.* AD 225 (St Peter Port harbour, Gazetteer C7)
122. Bowl, muddy grey sandy fabric with harsh feel, crudely decorated with burnished lines on exterior and burnished lines and starbust on interior (St Peter Port harbour, Gazetteer C7)
123. Bowl, grey with abraded surface, traces of vertical scoring on cordon, probably Thames-side/Upchurch late 1st–2nd century AD (Monaghan 1987, type 4A) (St Peter Port harbour, Gazetteer C7)
124. Small jar base, buff with gold mica at surface, grey interior, MDER, 1st century AD? (St Peter Port harbour, Gazetteer C7)
125. Flanged dish, grey-black abraded BB1 similar to Gillam 229, later 4th century AD (St Peter Port harbour, Gazetteer C7)
126. Bowl, oxidised sandy fabric with silver mica at surface although abraded (St Peter Port harbour, Gazetteer C7)
127. Jar, dark grey sandy handmade fabric patchily discoloured and sooted. Vessel interior very uneven due to finger impressions, exterior decorated by diagonal slashing (St Peter Port harbour,Gazetteer C7)
128. Small mortarium discoloured buff but once cream, quartz grit with some flint, Taverney (Vermeersch 1993). Kay Hartley comments that this is a 'Flanged mortarium with flange downturned almost to the body and thus something between a Gillam 255 (e.g. no. 72, above) and a collar type... probably late 2nd or 3rd century in date' (St Peter Port harbour, Gazetteer C7)
129. Mortarium, grey fabric with buff surface, no remaining grit, form Gillam 238. Kay Hartley comments that one production centre for these mortaria can be attributed to Noyon (Oise), but there will have been others in the Oise/Somme area of northern France (Hartley 1998, 200–6). It is securely dated to the period AD 65–100 (*e.g.* Cunliffe 1971, 171, nos 1 and 6). These mortaria are found throughout Britain and less commonly in northern France and Belgium. This sherd is discoloured to black, with magenta patches and has surface encrustation, all resulting from being in the sea; it would originally have been cream throughout and considerably lighter in weight. It would have had flint and quartz trituration grit (St Peter Port harbour, Gazetteer C7)

The samian ware

by B. R. Hartley and Brenda Dickinson

Editors' note: in the mid-1980s Brenda Dickinson and Brian Hartley examined the La Plaiderie samian, and in the late 1990s Brenda Dickinson examined the samian from the Bonded Store and a selection of other sites on Guernsey. Samian studies have advanced to the point where a detailed listing from such small sites might seem excessive. However, as these are the only samian assemblages of any size found to date in Guernsey, they are listed here in detail.

Abbreviations: CG = central Gaulish, EG = east Gaulish, SG = south Gaulish. Unless otherwise stated, CG = Lezoux and SG = La Graufesenque.

La Plaiderie

SUMMARY

The samian from La Plaiderie ranges from the Tiberio-Claudian period to the 3rd century. The material is divided

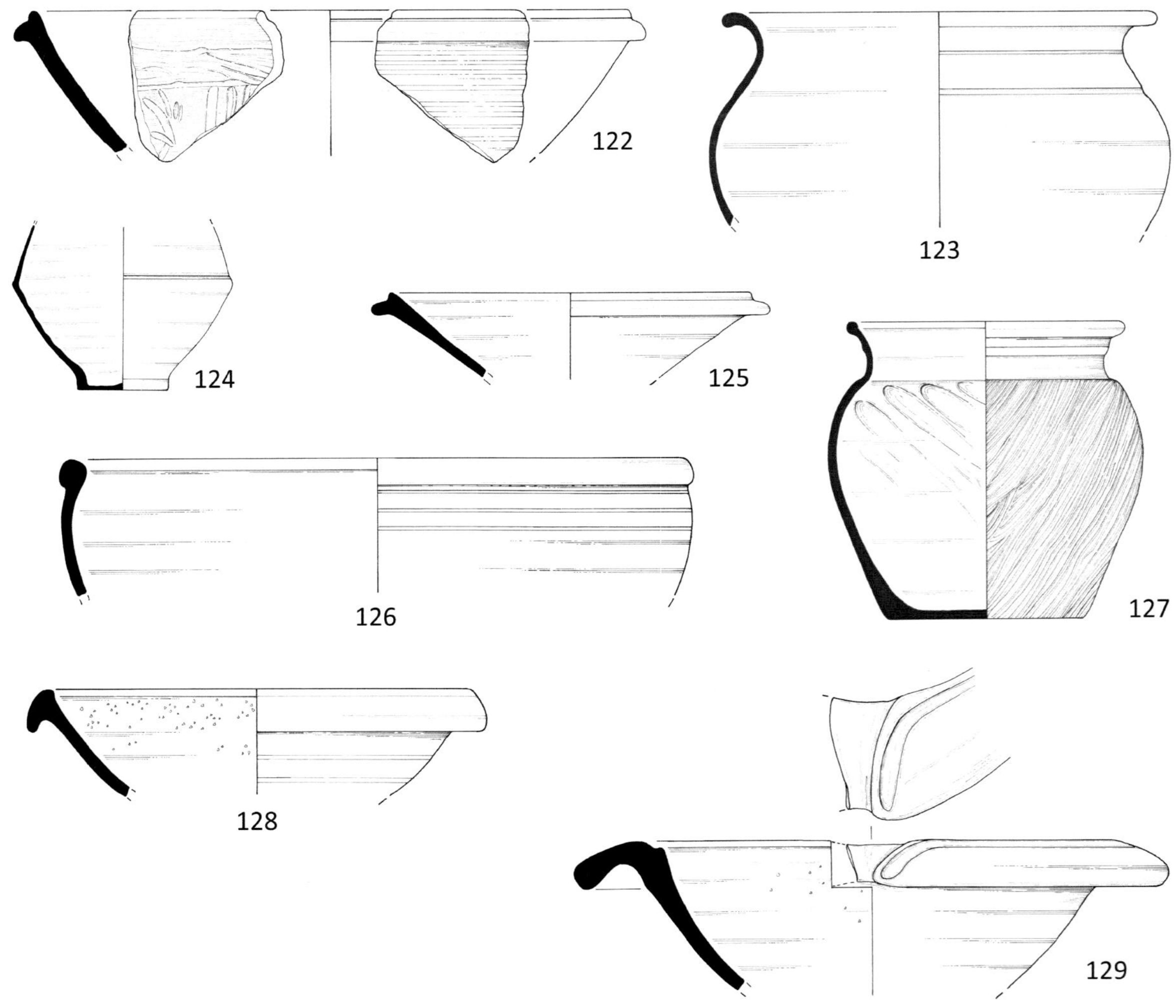

Figure 64 Coarsewares from other Roman sites. Scale 1:4.

into south Gaulish (12%), central Gaulish (1% from Les Martres-de-Veyre and 57% from Lezoux), and east Gaulish (31%) (Table 9). The 1st-century material comes mainly from La Graufesenque, but there are a few Montans vessels and two in characteristic 1st-century Lezoux fabrics. Montans ware, presumably shipped up the west coast, is common in north-west Gaul. First-century Lezoux ware also occurs in fair quantity in this area and is known from Jersey. The opening years of the 2nd century saw a little samian from La Graufesenque, Montans and Les-Martres-de-Veyre. However, the bulk of the 2nd-century material is obviously from Lezoux, though some of the remarkably high proportion of east Gaulish ware at the site will be contemporary with it. This includes material from Rheinzabern and the Argonne, with a little from Trier.

The extraordinary thing about the site is the overall percentage of east Gaulish ware, much of which is likely to be 3rd century, with Rheinzabern, the Argonne and Trier as the only identified sources. The problem is how and why such a high proportion of east Gaulish ware reached the Channel Islands, when comparable material seems to be largely lacking in Brittany and south-west Britain, as well as in Normandy west of the Seine. There are more unusual forms such as flagons, jars with 'cut-glass' decoration and 'black' samian than would normally be expected from one site. There is also a fairly high proportion of mortaria, but that is not uncommon on sites occupied in the late 2nd and 3rd century.

Catalogue

TRENCH 1

U/S Material ranging from the 1st to the 3rd century, mainly central and east Gaulish and of mid- to late Antonine and 3rd-century date. It includes a sherd of form Dr. 30 in F.50

F.1 Dr. –, SG. A scrap in pale cream fabric, with maroon-brown glaze, typical of Tiberio-Claudian Montans ware

F.6 i) Dr. 27, SG, Flavian or Flavian-Trajanic

Table 9 La Plaiderie: summary of samian vessel sources.

Industry	*Min. no. of vessels*	*Period*	*% of whole*
South Gaul	*34*		*11.9*
Montans	15	4 Tibero-Claudian	5.2
		2 Flavian-Trajanic	
		1 Trajanic	
		5 Trajanic or Hadrianic	
La Graufesenque	19	4 first century	6.6
		2 Neronian/early Flavian	
		2 pre-Flavian	
		3 early Flavian	
		1 Flavian	
		5 Flavian or Flavian/ Trajanic	
		2 Flavian/Trajanic	
Central Gaul	*164*		*57.3*
Les Martres-de-Veyre	2	1 Trajanic or Hadrianic	0.7
		1 early Antonine	
Lezoux	162	1 Tibero-Claudian	56.6
		1 Flavian?	
		4 Hadrianic	
		17 Hadrianic or early Antonine	
		1 early Antonine	
		23 mid- to late Antonine	
		11 late Antonine	
		104 Antonine	
East Gaul	*88*		*30.8*
Rheinzabern	30		10.5
Trier	8		2.8
Argonne	9		3.1
Unassigned	41		14.3

ii) With F.48, F.90, T1 L2 (4) and probably F.76, Dr. 37, CG. The ovolo (Rogers B153) and zig-zag borders suggest the work of Servus iv (Rogers' Servus II). The panels include: 1B) an ornamental balustrade (Rogers U263); 1C) a Cupid (O. 508 variant); 2) Pan to right (D.419 = O.717), over a box; 3) the balustrade, over a 'propellor' and a vase (Rogers T29). Other sherds show two double-bordered arcades, one with the 'propellor', the other with a Pan (D. 412 = O.710), partly obliterated by an inserted panel with bead and zig-zag borders and containing a discus-thrower (D. 400 = O.673). To the right is a leaf (Rogers H133) on a zig-zag stem. Various devices are used to divide the panels and support the arcades, such as a pillar (Rogers P21), a striated spindle with double chevron ends and a caryatid (D. 656 = O. 1199). The relationship between the various sherds is not clear. The bowl is almost certainly by Servus; cf. Sauvaget 1970, pl. iv for the ovolo, border, Pan, discus-thrower, arcades, column and box. A bowl from Colchester may be from the same mould and, if so, the decoration is much more varied than appears here. *c*. AD 160–200

F.8 Dr. 79, CG, mid- to late Antonine

F.8A i) Dr. 31, 33 and –, CG. Antonine
ii) Dr. 45 (Trier), 30 or 37 rim (Rheinzabern), a gritted samian mortarium (Rheinzabern) and a scrap, EG. Late 2nd or early 3rd century

F.9 Dr. 68, CG. A jar with black, faintly iridescent coating over pink-brown fabric. The decoration includes a band of rouletting over panels: 1) a double festoon; 2) a trifid motif in a small double medallion. The medallion appears on jars in the styles of Namilianus-Croesus and the Paternus v group (Bémont 1977, 230 and 185, respectively). Mid- to late Antonine

F.11/15 i) Dr. 37, in the fabric of Les Martres-de-Veyre, possibly with the Mercury D. 290, used there by Cettus, *c*. AD 135–160
ii) Dr. 36, CG. Hadrianic or early Antonine
iii) With F.73. Dr. 37, CG. A bowl with a large vine leaf (Rogers H13) in a winding scroll, together with a bird to right. The leaf was used by potters in the Cerialis ii-Cinnamus ii group, *c*. AD 130–170
iv) Dr. 31, CG, stamped MATERNINI: Maternianus i of Lezoux, where the die (2a) is known to have been used. The name is not entirely certain and could be Maternianus, if the final leaning N is not intended to be AN ligatured. All the other examples noted are on cups of Dr. 33. One is in a burial at Astwick, Bedfordshire, together with stamped vessels of Aucella (1a), Do[v]eccus i (13c), Marcrinus iii (1a) and Sacrillus (3a), all mid- to late Antonine potters, *c*. AD 160–190. Slightly burnt with heavily-worn footring

F.14 i) (Joining F.101) Dr. 18/31R, SG. Probably late 1st- or early 2nd-century Montans ware.
ii) Dr. 31 and – (two, one burnt), CG. Antonine. One of the unidentified sherds (unburnt) is perhaps from a disc-necked flagon
iii) Dr. 30 or 37, CG. Mid- to late Antonine
iv) Curle 21, EG. Late 2nd or early 3rd century

F.14B Dish and –, EG. Late 2nd or early 3rd century

F.16 Dr. 79 *etc*. CG. Mid- to late Antonine

F.18 Dr. 37, CG. In the style of Servus iv (Rogers' Servus II), with one of his ovolos (Rogers B153), a zig-zag border and a Pan (D. 419 = O. 717) in a double arcade. The decoration recalls his bowl in F.6, *c*. AD 160–200

F.20 Dr. 45, CG, *c*. AD 170–200

F.22 Dr. 37, CG. Antonine

F.23 Inkwell, CG. Antonine

F.32 i) Dr. 29 rim, SG. Before *c*. AD 85
ii) Dr. 37, SG. Flavian or Flavian-Trajanic
iii) Dr. 30 or 37 rim, EG (Rheinzabern). Late 2nd or early 3rd century

F.41 i) Dr. 30, SG. Flavian or Flavian-Trajanic
ii) Two fragments of Dr. 37, SG. The fabric is not impossible for Montans, where detached spirals were often used as fillers in the field, as here. The animal, apparently unrecorded, but deeply impressed, appears to be a bear. Probably 2nd century, *c*. AD 100–145
iii) Dr. 33 and – (three), CG. Antonine

F.43 i) –, SG. The cream fabric and purple-brown glaze suggest Tiberio-Claudian Montans ware
ii) A scrap of Argonne ware. Second half of the 2nd century

F.44 *Plain*
i) –, SG. First century
ii) Dr. 18/31, probably from Les Martres-de-Vayre. Trajanic or Hadrianic
iii) Dr. Curle 11 and a scrap, CG. Hadrianic
iv) Dr. 15/31 (?), 33 (a minimum of three) a dish, at least two jars and a handle, burnt, which may belong to one, CG. Antonine
v) Dr. 45 collar and a base fragment of gritted samian mortarium (worn), CG, *c*. AD 170–200
vi) A gritted samian mortarium, EG. Late 2nd or early 3rd century
vii) CG (mainly) and EG scraps. Mostly Antonine, though some could be early 3rd century
Decorated
viii) Dr. 29, SG, *c*. AD 70–85
ix) Dr. 30 or 37 base (small) and a jar with a scroll decoration, CG. Hadrianic or Antonine
x) Dr. 37, CG. Hadrianic or early Antonine
xi) Two joining sherds of Dr. 37, heavily eroded, in Argonne fabric. The decoration, which is closed by three uneven grooves, involves animals to the left, chasing each other, and a small leaf, perhaps heart-shaped, *c*. AD 150–200
xii) Two or three sherds from jars with 'cut-glass' decoration, CG. Antonine
xiii) An unusual flagon form, perhaps similar to Oswald and Pryce 1920, pl. lxxxii, 6 and 10, or a colour-coated oil-flask. Probably CG and Antonine
xiv) Dr. 37, EG. Probably Trier ware, with an ovolo with straight tongue turned to the right at the bottom, in the manner of Censor ii, Criciro vii and Dexter ii. Late 2nd or early 3rd century
xv) Dr. 37, EG. The ovolo (Ricken and Fischer 1963, E42 and a dog to right (*ibid*, T146a) were used at Rheinzabern in the late 2nd and early 3rd century. There is also a vertical series of bifid (?) motifs, upside-down, *c*. AD 180–240. Also three black and one orange colour-coated sherds

F.47 i) Dr. 30, SG. The ovolo, with straight tongue swelling to the right at the end, resembles one used at Brive (Moser and Tilhard 1987), though the bowl is in La Graufesenque fabric and the ovolo seems to have been used there, too. A saltire panel has a trifid motif in the top, between striated spindles. Flavian
ii)Two jars, one in 'black samian' fabric, CG. Antonine
iii) Dr. 37, EG. Late 2nd or early 3rd century

F.48 i) Dr. 30, in pale fabric, with purple-brown glaze. Probably Montans ware, with panels showing: 1) a saltire; 2) a kneeling stag (a variant of Hermet, pl.27, no. 2.); 3) a basal wreath of trifid (?) motifs. The style is probably derived from the Germanus i school at La Graufesenque. Cf. Hermet, pl. 101, nos 22, 24, 26, 27, 29. Late 1st or early 2nd century
ii) See F.50, iii
iii) Dr. 37 (two), CG. Hadrianic or early Antonine
iv) Dr. 31, 33, Curle 21 and two sherds from one vessel, with external groove, CG. Antonine
v) Dr. 37 (two: in the styles of Servus iv (see F.6) and the Paternus v group) and 79, CG. Mid- to late Antonine
vi) Dr. 45 and a gritted samian mortarium, CG, *c*. AD 170–200
vii) Dr. 37, EG. The tongueless ovolo (Ricken and Fischer 1963, E67) and bear (*ibid*, M126a) were used at both Heiligenberg and Rheinzabern by Reginus vi. Cf. Ricken 1948, Taf. 142, 14F and 21F. The fabric does not help to decide the provenance. *c*. AD 150–180
viii) Dr. 31, 37 (two, one from Rheinzabern), 45 (in Trier fabric), two gritted samian mortaria and a jar, EG. Late 2nd or early 3rd century
ix) Many CG and a few EG scraps, the latter including a sherd of Trier ware. Late 2nd and/or early 3rd century

F.48B i) Dr. 15/17, SG. 1st century
ii) Dr. 37, CG. In orange, micaceous fabric with orange-brown glaze and a coarse wavy line below a rosette-tongued ovolo. Hadrianic-Antonine

iii) Dr. 31, 33, 36 (two), 37 (two, one burnt), Curle 15 or 23, a gritted samian mortarium and several scraps, CG. Probably all Antonine
iv) Dr. 31R, CG. Mid- to late Antonine
v) Dr. 37, in what at first sight appears to be Rheinzabern fabric. However, none of the motifs can be traced precisely in Rheinzabern ware and it remains possible that this is a late CG bowl. Apart from the rosette, matched in the work of Marcus v, the only clue is in the plant, which is similar to (but probably not identical with) one used by Banuus. The bird was originally a Lezoux type, but as variants were also used at Rheinzabern, it does not help greatly. Late Antonine or early 3rd century
vi) Dr. 30 or 37, 43 (?), 45, a gritted samian mortarium, a cup, a flagon and a sherd with cut-glass decoration, EG, late 2nd or early 3rd century

F.50 i) Footring, perhaps 2nd-century Montans ware. Trajanic or Hadrianic
ii) Dr. 29/37, SG. The rim is beaded like form 37, but has the internal grooving of form 29, though it lacks external rouletting. There are also three external grooves above the decoration. Second-century Montans ware. Trajanic or Hadrianic
iii) Two sherds, with others in F.48, T1 L1 and T1 L2 (7), some joining. Dr. 30, CG. The rosette-tongued ovolo is probably Rogers B24. The panels include: 1) a small double medallion; 2) Apollo (D. 55 = O. 92); 3A) a bird to right, looking back, in a chevron festoon (Rogers F60); 3B) a band of chevrons; a sphinx to left (D. 497 = O. 857), among leaf-tips (Rogers J122, or the like); 4A) a seated Diana (D. 68 = O. 111); 4B) (probably joining) a hare to right (O. 2057). Elsewhere are a bird (O. 2317?) in a double medallion, following 4A, and an erotic group (Oswald, pl. XC, M), following 4B. The decoration recalls Les Martres-de-Veyre, though the bowl itself is in Lezoux fabric. It is almost certainly in one of the less common, and probably earlier, styles of Sacer i, who is thought to have started work at Les Martres. The festoon is on a stamped Dr. 30 from Dragonby and the ovolo and rosette are on another, from Cannstatt (Knorr 1905, taf. V, 5). Unstamped bowls in Sacer's style include the bird and medallion (Melandra) and the erotic group and hare (Heronbridge), *c*. AD 125–140.
iv) A flagon neck, CG? Cf. Oswald and Pryce 1920, pl. LXXXIII, 2. Second century?

F.51 Dr. 33 (?), EG. Late 2nd or early 3rd century

F.57 Dr. 37 (?), EG, almost certainly Argonne ware. Second half of the 2nd century

F.58 i) Dr. 37, CG. Hadrianic or early Antonine
ii) Dr. 30 or 37 rim, CG. Antonine
iii) Dr. 37, CG or EG. Second century
iv) Dr. 37, 45 (Trier?), two gritted samian mortaria, two jars and two scraps, EG. Late 2nd or early 3rd century
v) Two fragments from an EG bowl, with barbotine scroll-work on the outer wall. It belongs to the range Ludowici SMa-c and is most probably SMc. The fabric suggests an origin at Trier, where such vessels were found in the Massenfund (Huld-Zetsche 1972, Abb. 4, 11a). First half of the 3rd century.

F.64 i) A jar base and a scrap, CG. Antonine
ii) A CG 'black samian' jar, with bung foot. Antonine

F.69 A scrap of 1st-century samian, probably from Montans

F.69/66 i) Dr. 36, in cream fabric with brown glaze, probably early 2nd-century Montans ware
ii) –, CG. Second century
iii) A disc-necked flagon, CG. Antonine?
iv) A gritted samian mortarium, burnt, CG, *c*. AD 170–200
v) Dr. 31, EG, from the Argonne or Rheinzabern. Late 2nd or early 3rd century

F.73 i) See F.11/15, iii
ii) Dr. 31 and a scrap, CG. Antonine

F.76 i) Dr. 30 or 37 base, CG. Hadrianic or early Antonine
ii) A flake of Dr. 37, with the same column and zig-zag border as F.6, ii, and almost certainly from the same bowl.

F77 i) Dish, SG. First century
ii) –, CG. Hadrianic or early Antonine

F.79 Dish, with the quarter-round moulding of Dr. 15/17, but with a flat base outside the footring, as on Dr. 17. The pale orange, micaceous fabric and dull orange glaze are characteristic of 1st-century Lezoux ware. The form must be Tiberian or early Claudian

F.84 Dr. 31, CG. Mid- to late Antonine

F.85 Dr. 33, EG, from the Argonne or Rheinzabern. Late 2nd or early 3rd century

F.89 Dr. 18/31, slightly burnt, CG. Hadrianic

F.90 i) Dr. 18, SG. Neronian-Flavian
ii) Dr. 30 or 37, 31 (two), 33, 36, 37 (see F.6, ii), 46 and several scraps, CG. All apparently Antonine and some clearly after AD 160

F.94 i) A jar, EG (Rheinzabern). Late 2nd or early 3rd century.
ii) Dr. 37, EG. The ovolo (Ricken and Fischer 1963, E17) and vertical rows of squarish beads (*ibid*, 0256?) are on a stamped bowl of Iulius viii from Rheinzabern (Ricken 1948, Taf. 212, 16). Probably early 3rd century

F.95 Dr. 37, EG. Rheinzabern ware, with a freestyle scene, including a lion (Ricken and Fischer 1963, T8 variant?), boar (*ibid*, T74) and bear (*ibid*, T57?). Not assignable to a particular potter, but probably late 2nd century.

F.100 i) –, CG. Hadrianic or Antonine
ii) Jar, EG (Rheinzabern). Late 2nd or early 3rd century

F.101 i) See F.14
ii) Dr. 30, 33, 37, a fragment of a (gritted?) samian mortarium and – (two), CG, Antonine
iii) Dr. 31, Curle 21 (Rheinzabern) and –, EG. Late 2nd or early 3rd century

F.102 Dish, EG (Rheinzabern). Late 2nd or early 3rd century

F.105 i) Dr. 37, SG. The pale fabric and purple-brown glaze suggest Montans ware. The basal wreath probably consists of rosettes, as on a 2nd-century bowl from Richborough. Trajanic or Hadrianic
ii) Dr. 31 (two), Curle 21 and a jar, CG. Antonine
iii) Dr. 38 (?), CG. Mid- to late Antonine

F.108 i) Dr. 31, 38, Curle 15, a dish and –, CG. Antonine
ii) Dr. 45, CG, *c*. AD 170–200
iii) Dr. 30 or 37 and 45, EG. Late 2nd or early 3rd century

F.110 Dr. 37, CG. The decoration includes a naked warrior with shield, apparently not otherwise recorded, and a coarse wavy line above. Hadrianic-Antonine

L2 i) Dr. 30 rim, SG. Neronian or early-Flavian
ii) Dr. 29 (two), SG, *c*. AD 70–85
iii) Dr. 35, in orange, micaceous fabric, with moderately glossy orange glaze. First-century Lezoux ware, probably Flavian
iv) Dish, in pale buff fabric, with purple-brown glaze. Probably 1st-century Montans ware
v) Dr. 37, SG. The trident-tongued ovolo is on a stamped bowl of Sulpicius from Wilderspool. The decoration includes a panel with a satyr (O. 597) in a thick chevron arcade with a central boss. Cf. Jacobs 1913, no. 8 for the same figure in a different arcade, but with the same batons attached, *c*. AD 80–110
vi) Dr. 30 or 37, SG. Flavian or Flavian-Trajanic. See F.50
vii) Dr. 18/31R, 37, Curle 15 and a 'black samian' jar, with non-metallic coat, CG. Hadrianic or early Antonine
viii) Dr. 30 or 37 (six rims, two burnt), 31 (at least 10), 33 (at least six), 37 (two, one burnt), 38, 44, 72 *etc*, a jar with black coat and appliqué leaves and – (five), CG. Antonine
ix) Dr. 30 or 37, 31R, 37 (two, in the styles of Servus iv (see F.6) and the Paternus v group), 79 (two) and 79 or Ludowici Tg, CG. Mid- to late Antonine
x) A gritted samian mortarium, CG, *c*. AD 170–200
xi) Dr. 37, EG. The ovolo (Ricken-Fischer, E17) and pan-mask (*ibid*, M9) in a chevron arcade (*ibid*, KB126) are all on bowls from Rheinzabern in the style of Florentinus (Ricken 1948, Taf. 113, 16; 114, 9). Late 2nd century
xii) Dr. 31, 33 (Argonne), 37 (five?), 43 (at least two), 45 (at least four, one from Trier, two or more from Rheinzabern and one perhaps from the Argonne), Ludowici Ti', a jar and several scraps, EG. Late 2nd or 3rd century, mostly Rheinzabern ware. Also two colour-coated sherds

L2/L3 Two joining sherds of Ludowici form Ti' variant, larger and shallower than usual. The fabric strongly suggests an origin at Rheinzabern. Late 2nd or early 3rd century.

L3 i) Dr. 27, SG, drilled for riveting. Probably pre-Flavian
ii) Dr. 30, SG. First century
iii) Dr. 18/31R and 33a, CG. Hadrianic
iv) Dr. 31 (five), 33 (four), 37?, Curle 21, Curle 23 and a dish or bowl, CG. Antonine
v) Many CG scraps. Second century
vi) Dr. 37, EG. A double medallion contains a kneeling stag (O. 1705B), as used at Lavoye (Ricken 1934, Taf. XII, 49). Second half of the 2nd century
vii) Dr. 43 (with collar decorated *en barbotine* wine birds and tendrils) and 45 (with grit extending up to the inside of the collar), both from Rheinzabern. Late 2nd or early 3rd century
viii) A jar with 'cut-glass' decoration, probably Trier ware. Late 2nd or 3rd century
ix) A dish and a dish or bowl rim, shaped as a disc with a hole in the middle, EG. Late 2nd or 3rd century

L3 area beneath F.1
i) Dr. 37 or, more probably, 29, SG. The yellowish-cream fabric and purple-brown glaze suggest 1st-century Montans ware. Probably pre-Flavian
ii) Dr. 37, CG. A panel with wavy-line border contains a beaded ring (Rogers C290) and probably has a beaded rosette at the bottom of the border. The next panel contains a satyr with double flute (D. 311 = O. 610). Not assignable to a particular potter, though the maker was clearly a member of the Quintilianus i group, *c*. AD 125–150
iii) Dr. 30 or 37, 31, 33, 37, 38 or 44, a 'black samian' jar and several scraps, CG. Antonine
iv) Dr. 30 or 37 and 32, both from Rheinzabern, and a jar in Trier fabric, EG. Late 2nd or 3rd century

L3 associated with F.20/21
i) Dr. 30 or 37 (burnt), 31 and 38, CG. Antonine
ii) –, CG. Hadrianic or Antonine

L3 F.47 i) Dr. 37, SG. Flavian or Flavian-Trajanic

ii) Dr. 30 or 37 rim, SG. The yellow-cream fabric and brown glaze suggests Montans ware. Probably Trajanic or Hadrianic
iii) A jar and – (two), CG. Hadrianic or Antonine
iv) A jar with 'cut-glass' decoration, CG, *c.* AD 150–200
v) A gritted samian mortarium, very worn inside, CG, *c.* AD 170–200
vi) – (three), EG (Rheinzabern). Late 2nd or early 3rd century
vii) Dr. 36, heavily burnt. Undatable

L3 inside Building 2, cut by kilns
i) –, SG. First century
ii) –, CG. Hadrianic or Antonine
iii) –, burnt. CG. Antonine
iv) Dr. 37, EG. Late 2nd or 3rd century

L4 i) –, SG. Flavian or Flavian-Trajanic
ii) – (three), CG. Hadrianic or Antonine
iii) Dr. 30 or 37 (burnt), 31, 33 and 38, CG. Antonine
iv) Dr. 45, with lion's-head spout (Rheinzabern or Argonne) and – (three, two Rheinzabern, one Argonne), EG. Late 2nd or early 3rd century

L4 east of F.8
Dr. 37, CG. Hadrianic or early Antonine

L4 beneath F.47
i) – (three), CG. Hadrianic or Antonine
ii) Dr. 30 or 37 and a dish or bowl, CG. Antonine
iii) Dr. 79 *etc*, EG. Probably late 2nd century. Also a colour-coated sherd

F.116 i) Dr. Ludowici Ti' variant, EG (Rheinzabern). Late 2nd or early 3rd century
ii) –, EG (Argonne). Second half of the 2nd century

F.123 Dr. 29, SG. The pale fabric and brown glaze suggest an origin at Montans. Both surviving panels in the lower zone have rows of leaf-tips, one with an animal among them. Probably mid-1st century

T2 i) Dr. 37, SG. Flavian-Trajanic
ii) Dr. 30 or 37 (with internal groove below the lip), 37 and –, SG. Probably Montans ware, but not closely dateable
iii) Dr. 18/31 or 31 and 36, CG. Hadrianic or early Antonine
iv) Dr. 31, CG. Early Antonine
v) Dr. 31 (five), 36 and four jars, one with 'cut-glass' decoration, CG. Antonine
vi) Dr. 31 (two), 31R and 79, CG. Mid- to late Antonine
vii) Dr. 45 and a gritted samian mortarium, CG, *c.* AD 170–200
viii) Many CG scraps, mainly Antonine
ix) EG ware of late 2nd- and early 3rd-century date, with forms 31R, 33, 37 (at least four, one heavily burnt), 43 (with barbotine vegetation on the collar), 45, burnt (Trier), Ludowici Tb, two jars, one with moulded gadroons, the other with 'cut-glass' decoration, two gritted samian mortaria (from the Argonne and Rheinzabern) and several scraps.

L4 (small-find 380) A cup (Dr. 33?), stamped] DΛ[. Almost certainly a stamp of Daccius ii of Lavoye, to judge by the orange fabric and glaze. The potter worked in the early to mid-Antonine period, stamping forms such as 18/31 and 80

The Bonded Store

SUMMARY

The catalogue below consists of a maximum of 489 vessels, including unidentified forms. The dominance of central Gaulish products from Lezoux is obvious (Table 10). Vessels represented by more than one sherd are shown as, for example, Dr. 37 (1/2), *i.e.* two sherds from one vessel.

Catalogue

AREA A

A1003 i) –, CG. Hadrianic or Antonine
ii) Walters 79 or Ludowici Tg, CG, with stamp of Cobnertianus. *c.* AD 160–90

A1004 i) Dr. 15/17, SG. Neronian or early Flavian
ii) Dr. 36 (?) (rim), SG. Flavian or Flavian-Trajanic
iii) Curle 15 (rim) and a dish or bowl, CG. Hadrianic or Antonine
iv) Dr. 18/31 (rim) and Curle 11 (rim), CG. Hadrianic or early Antonine
v) Dr. 31 (base and footring), Curle 23 (rim) and 'black samian' jar, CG. Antonine
vi) Dish (?), EG (Rheinzabern). Late 2nd or first half of 3rd century

A1005 Curle 23, SG (Montans). Trajanic-Hadrianic

Table 10 The Bonded Store: summary of samian vessel sources.

Samian source	*No. sherds*
La Graufesenque	29
Montans	36
Banassac	4?
Lezoux	369
Lezoux or EG	1
Argonne	16?
Argonne or Rheinzabern	4
Heiligenberg?	1?
La Madeleine	4?
Rheinzabern	22
Trier	2?
East Gaulish unspecified	1?

Based on a maximum of 489 pots, including unidentified forms.

A1010 i) Curle 23 (rim), CG. Mid to late Antonine
ii) Ludowici Tb variant (with fluted rim), EG (Rheinzabern). Late 2nd or first half of 3rd century
A1204 i) Dr. 18 (?) and 18/31 (base and footring), SG. Flavian or Flavian-Trajanic
ii) Dr. 27 (footring), CG. Hadrianic or early Antonine
iii) Dr. 36? (base and footring), Curle 15 or 23 (base and footring) and – (four), CG. Hadrianic or Antonine
iv) Dr. 37 (two) and Curle 15 or 23, CG. Antonine
v) Walters 79 (rim), burnt, CG. Mid- to late Antonine
vi) Dr. 31 (rim) and 33 (base and footring), EG (Argonne). *c*. AD 150–200
vii) Dr. 37 (two), EG (Rheinzabern). Late 2nd or first half of 3rd century

A2003 i) Dr. 18 (?), SG (Montans?). First century
ii) Dr. 30 or 37 (rim), SG. Flavian or Flavian-Trajanic
iii) Dr. 18/31 or 31 (rim), 37, dish or bowl (slightly burnt), an enclosed vessel, a rim, a footring and – (six), CG. Hadrianic or Antonine
iv) Dr. 27 (?) and Curle 11 (flange), CG. Hadrianic or early Antonine
v) Dr. 31 (two, one rim, one footring), 33 (two, one rim, the other burnt) and a jar, CG. Antonine
vi) Dr. 33, 30 or 37 and Walters 80, CG. Mid- to late Antonine
vii) Dr. 45 collar (small), CG. *c*. AD 170–200
viii) (associated with A2007) Dr. 18/31R (base and footring), slightly burnt, CG. Hadrianic or early Antonine
ix) Walters 80 (complete profile), CG. Mid- to late Antonine

A2004 –, CG. Hadrianic or Antonine

A2007 i) Dr. 46 (rim), CG. Hadrianic or early Antonine
ii) Dr. 30 or 37 (?), CG. Hadrianic or Antonine
iii) Dr. 31 (rim), Curle 15? (rim) and dish or bowl, CG. Antonine
iv) Dr. 31 (two, rims), EG (Rheinzabern). Late 2nd or first half of 3rd century
v) Ludowici RSMa or RSMb (collar), EG (Rheinzabern). First half of 3rd century
vi) Dr. 37, CG. Hadrianic or Antonine

A2015 Dr. 30 or 37 and cup or bowl, CG. Hadrianic or Antonine

A2016 Dr. 33 (rim), EG (Argonne or Rheinzabern). Antonine or first half of 3rd century

AREA B

B U/S i) Dr. 33, CG. Antonine
ii) Dr. 37, CG, style of Rogers's P-16. Early Antonine

B1003 Cup, CG. Hadrianic or early Antonine

B1204 i) –, CG. Hadrianic or Antonine
ii) Dr. 33 (two), CG. Antonine
iii) Curle 21, CG. *c*. AD 150–200
iv) Dr. 31R, CG. Mid- to late Antonine

B2003 i) Walters 79/80 (1/4, one rim, one footring), CG. Mid- or late Antonine
ii) Dr. 31 (footring), CG. Mid- to late Antonine
iii) (under chalk) Dr. 30 or 37 (1?/2, one rim), CG. Mid- to late Antonine

B2026 i) Dish or bowl (two), CG. Hadrianic or Antonine
ii) Dr. 27 (1/2, one rim), CG. Early Antonine
iii) Dr. 37, CG. Late Antonine

B2032 Dr. 27g, SG. Neronian or early Flavian

B2044 i) Dr. 31 (rim) and 33 (rim), CG. Antonine
ii) Dr. 31 (rim), with remains of a rivet, EG (Rheinzabern). Late 2nd or first half of 3rd century

B2045 i) Dr. 36, CG. Hadrianic or Antonine
ii) Dr. 31 (rim), EG (Rheinzabern). Late 2nd or first half of 3rd century

B2048 i) Curle 11 (flange), CG. Hadrianic
ii) Dr. 46 (rim), dish or bowl and – (footring), CG. Hadrianic or Antonine

B2049 Dr. 31 (base and footring), CG. Antonine

B2051 Dr. 38 or 44 (footring), heavily burnt, CG. Antonine

B2054 i) – (two), CG. Hadrianic or Antonine
ii) Dr. 37, CG. Antonine

B2061 i) Dish (footring), CG. Antonine
ii) Dr. 32 *etc*. (base and footring), EG (Rheinzabern). Late 2nd or first half of 3rd century

B3003 i) Dr. 31 (rim) and 33, CG. Antonine
ii) Dr. 15/31 (rim) and 31 (with graffito X on outside, after firing), CG. Mid-Antonine

B3004 i) Dr. 18/31 or 31 (rim) and 30 (rim, joining sherd in B3005), CG. Hadrianic or Antonine
ii) Dr. 31 (rim), 33 and dish or bowl, CG. Antonine
iii) Gritted samian mortarium, CG. *c*. AD 170–200. Grits lightly worn
iv) – (1?/2), EG (Argonne or Rheinzabern). Antonine or first half of 3rd century

B3005 i) Ritterling 8 (rim), SG (Montans). Claudian or early Neronian
ii) Dr. 30 or 37 rim, CG. Hadrianic or Antonine. Joins a sherd in B3004
iii) Dr. 37, CG. Hadrianic or early Antonine
iv) Dr. 36 (?) and 37 (probably shaped as a counter), CG. Mid-Antonine
v) Dr. 37, CG. Mid- to late Antonine

AREA C

C1003 i) Dish, SG (Montans). Claudio-Neronian
ii) Ritterling 8 (footring), SG. Neronian
iii) Dr. 30 or 37 (two, one rim) and dish or bowl, CG. Hadrianic or Antonine

iv) Dr. 30 or 37 rim, Curle 11 (rim) and Curle 15 (rim), CG. Hadrianic or early Antonine
v) Enclosed vessel, with barbotine decoration, and dish, CG. Antonine
vi) Dr. 45 and a gritted samian mortarium, CG. *c.* AD 170–200
vii) Dr. 33 (two, one rim), EG (Argonne). *c.* AD 150–200
viii) Dr. 37, EG (Rheinzabern). Late 2nd or first half of 3rd century

C1003a i) –, burnt, CG. First century
ii) Dr. 36 flange, CG. Trajanic
Iii) –, CG. Trajanic or Hadrianic
iv) Dr. 33 (1/2) and –, CG. Hadrianic or Antonine

C1004 i) Dr. 35, CG. Hadrianic or Antonine
ii) Dr. 18/31R (rim), CG. Hadrianic or early Antonine
iii) Dr. 33 (rim), CG. Antonine

C1005 i) Dr. 15/17, SG (Montans). Pre-Flavian
ii) Dr. 37, SG. *c.* AD 85–110
iii) – (two), CG. Hadrianic or Antonine
iv) Curle 11 (flange), CG. Hadrianic
v) Dr. 18/31 or 31 and 18/31R (rim), CG. Hadrianic or early Antonine
vi) Dr. 31 (rim) and 33 (rim), CG. Antonine
vii) Curle 23 (rim), SG (Montans). Hadrianic or early Antonine

C1006 i) Dr. 15/17 (rim), burnt, SG. Pre-Flavian
ii) Dr. 15/17 or 18, SG. Neronian or early Flavian

C1065 Dr. 31, CG. Antonine

C1068 i) – (two), SG (Montans). Claudian or Neronian
ii) Dr. 18/31R and 37, CG. Hadrianic or early Antonine
iii) Curle 15 or 23, CG. Antonine

C1070 i) Dish or bowl, CG. Hadrianic or Antonine
ii) Dr. 18/31R and Curle 15 or 23, CG. Hadrianic or early Antonine
iii) Dr. 33 (two, rims), CG. Antonine
iv) Dr. 45 (collar), CG. *c.* AD 170–200

C1071 i) Dr. 31R, burnt, CG. Mid- to late Antonine
ii) –, EG (Argonne). *c.* AD 150–200

C1077 Walters 79 or Tg, CG. Mid- or late Antonine

C1079 Dr. 15/17 (rim), SG. Neronian

C1080 Curle 11 (flange), SG (Montans). Early Flavian

C2002 Dr. 33 (1/2, joining), CG. Late Hadrianic or early Antonine

C2003 i) Dr. 29 (?), CG. Neronian
ii) Dr. 36 (flange), CG. Trajanic
iii) Dr. 33, 35 or 36 (flange) and – (two), CG. Hadrianic or Antonine
iv) Dr. 18/31 and 30 or 37 (rim), CG. Hadrianic or early Antonine
v) Dr. 35, without barbotine leaves on the flange, CG. Antonine
vi) Curle 21 (1/2, one rim), CG. *c.* AD 150–200
vii) Dr. 33 (rim), CG. Mid- to late Antonine
viii) Dr. 45 (collar), CG. *c.* AD 170–200
ix) Dr. 33 (rim), EG (Argonne). *c.* AD 150–200
x) Dr. 31R (rim, burnt), Curle 21 and a dish, EG (Rheinzabern). Late 2nd or first half of 3rd century

C2004 i) Dr. 33 (three, one rim) and 35 or 36 (flange), CG. Hadrianic or Antonine (Fig. 65.4)
ii) Dr. 18/31 and 18/31R, CG. Hadrianic or early Antonine
iii) Dr. 46 (1/2, one rim), CG. Antonine
iv) Dr. 31R, CG. Mid- to late Antonine
v) Dr. 37, EG (Lavoye). *c.* AD 150–200
vi) Dr. 36, CG, burnt on flange. Flavian or Flavian-Trajanic
vii) Dr. 37, EG (Lavoye). All internal glaze removed and three indentations made, probably by stirring. Second half of 2nd century

C2005 i) Dr. 27 (rim), SG (Montans). Claudio-Neronian. From same vessel as C2097
ii) Dr. 36 flange, SG. Neronian or early Flavian
iii) Dr. 15/17, SG. Pre-Flavian
iv) Dr. 33 (rim), EG (La Madeleine). Hadrianic-Antonine

C2006 Dr. 27g (footring), SG. Claudio-Neronian

C2080 –, CG. Probably pre-Flavian

C2090 i) Small bowl (footring), SG (Montans), joining a sherd in C2093. Late 1st or early 2nd century
ii) Dish (footring), CG. Hadrianic or Antonine
iii) Flagon neck (burnt), CG. Second century

C2093 i) Small bowl, SG (Montans), joining a sherd in C2090. Late 1st or early 2nd century
ii) Dr. 18/31 or 31 (rim), CG. Hadrianic or early Antonine

C2094 i) Dr. 15/17 (rim), burnt, and 15/17? (rim), SG (Montans). Claudio-Neronian
ii) Dr. 30, SG (Montans). First century
iii) –, SG. Pre-Flavian
iv) Dr. 37, SG (Montans). First half of 2nd century
v) Dr. 37 and flat dish, CG. Hadrianic or early Antonine
vi) Dr. 30 and – (five, one footring), CG. Hadrianic or Antonine
vii) Dr. 37, CG, style of the Cerialis ii–Cinnamus ii group. *c.* AD 135–65
viii) Dr. 30 or 37 (rim), 31, 33 (rim) and 33 (burnt), CG. Antonine
ix) Dr. 31 (rim), CG. Mid-Antonine
x) Curle 21, CG. *c.* AD 150–200
xi) Dr. 31, 31R (three, one rim) and Walters 79/80 (heavily burnt), CG. Mid- to late Antonine
xii) Curle 21 (rim), EG (Argonne). *c.* AD 150–200. Mid- to late Antonine
xiii) Cup or bowl, burnt. Undatable

xiv) Dr. 31R (full profile), CG. Mid- to late Antonine. Footring heavily worn
xv) Dr. 33 (full profile), CG, with stamp of Agileito (Fig. 65.2). Hadrianic-Antonine

C2097 i) Dr. 27 (rim), SG (Montans), Claudio-Neronian. From same vessel as a sherd in C2005
ii) Dr. 37, SG (Montans). Flavian or Flavian-Trajanic (Fig. 65.1)
iii) Dr. 18/31 or 31 (footring), CG. Hadrianic or early Antonine

C3003 Dr. 18/31R (rim) and 33, CG. Hadrianic or early Antonine

C3012 i) Dr. 31 (rim), slightly burnt, SG (Montans). Early Antonine
ii) Dr. 38, CG. Antonine

C3013 i) Dr. 18/31 or 31, CG. Hadrianic or Antonine
ii) Dr. 33 (rim), 38 or 44 and a jar (Déchelette 66?), CG. Antonine

C3014 Dr. 33 (?), CG. Hadrianic or Antonine

C3017 i) –, SG (Montans). Claudio-Neronian
ii) Dr. 36 flange, SG (Montans). First half of 2nd century
iii) Dr. 36 and – (four), CG. Hadrianic or Antonine
iv) Dr. 30 or 37 (rim), 33 (two, one rim) and 38 (flange), CG. Antonine
v) Dr. 32 (rim), EG (probably Heiligenberg). Antonine
vi) Footring, EG (Argonne). *c.* AD 150–200
vii) Dr. 37, CG. Mid- or late Antonine. Shaped as a counter (Fig. 65.3)

C3018 Dr. 33 (rim), CG. Mid- to late Antonine

C3021 Dr. 30 or 37 (rim), CG. Antonine

C3022 i) –, SG (Montans). First century
ii) Dr. 18 (rim), SG. Flavian
iii) Dr. 33 (1/2, joining rims), CG. Hadrianic or early Antonine
iv) Dr. 36 or 38 or 44, EG (La Madeleine). Hadrianic-Antonine. Internal glaze ground away
v) Curle 21, CG. *c.* AD 150–200
vi) Dr. 30 or 37, EG (probably Argonne). *c.* AD 150–200

C3023 i) Jar, CG. Hadrianic or Antonine
ii) Dr. 33 (three, rims), CG. Antonine

C3024 i) Dr. 35 (with or without a pedestal), SG (Montans). First century
ii) Dr. 18/31 or 31, CG. Hadrianic or early Antonine
iii) Dr. 33 (1/2, joining), CG. Antonine

C3026 i) Dr. 15/17 (?), SG (Montans). First century
ii) –, CG. Hadrianic or Antonine
iii) Dr. 38 or 44 (rim) and 38 or 44 (base and footring, with all internal glaze gone), CG. Antonine

C3030 Dr. 33 (base and footring), SG (Montans). Trajanic to early Antonine

C3033 i) Dr. 36 (flange) and –, CG. Hadrianic or Antonine
ii) Cup, CG. Hadrianic or early Antonine

C3034 i) Dish, SG. Flavian or Flavian-Trajanic
ii) –, CG. Hadrianic or Antonine

C3036 i) –, SG. First century
ii) Dr. 30R, CG. Late 1st or early 2nd century. Burnt

C4001 U/S Dish, CG. Hadrianic or Antonine

C4003 i) Dr. 18/31 or 31 (rim) and –, CG. Hadrianic or Antonine
ii) Dr. 31, 37 and dish or bowl, CG. Antonine
iii) Curle 21 (?), CG. Mid- or late Antonine. Some internal glaze removed by stirring
iv) Dr. 45 (collar), CG. *c.* AD 170–200

C4014 i) Dish or bowl, CG. Hadrianic or early Antonine
ii) Dish or bowl and cup, CG. Hadrianic or Antonine
iii) Dr. 38 or 44 (rim) and enclosed vessel, CG. Antonine
iv) Dr. 37, CG. Mid- to late Antonine. All internal glaze removed and two indentations made, probably by stirring

C4015 i) Dr. 31 (rim), CG. Antonine
ii) Curle 21? (footring), CG. *c.* AD 150–200
iii) Dr. 31 (base and footring), EG (Argonne). *c.* AD 150–200. Heavily abraded inside and out

C4022 Dr. 31 (rim), CG. Mid-Antonine

C4035 Dr. 37, SG (Banassac). Trajanic-Hadrianic

C4038 Dr. 30 (rim), 35 (rim, without barbotine) and 35 or 36 (rim), CG. Hadrianic or Antonine

C4102 i) Dish, CG. Late 1st or early 2nd century
ii) –, CG. Hadrianic or Antonine
iii) Dr. 27 rim, CG. Hadrianic or early Antonine
iv) Dr. 31 (footring), CG. Antonine

C4103 Dr. 33 (rim), CG. Hadrianic or early Antonine

C4114 Dr. 37, burnt, EG. Late 2nd century?

C5001 Dr. 31 or 31R, CG. Mid- to late Antonine

AREA D

D U/S Bowl, burnt, CG. Antonine. Glaze ground off inside

D1 U/S i) –, CG. Hadrianic or Antonine
ii) Dr. 30 or 37 (footring) and 46? (base and footring), Antonine

D1002 i) Dr. 27 (rim), CG. Hadrianic or early Antonine
ii) Dr. 37, CG. Hadrianic or early Antonine?
iii) Dr. 33 (rim), CG. Antonine
iv) Dr. 31, CG. Mid- or late Antonine

D1002/1004
Dr. 46 (?), CG. Antonine. Heavily burnt, unstamped or stamp eroded away

D1004 i) Dr. 37 and –, CG. Hadrianic or Antonine
ii) Curle 15 or 23, CG. Antonine
iii) Dr. 31 (1/2, one rim), CG. Mid-Antonine
iv) Curle 21, CG. *c.* AD 150–200
v) Flat dish, EG (Rheinzabern). Mid-Antonine

D1007 i) Dr. 29 (?), SG (Montans). Claudio-Neronian. Joining A2009
ii) Rim, CG. Hadrianic or Antonine

D2002 i) Flange and –, SG (Montans). Pre-Flavian
ii) –, CG. Hadrianic or Antonine

D2005 i) Dr. 18/31 or 31 (rim), 30, 30 or 37 (base and footring), 33 (2, one base and footring), Curle 15 (rim) and – (five), CG. Hadrianic or Antonine
ii) Jar, CG. Antonine
iii) Dr. 45 collar, CG. *c.* AD 170–200
iv) Dr. 37, EG (Argonne), with glaze ground away inside. Second half of 2nd century
v) Dr. 31 (1/4, one rim), EG (Rheinzabern). Late 2nd or first half of 3rd century
vi) Dr. 37, CG, style of Attianus ii. *c.* AD 125–145
vii) Dr. 31, CG (Lezoux), with stamp of Magio i. *c.* AD 160–90
viii) Dr. 37, EG, style of Maiiaaus of Trier. Late 2nd or first half of 3rd century

D2006 Dr. 30 or 37, CG. Hadrianic or Antonine

D2008 Cup (?), CG. Hadrianic or Antonine

D2009 i) Dr. 29 (?), SG (Montans). Claudio-Neronian. Joining A2007
ii) –, SG (Montans). First century
iii) – (1/3), SG. First century
iv) Dr. 35/36 (flange), SG (Montans). First half of 2nd century?
v) Dr. 37, SG (Montans?). First half of 2nd century
vi) Dr. 27 rim, burnt, CG. Hadrianic or early Antonine
vii) Dr. 37, SG (Montans). Flavian or Flavian-Trajanic

D2010 i) Dr. 15/17 or 18, SG. Flavian or Flavian-Trajanic
ii) Dish, CG (Lezoux). Flavian
iii) Curle 21, EG (Argonne or Rheinzabern). All glaze ground or eroded away. *c.* AD 150–250

D3001 i) Dr. 18/31 or 31 rim, CG. Hadrianic or early Antonine
ii) Dish or bowl, CG. Antonine
iii) Dr. 31, EG (Argonne). All glaze ground or eroded away. *c.* AD 150–200

D3003 i) Dr. 37, SG. Flavian or Flavian-Trajanic
ii) Dr. 30 or 37, CG. Hadrianic or Antonine
iii) Dr. 38 rim, heavily burnt, CG. Late Hadrianic or early Antonine
iv) Curle 21, EG (Rheinzabern). Late 2nd or first half of 3rd century
v) Dr. 37, CG. Flavian or Flavian-Trajanic
vi) Dr. 37, EG (Rheinzabern). Late 2nd or first half of 3rd century

D3004 i) –, SG. First century
ii) Cup, CG. Hadrianic or Antonine
iii) Dr. 38 (flange) and a bulbous beaker, CG. Antonine
iv) Dr. 18/31R (rim) and 33 (rim), CG. Hadrianic or early Antonine
v) Dr. 31 (rim), CG. Mid- to late Antonine
vi) Dr. 31R, CG. All internal glaze ground or eroded away. Mid- to late Antonine
vii) Dr. 45 (collar) and gritted samian mortarium (base and footring, all internal glaze ground away), CG. *c.* AD 170–200
viii) Dr. 31R, EG (Rheinzabern). Late 2nd or first half of 3rd century
ix) Dr. 37, SG (Montans). Trajanic to early Antonine

D3005 i) Dr. 42 (rim, with part of a strap-handle), CG. Hadrianic or early Antonine
ii) Dr. 33 (rim), CG. Hadrianic or Antonine

D3007 Dr. 18/31–31 (1/2 joining, one rim), CG. Early Antonine

D3008 Dr. 37, SG (Montans). Trajanic to early Antonine

D3010 Dr. 31R rim, CG. Mid- to late Antonine

D4001 i) Dr. 18/31R (rim) and 42 (rim, with strap-handle), CG. Hadrianic or early Antonine
ii) Dr. 30 or 37 (rim), CG. Antonine
iii) Dr. 18/31–31 (1/2, one base and footring), EG (Argonne). Early Antonine
iv) Footring, EG (Argonne). *c.* AD 150–200
v) Dr. 37, CG, in the style of Doeccus. *c.* AD 165–200

D4002 i) Dr. 30 (rim), CG. Neronian-Flavian
ii) –, SG (Montans). First half of 2nd century
iii) Dr. 18/31 or 31 (rim) and Curle 15 (rim), CG. Hadrianic or early Antonine
iv) Dr. 18/31 or 31 (rim), Déchelette 64 (?) and –, CG. Hadrianic or Antonine
v) Dr. 30 or 37 (rim), 46 and a jar, CG. Antonine
vi) Dr. 15/31, 31R and Curle 21, CG. Mid- to late Antonine
vii) Dr 31 (1/2, joining), EG (Argonne or Rheinzabern). Antonine or first half of 3rd century
viii) Dr. 37, EG (Rheinzabern). Late 2nd or first half of 3rd century. Worn inside

D4003 i) Dr. 27, SG (Montans). First half of 2nd century
ii) Dr. 33 and 37, CG. Hadrianic or early Antonine
iii) –, CG. Hadrianic or Antonine
iv) Cup, CG. Antonine

D4005 Jar, CG. Flavian or Flavian-Trajanic

D4007 –, CG. Hadrianic or Antonine

Samian from other sites in Guernsey and Herm

by Brenda Dickinson

Cross-references are supplied to the Gazetteer in this volume. Excavation finds post-2001 are not included here. Abbreviations as for reports above; GMAG indicates an accessioned item at Guernsey Museum.

La Varde, Vale (Gazetteer A1)

GMAG 3386b Dr. 36 (flange), CG. Hadrianic or Antonine (Burns and Burns 1985, fig. 3.13)

GMAG 3386c Dr. 35/36, CG. Hadrianic or Antonine (Burns and Burns 1985, fig. 3.14)
GMAG 3386d Dr. 37, CG. Hadrianic or Antonine (Burns and Burns 1985, fig. 3.15, wrongly labelled as Herm)
GMAG 3386e Dr. 30, CG. Flavian (Burns and Burns 1985, fig. 3.16, wrongly labelled as St Sampson's Harbour)
GMAG 3386f Dr. 37, CG. Antonine
GMAG 3386g Dr. 33 (rim), CG. Hadrianic to mid Antonine (Burns and Burns 1985, fig. 3.12)
GMAG 3386h Dish or bowl, EG (La Madeleine?). Hadrianic-Antonine
Dr. 15/31 (rim), 33, dish and dish or bowl, CG. Antonine
GMAG 3386i Dr. 37 (rim), CG. Hadrianic or Antonine
GMAG 3386j Dr. 18/31 or 31, CG. Hadrianic or Antonine
Dr. 27 (?), CG. Hadrianic or early Antonine?
Curle 21 (?), CG. *c*. AD 150–200
GMAG 3386k – (1/2), CG. Antonine. Decorated with a barbotine animal
GMAG 3386l –, SG. First century
Cup (?), SG (Banassac?). Trajanic to early Antonine
–, (three), CG. Hadrianic or Antonine
Dr. 31R and dish or bowl, CG. Mid- to late Antonine
Dr. 18/31R, burnt, CG or EG. Second century
–, EG (Argonne or Rheinzabern). Late 2nd or first half of 3rd century
GMAG 3386l? Curle 15 or 23, SG. Flavian or Flavian-Trajanic
Dish, burnt, SG (Banassac?). Trajanic to early Antonine
– (two), CG. Hadrianic or Antonine
Dr. 33, CG. Antonine

NB: the GMAG collection includes several more unclassified scraps of samian from La Varde.

Le Creux ès Faïes, St Peter's (Gazetteer A3)
GMAG 3052 Dr. 30 or 37 (rim), CG. Hadrianic or Antonine. Shaped as a pierced disc, heavily cross–hatched on the back, after shaping

Le Tranquesous, St Saviour (Gazetteer A10)
TRS 76 Dr. 30 or 37 rim, SG. Neronian or early Flavian

The Pollet, St Peter Port (Gazetteer A12)
PO 80 T2 L5 Dr. 37, SG (Montans). First half of 2nd century
Dish or bowl, CG. Hadrianic or Antonine
Dr. 31, EG (Rheinzabern). Late 2nd or first half of 3rd century
PO 80 T3 L5 Dr. 37, CG. Hadrianic or Antonine
Dr. 44, CG. Antonine

Grandes Rocques, Castel (Gazetteer A16)
GR86 S/L1 14 Cup, very heavily burnt. Probably CG and 2nd century, if samian at all

Royal Hotel, St Peter Port (Gazetteer A23)
RHS 99 Curle 15 rim, CG. Hadrianic or early Antonine
RHS 01 T4 L3 Cup, SG (Montans). First century
–, CG. Hadrianic or early Antonine
Dr. 31 (base and footring), CG. Antonine
RHS 01 T4 L4 Enclosed vessel (?), SG. Flavian or Flavian-Trajanic
RHS 01 T4 F80 Dr. 30 or 37 (rim), CG. Hadrianic or early Antonine

Route de Carteret, Castel (Gazetteer A24)
RDC 00 B113 Cup or dish (1/2), CG. Hadrianic or Antonine
RDC 01 B119 Cup (footring), CG. Hadrianic or early Antonine

Herm (Gazetteer B9)
GMAG 3387 Dr. 33 (1/3 rims, two joining), CG. Mid- to late Antonine
Dr. 33 (rim), EG (Rheinzabern?). Late 2nd or first half of 3rd century
Footring, EG (Argonne?). *c*. AD 150–200
–, EG, late 2nd or first half of 3rd century
GMAG 3388a Dr. 37, EG (Rheinzabern). Mid- to late Antonine
GMAG 3388b/c Dr. 31, CG. Mid- to late Antonine

La Salerie, St Peter Port (Gazetteer B20)
Dr. 18/31 (base and footring), SG (Montans). First half of 2nd century (Burns and Burns 1985, fig. 3.10)
Dr. 30 or 37 (rim), EG (La Madeleine). Hadrianic-Antonine (Burns and Burns 1985, fig. 3.11)
Dr. 30 or 37 (rim), CG. Antonine (Burns and Burns 1985, fig. 3.9)

Cow Bay, St Peter Port, 1983 (Gazetteer B21)
GMAG 1984.125
Dr. 31, Curle 15 or 23 (two) and Curle 23 (rim), CG. Antonine
Dr. 37 (rim), SG (Montans). Hadrianic-Antonine (Burns and Burns 1985, fig. 3.1)
Curle 23, CG. Antonine (Burns and Burns 1985, fig. 3.3)
Curle 21, EG (Rheinzabern). Late 2nd or first half of 3rd century
Dr. 31R, CG. Mid- to late Antonine
Curle 23 (base and footring), CG. Mid- to late Antonine (Burns and Burns 1985, fig. 3.8)

Dr. 18/31 (rim), CG. Hadrianic or early Antonine

Dr. 38 or 44 (base and footring), CG. Antonine

Cow Bay, St Peter Port, 1985 (Gazetteer B21)

-	Hemispherical bowl, CG, but not necessarily Lezoux ware. Unstamped, but with ring incised in base, and with fluting under the base. Second century
CB974	Dr. 31R (rim), CG. Mid- to late Antonine
CB975	Flat dish (base and footring), CG. Early Antonine. Perhaps an early variant of Walters 79 or Ludowici Tg

Cow Bay, St Peter Port, 1997 (Gazetteer B21)

CB973	Dr. 37 (rim), SG (Banassac?), with blurred decoration. Trajanic to early Antonine
-	Dr. 33, CG, with stamp of Macrinus iii of Lezoux. *c.* AD 150–80
-	Dr. 38 (?) flange, EG (Trier?). Late 2nd or first half of 3rd century?

Cow Bay, St Peter Port, 2001 (Gazetteer B21)

-	Curle 15 (rim), CG. Hadrianic or early Antonine

Dredged off harbour (St Sampson's?), 1860 (Gazetteer B35)

GMAG 3386a	Dr. 35 (flange), CG. Hadrianic or Antonine. The barbotine leaves on the flange seem to have been made from a lighter clay than the cup itself. Note: this vessel is definitely samian ware; it was previously published as a probable late Romano-British product of the Oxfordshire kilns (Burns 1986, 659, no. 17)

St Peter Port harbour (Gazetteer C7)

1655	Curle 21, CG. *c.* AD 150–200
2544	Dr. 31 (footring), CG. Antonine
G4803	Déchelette 72 (base and foot ring, slightly burnt), CG. *c.* AD 150–200
unmarked	Dr. 31 (footring), CG. Antonine
	Dr. 37, CG, style of Albucius ii. *c.* AD 150–180

St Peter Port harbour, sea bed (Gazetteer C7)

G5749–49a	Curle 23, CG. Mid- to late Antonine. Unstamped, but small boss in the centre of the base, surrounded by fluting.

CATALOGUE OF DRAWN SAMIAN (FIG. 65)

Bonded Store

1. Dr. 37, SG (Montans), context C2097
2. Dr. 33, CG, with stamp of Agileito, context C2094
3. Dr. 37, CG, sherd showing cherub (?) converted to counter, context C3017
4. Dr. 33, CG, base sherd with stamp SEXTIMA, context C2004

Other sites

5. Dr. 33, base with stamp DIVICA, St Peter Port harbour (Gazetteer C7).

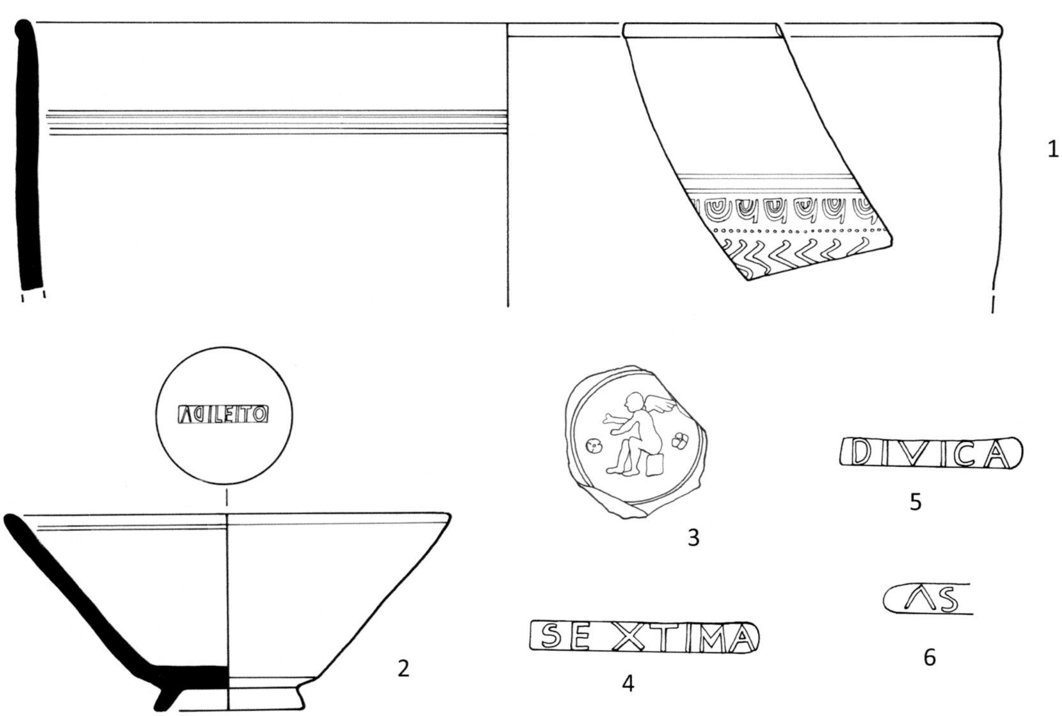

Figure 65 Samian from the Bonded Store and other sites. Scale 1:2 (nos 1–3), 1:1 (nos 4–6).

6. CG, stamp of ASIATICUS, St Peter Port harbour (Gazetteer C7)

Roman pottery from other sites in Guernsey and Herm

by Jason Monaghan

The pottery was viewed by hand on a 'spot dating' basis, which did not involve fabric analysis beyond recognition of broad traded types. The unstratified or residual nature of most of the sherds made more sophisticated analysis redundant for this exercise. Some had previously been examined by Mark Wood and commented on in his work. The material from La Varde, plus some other harbour material, was published by Burns and Burns (1985) and some maritime finds by Monaghan (1988 and 1990).

Most of the harbour or maritime ceramic finds showed some degree of abrasion and many had marine growths upon them. It cannot be ascertained whether the harbour finds came from shipwrecks, were discarded overboard from ships, come from disturbed land sites or were simply dumped in the sea. They represent a random sample of the pottery in use in Guernsey between the 1st and 4th centuries AD. The predominant fabrics are a variety of greywares, probably from northern Gaul. Fittingly for a harbour, there are a significant number of amphora sherds. Harbour finds have tended to include more complete vessels than the land sites. Underwater finds other than the pierheads wreck ('Asterix') have chiefly comprised amphorae, with major concentrations at Little Russel 'site A' (Gazetteer C4) and 'site B' (Gazetteer C2).

Much of the material from terrestrial sites was small and abraded, indicating high residuality (Table 11). Away from the harbour there were far fewer amphorae, and mortarium sherds were very rare. At 9% of terrestrial and littoral finds, samian is by far the most important fineware, although it may have been more easily spotted during the fieldwalk and beachwalk activities. A significant number of sherds in iron-free fabrics appeared to come from flagons, and there were instances of white-slipped oxidised flagons as well. Fabrics are, however, very mixed, showing a diversity of sources beyond the island. Small near-black sherds could not easily be distinguished between true black-burnished ware, its Iron Age predecessor and possibly similar Gaulish pottery.

Cow Bay (Gazetteer B21) yielded a fair cross-section of Guernsey's Roman ceramics, including the noticeable north Gaulish greyware with its light core and sometimes burnished bands. It also yielded examples of the other northern Gaulish grey fabrics which seem to have been a staple of the island. A large piece of terra nigra, and a second found loose in the harbour nearby, represents the early pottery trade.

Both the Savoy (Gazetteer A26) and Royal Hotel (Gazetteer A23) sites yielded similar selections of small sherds of Roman pots, suggesting these may not themselves have been important Roman sites, yet were in the vicinity of such sites which had been extensively disturbed and possibly completely destroyed.

At 209 sherds plus 290 possibly Roman scraps, the Royal Hotel yielded the largest assemblage away from the well-stratified Roman sites. With a high percentage of oxidised sherds, vessels which are apparently flagons, and a high count of 'white' sherds (if they are not post-Roman), there is a suggestion of a highly disturbed cremation cemetery. The presence of micaceous wares and the general absence of BB1 and the Tripod Bowl fabric indicates an early date span, probably 1st to 2nd century. The small amount of tile and the absence of amphorae support this idea. Mortaria are also absent, but are pretty rare in Guernsey overall. Quite a lot of the sherds are rounded, indicating that they have been in the sea or at least on the beach. A large number of very small oxidised scraps were difficult to identify with any certainty, so are excluded from the summary table. Samian is suitably well represented at 10% of sherds, although rather more than this would be expected if it was a classic cemetery with three or four funerary vessels per burial.

Due to the small size and residual nature of most of the sherds at the Royal Hotel, it is possible that a number identified as Roman white ware could be a late/post-medieval white ware such as Beauvais. Likewise small oxidised sherds are often difficult to identify when residual in later contexts. Some of the thinner oxidised sherds are possibly abraded samian.

Graffiti

by R. S. O. Tomlin

Two sherds (nos 1–2, below) found in the same context (C2094) at the Bonded Store bear inscriptions, and there is an inscription on a mortarium from Trench 1, F.69 at La Plaiderie (no. 3). These are likely to represent the earliest personal names recorded from Guernsey.

1. Wall sherd of a flagon in dark fabric with pink oxidised surface, scratched above the shoulder after firing:

   [...]V͡ΛT

Probably *Vat(...)*, an abbreviated personal name.

Although broken to the left, the graffito is probably complete, with V ligatured to 'open' A. The reading [.] MT is just possible, with incomplete M; this would be the name of a Roman citizen reduced to its three initials, but it seems most unlikely. For other examples of the abbreviation VAT, see *RIB* II.7, 2501.573 (London) and II.8, 2503.598 (Old Winteringham). Possible names are all

Table 11 Summary of pottery from small terrestrial sites.

Site	*A*	*M*	*W*	*O*	*G*	*F*	*B*	*N*	*S*	*C*	*X*	*T*	*Q*	*n*
La Varde (A1)	1			1	2				23				1	
Le Déhus (A2)				1										
Le Creux ès Faïes (A3)									2				1	
Lihou (A4)	2											1		a
Castel Church (A6)				2					1			732		b
Cobo (A9)	1											1	2	
Le Tranquesous (A10)	11		20	161	4	2	2	21	1		67		4	c
The Pollet (A12)									5					
King's Road (A13)	19				3		1	3	1		9			
Grandes Rocques (A16)				1					1					
Albecq (A17)					1	1								
Lefebvre Street (A18)	1		1	4	2	1		1	2	2				
Sunrise Cottage (A20)												1		
Fort Grey (A21)								1				2	1097	d
Fisherman's B'h (A22)	1		4	4	4	4	15	2		1	1	3	523	e
Herm (A22?)	1			3	3	1	1		3				10	f
Royal Hotel (A23)			24	90	50	14	2	1	20	6	2	7	15	g
Route de Carteret (A24)				1					3					
Les Canichers (A25)			4	1	7	1			1			1		
Savoy Hotel (A26)	1		8	13	26	8	1		6	3	2			h
St Peter P. School (A27)				2					2			2		
Jethou (A28)							1							
West of airport (A30)	2			11	1	3		2				4		i
Les Vardes quarry (A31)					1			1					3	
St Martin's Ch.(A32)									1					
St Tugual's Ch. (A33)								1						
Le Tertre (A34)				1										
Le Maresquet (A35)												1		
Rue des Prevosts (B10)											1			j
Les Arquets (B11)				1		1								
R. des Saumarez (B12)				2										
La Terre Norgiot (B13)			1	10	1	1	1				3			k
Jerbourg (B14)				1										
Les Prevosts (B15)				1										
Les Paysans (B16)				1										
Fort Le Marchant (B18)			2	1	4	1	3							
Cow B. (B21)/SPPH (C7)	74	7	4	34	85	12	15	14	26	7	12	33	1	l
Jethou (B22)					1									
Bailiff's Cross (B24)			1	7	2							18		m
Herm (B25)							1							
Le Neuf Chemin (B26)					2									
L'Ancresse (B27)	1													
L'Ancresse (B28)	1													

Table 11 Summary of pottery from small terrestrial sites. (Continued)

Site	*A*	*M*	*W*	*O*	*G*	*F*	*B*	*N*	*S*	*C*	*X*	*T*	*Q*	*n*
L'Erée (B30)					1									
Perelle Bay (B31)		1												
Le Crocq (B32)				1										
La Villiaze (B33)				1										
													total (pot)	
terrestrial totals	116	8	69	356	200	50	43	47	98	19	97		1103	
%	10.5	0.7	6.3	32.3	18.1	4.5	3.9	4.3	8.9	1.7	8.8		100	

The table includes only sherds which have been available for examination, and not (for example) those sites with antiquarian records of Roman sherds which cannot now be verified.

Key:

A: amphora; M: mortaria; W: 'white/cream' fabrics; O: oxidised; G: grey coarse; F: fine grey; B: black-burnished, BB1, BB2 and imitations; N: north Gaulish greyware; S: samian; C: colour-coated ware; X: other recognisable; T: tile; Q: briquetage; n: note.

Notes:

a) possibly a few more pieces of tile.

b) totals to 2012 inclusive; additional material has been recovered more recently.

c) all X type pottery is terra nigra.

d) combines Cunliffe excavations of 1999 with antiquarian and recent finds.

e) combines Cunliffe excavations of 1999 with antiquarian and recent finds. X is terra nigra.

f) antiquarian finds probably from the Fisherman's Beach site.

g) X is two mica-dusted sherds; also 290 scraps not identified.

h) X is one shell-tempered greyware sherd, one imitation samian sherd. Also 15 unidentified scraps.

i) also six unidentified scraps.

j) X is terra nigra.

k) X is terra nigra.

l) Combines beach finds from Cow Bay (B21) and harbour finds principally made by diving in the 1980s/90s (C7). Some of the latter (in particular the amphorae sherds) may come from the Little Russel A wreck (Gazetter C4). X includes four *céramique à l'éponge* (probably from A15), two terra nigra, two Argonne, and four MDER.

m) oxidised sherds and tile not all convincingly identified.

rare; in Britain they include *Vatta* (*RIB* 610) and *Vatiaucus* (*RIB* II.3, 2432.4).

2. Wall sherd in pink fabric, scratched after firing:

[…]I VI[…]

The third letter is a downstroke broken at the top, which is therefore incomplete; possibilities such as II = E, M or N, cannot be excluded. Its closeness to V suggests that V was preceded by a space, which would imply that the first I is the end of another name in the genitive case. Since the scratches all seem to be by the same hand, it is possible that the owner had two names, for example [IVL]I VI[IRI], or even that his name was followed by a numeral VI[...], but the latter would be unlikely. But since so little survives, the question remains open.

3. Mortarium, exterior, scratched after firing (Fig. 62.97):

DIV I.S

DIV is likely to be the abbreviated name of the owner, and the likeliest is the Celtic name DIVIXTVS. Any other name in Diu- is very rare indeed. I.S is less certain, but ought to be the numeral '1' followed by s(emis), for 'half', i.e. recording 'one and a half' units. There is no obvious correlation to the size or volume of the vessel, however, and thus the interpretation remains somewhat uncertain.

5

Other finds

Roman brick and tile

by Jason Monaghan

The Bonded Store

Almost 80kg of Roman brick and tile was recovered from the site (Table 12). Much was clearly residual, mixed with some medieval tile and a fair amount of post-medieval (Victorian) brick. The tile was considerably fragmented, with the weight per piece being only 45g compared to 131g at Castel Church (see below). There were 985 fragments with an average weight of 12 grams each that could not be identified as a particular form, and indeed could include some abraded pottery, brick or briquetage. Very few match breaks were observed, suggesting considerable disturbance and redeposition. Flat bricks were indistinguishable from pieces of floor tile so both are combined.

FABRICS

No fabric analysis was performed during the main research, although Phil Mills kindly commented on a number of fabric samples; no sources could be identified and his report is in the archive. The tile was predominantly in a range of terracotta fabrics, but 36 were identified in a variety of off-white iron-free fabrics (Table 13). The most striking feature is the abundance of a strange 'light' fabric making up a quarter of the sherd count and a fifth of the weight. Mills suggested that this was more akin to mudbrick than properly fired ceramic. This lightweight material occurred in both imbrices and tegulae, and was spread across many contexts. Its average sherd weight was 34g compared to 49g for the regular fabrics. The 'mudbrick' tile was virtually inclusion-free and varied in colour from off-white through light grey, light yellow and light terracotta shades. In the hand it feels almost the weight of wood. It is soft, shatters and erodes easily, so the abundance of this tile suggests it came from

Table 12 The Bonded Store: summary of brick and tile.

	No.	*g.*	*% no.*	*% wt*	*wt g/sherd*
flat	10	1767	1.3	2.6	176
imbrex	254	16,767	32.6	24.8	66
tegula	514	49,082	66.1	72.6	95
fragments	985	12,083	excluded	excluded	12
Total	1763	79,699	100	100	45

Table 13 The Bonded Store: summary of tile fabric types.

	No.	*g.*	*wt g/sherd*
'terracotta'			
flat	10	1767	176
imbrex	156	11,956	77
tegula	320	39,112	122
fragments	780	9788	13
subtotal	1266	62,623	49
'iron free'			
imbrex	18	1165	65
tegula	5	255	51
fragments	13	211	16
subtotal	36	1631	45
'light'			
imbrex	80	3646	45
tegula	189	9715	51
fragments	192	2084	11
subtotal	461	15,445	34
Overall total	1763	79,699	45

a building in very close proximity. Its ratio of imbrex to tegula weight is 38%, suggesting that a whole building was tiled in this material. A *tegula* found at the Canichers, St Peter Port, in 2001 was in a similar but not identical light fabric, as were a few pieces from La Plaiderie.

FORM

The ratio of tegulae to imbrices on an intact building is close to 1:1, with perhaps 5–10% more tegulae than imbrices unless imbrices were also used as ridge tiles, which would make the expected numbers even. However, an imbrex will break into fewer pieces than a larger tegula and will be only approximately 40% its weight. The weight of imbrices found at the Bonded Store was 34% of the weight of tegulae, close to the proposed ideal of 40%, indicating that a properly roofed building was in the vicinity.

Of the tegulae, 32 corners were noted in both light and terracotta fabrics (Table 14). There was a marked preference for Warry Type B6 corners for the terracotta tiles (Warry 2006, 44), whereas the light fabric favoured Type C5, although neither was exclusive. One of the light C5 corners could indeed have been modified from a B6. Warry puts C5 as a later type than B6, although they clearly co-existed. Three 'signatures' were observed on tegulae. One tegula had a faint impression which could be a stamp.

None of the tegulae had nail holes, as was also the case at the Castel Church. Warry (2006, 103) noted the frequency of nail holes on tegulae from civilian sites he surveyed (one tile in four) compared with a general absence of nail holes from legionary sites of the 1st and 2nd centuries. The substantial amount of tile found at the assumed late Roman fort at the Nunnery between 2008 and 2012 has likewise yielded no nail-holes. No tile-stamps have been definitely recognised on any Guernsey or Alderney site to date, despite the clear military activity in Alderney.

OTHER TILE AND BUILDING MATERIALS

There were few clearly identifiable flat bricks/floor tiles (pedales/bipedales), no indication of hypocaust pilae, and only suggestions that two fragments may be from box tiles. One fragment may have come from an antefix but could equally be a pottery handle. Other ceramic building material included 33 pieces of daub and one piece of *opus signinum*, totalling 1.7kg.

Table 14 The Bonded Store: summary of tegula corner types.

	left upper	*right upper*	*left lower*	*right lower*	*lower cut–out types (Warry 2006)*
terracotta	2	6	5	8	B6×9; C5×2; D1×1
iron free	–	–	1	–	C5×1
light	1	3	2	4	B6×2; C5×4

A large amount of Victorian and some medieval brick was found, making it difficult to distinguish the pieces of true Roman brick amongst the residual.

WATER-ROLLED OR BURNED TILE

Several contexts featured tile and/or pot which had been rolled in water, including A1203, A2204, C1002, C1004, C1066, C2004, C2092, D2002, D2005, D2009 and D3002. This indicates that this was residual material coming up from the beach – mostly in the post-Roman period. Seven tiles showed signs of burning, but in no significant concentration.

FRAGMENTATION

The fragmentation differs sharply between areas (Table 15). The light 'mudbrick' fabric is distributed across the site, but there is little in Area D, where it all occurs in post-Roman layers. It shows a similar fragmentation to the other fabrics across the areas. In Area B it is mainly in post-Roman contexts except B1204 and B1205, which are at least 3rd century. In Area A, it is all in post-Roman contexts (although A2007 is re-deposited Roman). In Area C, much is again residual, but there is a concentration in Period 2 (C2004) and in the higher Roman contexts in Trench 3 (Table 16). This suggests a late date for the destruction of this building, if not its construction.

Table 15 The Bonded Store: summary of tile fragmentation by area.

	Area A	*Area B*	*Area C*	*Area D*
all fabrics	166	151	1091	346
total weight/g	9963	12,904	50,408	7178
wt g/sherd	60	85	46	21
% all sherds	9.5	8.6	62	20
% weight	12	16	63	9
'light' fabric	69	40	332	18
'light' weight/g	2163	1942	10,837	432
'light' wt g/sherd	31	49	33	24
'light' as % of all weight	22	15	21	6

Table 16 The Bonded Store: summary of tile distribution by phase.

	Phase 1	*Phase 2*	*Phase 3*	*Residual*
all Areas				
sherds	153	1020	135	478
weight/g	6024	42,584	4467	31,363
weight g/sherd	39	42	33	66
Area C only				
sherds	29	765	111	198
weight/g	2267	35,845	3776	12,145
weight g/sherd	78	47	34	61

All the tile is residual in Area A except A1204. In Area C there is none in the lower levels of Trench 1, but a little in the Roman layers above. Area C Trench 3 contained the best stratified tile on the site, down to the hoggin layer C3035 and C3039. The large average sherd size amongst the residual pottery indicates the upper layers were disturbed on a limited number of occasions rather than extensively re-worked.

Castel Church (CCH 99, CCH05 and CCH12)

Some 58kg of Roman tile was derived from a number of shallow trenches excavated beneath the nave of Castel Church in 1999. Additional material was collected in January 2005 from lighting pits and cable trenches dug outside the church around the north of the nave. No material came from pits dug on the south side in 2005. In 2012 a pipe trench was mechanically dug from outside the church, running downhill to the north. Another haul of Roman tiles and *opus signinum* fragments was extracted from the spoil which lay parallel to the trench. No obvious stratigraphy could be seen in the walls of the trench.

It is likely that all this material is residual in medieval or post-medieval levels, although some of the 1999 contexts did not contain any confirmed post-Roman finds. One striking observation is that very little Roman pottery was found, despite the overall quantity of tile being similar to that found at the Bonded Store. Pottery sherds are smaller and more mobile than large pieces of tile and would be expected to be more easily disturbed and moved 'upwards' in the stratigraphic sequence by later activity. It suggests disturbance of destruction deposits rather than of deep Roman stratigraphy. In turn it holds out hope there is a relatively undisturbed site beneath the churchyard.

It is unlikely that the material found beneath the nave in 1999 was an *in situ* Roman deposit, given the loose nature of the ground from which the bulk of the tile came. It is more likely to have been material disturbed via robbing, foundation digging, or pit digging in the post-Roman period.

Some of the tiles are in large pieces, yet there are very few match breaks either within or between contexts. This in itself suggests considerable disturbance from their original deposit, but not the kind of repeat disturbance which would smash up the tiles into small pieces. The fact that many tiles still have quite fragile mortar adhering supports this.

The material recovered from the graveyard in 2005 supports the picture of Roman debris spreading down the hill to the north. Given many centuries of grave-digging, however, this material could have been disturbed from a considerable depth or moved some distance horizontally. Again, no Roman pottery was found.

In 2012, the pipe trench went deeper than the 2005 trench and resulted in another 20kg of tile being brought up, plus 107 *opus signinum* fragments totalling 3.4kg. Some of this was quite broken up by what is presumably repeated disturbance by grave-digging. Some pieces of tile and *opus signinum* were still attached to mortar, suggesting they have not travelled far. The finds tailed-off further down the hill where it is known that the graveyard was 'made up' by several feet in early modern times to accommodate a new tier of burials. This is confirmed by the greater quantity of post-medieval material found to the north (downhill) of the cemetery path. Four Roman pot sherds were found in spoil from this trench.

THE ROMAN BUILDING(S)

The tile is of a fairly homogenous nature, including tegulae and imbrices from the roof and pedales/bipedales from the floor or walls. This homogeneity indicates that the source material was a single building or closely related group of buildings constructed at a similar date. A small amount of daub was recovered, plus grey-white mortar and a pinker mortar which may rank as *opus signinum*. Most of the *opus signinum* came from the 2012 trench. One piece of granite found in 2012 had mortar adhering, with a thin sliver of tile, suggesting that was from a 'bonding' course. Some of the 2012 imbrices have *opus signinum* on top of their curved surfaces, and one has a layer of *opus signinum* below the grey mortar. Some pieces are shaped to suggest tile was once in contact. This opens up questions as to what exact structure this material came from. One, possibly two, pieces of box tile were found. Four tegulae and two imbrices showed signs of burning or overheating, but this is not sufficient to draw any conclusions.

Fragments of plaster were recovered and many tiles had thick mortar on the outer surface. None of this showed any indication of painting or decoration.

The repeat findings of tile on the site, and the quantity of tile found, points to a substantial building once standing on the platform where the church now stands, or very close nearby. It is possible that the building was levelled out, the rubble being quarried for materials, explaining why mainly larger pieces of tile are found in this location, having been robbed out, then subsequently dumped again. There is no evidence to suggest that the site was a kiln site or tile warehouse.

A statue-menhir which stands on the site has been described by Professor Colin Renfrew as possibly the oldest sculpture in the British Isles. Taken with the later choice of the site for a church, this strongly suggests that the Roman building may have been a temple. However, the elevated position and the excellent views to the north also offer the site as being a good position for a small fort or signal station such as is found at the Nunnery, in Alderney (Monaghan 2011–12). Indeed, there is a similarity in the material found on both sites, namely a good deal of residual Roman tile in later layers but not much Roman pottery. John McCormack has also pointed out (pers. comm.) that it is

Table 17 Castel Church: summary of tile.

	No.	Weight/g	% no.	% weight	Weight g/ sherd
1999					
flat	79	30,374	18	52	384
imbrex	113	8099	25	14	72
tegula	189	18,970	42	32	100
other	64	1026	14	2	16
Total	445	58,469	99	100	131
2005					
flat	4	2787	13	47	–
imbrex	4	368	13	6	–
tegula	23	2789	74	47	–
other	0	–	–	–	–
Total	31	5944	100	100	–
2012					
flat	80	6559	34	32	82
imbrex	29	3111	12	15	107
tegula	120	9953	52	49	83
other	4	421	1	2	105
scraps	23	834	excluded	excluded	–
Total	256	20,986	99	99	–

the only Guernsey churchyard that was originally square, possibly echoing an original Roman plan. Perhaps the ruin of this Roman building – *castrum* or *castellum*? – lies behind the legendary 'Castel' which gives the church and the parish its name.

QUANTITATIVE ANALYSIS

Some 445 pieces of tile were recovered in 1999, a further 31 in 2005, and 256 in 2012, plus 2kg of small fragments of indeterminate date which were discarded (Table 17). Floor tiles and 'flat bricks' could not be wholly distinguished and a number of smaller fragments classed as tegula could instead have been from floor tiles or bricks.

IMBRICES

In the 1999 dig, the weight of imbrices was *c*.43% the weight of the tegulae. This indicates that a properly roofed building was in the vicinity and there has been no 'sorting' in ancient times to separate tegulae from imbrices. The ratio is 31% in the 2012 trench.

TEGULAE

The tegulae are of standard type, and as at the Bonded Store, none has a nailhole. Five tegulae found in 1999 exhibited 'signatures', plus three more from the 2005 finds. Of the 20 recovered lower corners, 14 had cut-outs of Warry Type B6 and four incomplete pieces could also be Type B. The single type D16 had a flange with an irregular profile, such that a tile maker aiming at a B6 could easily have ended up with a D16 by accident. Warry dates Type B primarily to the 2nd century.

FLAT BRICKS

An interesting proportion of the tiles are flat bricks, smaller ones of 'pedales' size and thick pieces which are assumed to be bipedales. No examples were found of these stacked, as if functioning as hypocaust pilae. Some 42 pieces (half the collection) had mortar or plaster on one or both sides. It is likely therefore that these have been used as bonding courses in a wall. The more intact flat bricks are mostly pedales, roughly 33mm thick and 290mm square (i.e. slightly smaller than a Roman foot). The most complete example came from 1999 (context 022), with a whole edge and two corners preserved. This indicates that an intact tile would weigh approximately 6kg.

Three of the flat bricks were up to 65mm thick and all examples were delaminating. These are probably huge bipedales. The 2012 trench produced fragments of a similar delaminating fabric which included many plate-like shards of fired clay within its fabric. Some of this material was sintered.

FABRICS

The fabric of the majority of the tiles is unremarkable, being various shades of terracotta, with moderate sandy inclusions. The flat bricks are particularly homogenous. A small number of tiles were in aberrant fabrics with higher shell or mica content and some were made in low-iron clay, resulting in pale pink or off-white colouration.

La Plaiderie

Building materials from La Plaiderie were retained selectively on-site, and it is not known to what extent or on what basis they were 'weeded', so a complete record cannot be compiled. Therefore the tile has not been fully quantified for this report, but a review of the boxes of tiles and items on display was undertaken. Some 22 boxes of tile from La Plaiderie remained, of which 20 were exclusively Roman. This compares with 12 boxes from the Bonded Store. Just over 2000 sherds were noted on the record sheets and context T1 F.44 alone yielded 1253 pieces. The original quantity recovered was undoubtedly more than at the Bonded Store.

The material included a small proportion of tiles in the 'light' fabric seen at the Bonded Store. Most tiles fabrics were variations on terracotta, with a coarse sandy fabric being particularly noticeable. The remaining tile examined included:

6 tegulae with 'signatures'
4 tegulae with paw-prints: three dog, one sheep/goat
7 upper right corners of tegulae
14 upper left corners of tegulae
17 lower right corners of tegulae
19 lower left corners of tegulae
2 uncertain lower corners of tegulae
1 nail hole in small sherd of unusual light pink fabric

Tegula cut-out types amounted to 21 of type C5, six of type B6 and ten which were incomplete on the outer edge so could be either C5 or B6. There is clear similarity with both the Bonded Store and Castel Church in the choice of cut-out design and the absence of nail-holes; the only nail-hole in fact coming from a tile of an unusual fabric. As Type C appears to be a later 2nd- and 3rd-century product, a preponderance of Type C at the Plaiderie suggests a later date.

Romano-Celtic Ship PPPH1

The Roman ship from St Peter Port harbour sank *c.*AD 280 (Gazetteer A15). A total of 235 pieces of tile weighing 93.9kg were recovered from the area of the rear hold and the immediate seabed, amounting to:

171 pieces of tegulae, including several with match-breaks
52 pieces of imbrices, with only one match-break
8 box-flue tiles, with one match-break
5 flat brick/floor tiles

Of the 23 tegula lower corners, those available to study amounted to ten of Warry form C5, two were indeterminate B6 or C5, and four were B6 (i.e. both corners of the two reconstructed tiles illustrated in Rule and Monaghan 1993). Two fragments bore dog paw-prints and 13 tegula bottom edges had 'signatures', which were all different. A variety of fabrics was found on the Roman ship, which was clearly not 'local' in terms of its origin. The tile appeared to be part of the ship's structure, rather than cargo.

Briquetage

by Jason Monaghan

The Bonded Store

Briquetage is the name given to low-fired ceramics used in the boiling of salt, generally found in a highly fragmented state. The briquetage was partly sorted by Mark Wood, from fragments found in pottery bags, then partly by Jason Monaghan from pieces extracted from the building materials bags.

FORM AND FABRIC

The briquetage is found in various shades of red/brown through to orange/buff. It is handmade, friable and coarsely tempered with beach sand. A typical range of objects was found including both cylindrical and semi-rectangular boiling vessels, pads, props and shapeless squeezes. Some pieces of hearth or furnace have also become mixed with the briquetage, from which it is barely distinguishable. Likewise some smaller sherds classified as PRE (prehistoric) by Wood are also indistinguishable from those he classed as BQ (briquetage), and have been accounted for here.

DISTRIBUTION ON THE SITE

The briquetage is much less widely spread than the tile, with a greater concentration in Area C (Table 18) (although 61% by count, 62% by weight of tile was also in C). The impression is that salting activity took place on the site from the Iron Age through Phases 1 and 2. However, given the high level of residuality shown on this site it

Table 18 The Bonded Store: summary of briquetage quantity and weight by area and phase.

				Phase				
Area	*Pre-*	*Iron Age*	*1*	*2*	*3*	*Post-Roman*	*Total*	*% by area*
Quantity								
A	–	0	0	0	–	1	1	0.1
B	–	300	34	84	–	33	451	15.7
C	–	113	946	871	147	46	2123	74.1
D	5	18	243	13	0	11	290	10.1
Total	5	431	1223	968	147	91	2865	100
Weight/g								
A	–	0	0	0	–	8	8	<0.1
B	–	1900	221	350	–	236	2707	13
C	–	898	6852	7179	909	336	16,174	77.5
D	30	225	1546	69	0	107	1977	9.5
Total	30	3023	8619	7598	909	687	20,866	100

is useful to compare briquetage finds versus the Iron Age pottery distribution (Table 19). The briquetage is shown, if anything, to have an earlier bias than the IA/LIA pottery and certainly mirrors its residuality in Phases 2 and 3. Salting was therefore most likely an activity of the late Iron Age/Phase 1.

Table 19 The Bonded Store: summary of briquetage and prehistoric pottery sherd count.

	Phase						
	Pre-	*Iron Age*	*1*	*2*	*3*	*Post-Roman*	*Total*
sherd count							
briquetage	5	431	1223	968	147	91	2865
IA pottery	0	26	59	88	10	81	264
% of total							
briquetage	<1	15	43	34	5	3	100
IA pottery	0	10	22	33	14	31	100

A whole group of contexts contain briquetage but no tile, particularly in the stratigraphy from C4118 (Iron Age) to C4043 (Phase 1). There is a match link between C4048 in Phase 1 and C3036/C3034 in Phase 2, suggesting a similar history towards the bottom of the C Trench 3 and Trench 4 contexts. Context C1082, the furnace, also yielded many pieces of briquetage, suggesting that the 'furnace' may have been a salt-boiling area (or that furnace debris is indistinguishable from briquetage in this area). Contexts C3032, C3033, C3034 and C3035 from Roman Phase 2 and C3039 from Phase 1 contain interesting pieces of briquetage including props and parts of straight-sided boiling vessels (Fig. 66).

Catalogue of illustrated briquetage (Fig. 66)

1. Salting vessel, part of base and side (context C3039)
2. Salting vessel, similar form to no. 1 (context C3034)
3. Prop of hand-squeezed clay (context C3039)
4. Prop of hand-squeezed clay (context C3034)
5. Prop of hand-squeezed clay (context C3034)
6. Hand-brick (context C3034)

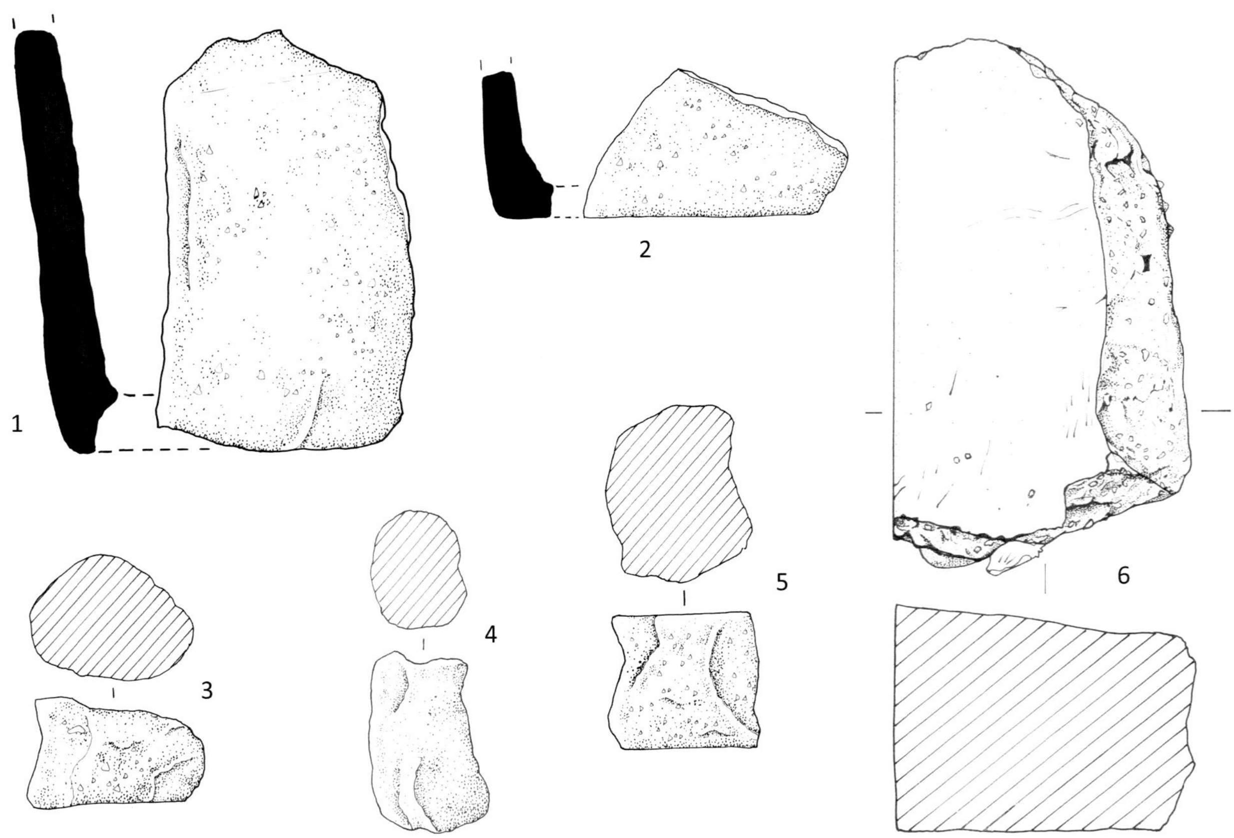

Figure 66 Briquetage from the Bonded Store. Scale 1:2.

Roman coins and coin moulds from La Plaiderie

by Cathy King and George Boon

The Roman coins were identified by Dr Cathy King of the Ashmolean Museum. Comments on the coin moulds were made by the late George Boon in 1984 and 1993. All coins are bronze unless otherwise noted.

Coins

Listed by small-find number:

10. Illegible, sestertius, probably late 2nd/early 3rd century AD (T1/F.20)
21. Silver denarius, Salonina, SALONINA AVG/IVN, AD 253–68 (T1/L2)
22. As or dupondius, early 2nd century AD, perhaps Trajan (T1/F.15)
27. Fragment of probable Roman coin; this coin was later stolen (T1/L2)
71. Illegible, possibly 4th century AD (T1/F.48)
83. Sestertius, Antoninus Pius, rev. Victory inscribing shield, mint of Rome, AD 161–80 (T1/L2)
92. Illegible, probably Roman (T1/L2)
112. Sestertius, Marcus Aurelius, AD 161–80 (T1/F.65)
125. Victorinus, rev. standing female figure, AD 268–70 (T1/F.47)
264. Sestertius, Marcus Aurelius, AD 163–64, *RIC* 861 (T2/F.121)

Coin moulds

Listed by small-find number:

17. One coin mould fragment, 'antoninianus of Gordian III AD 238–44 (obverse) and Philip I AD 244–49 (reverse), with the legend ANNON' (Boon, pers. comm.) (T1/L2)
18. One coin mould fragment, 'obverse of a denarius of Severus Alexander (AD 222–35), and the reverse is almost certainly from another coin of his which can be dated to AD 225' (Boon, pers. comm.) (T1/L2)
386. Four coin mould fragments, including 'part of an obverse impression of a denarius' (Boon, pers. comm.) (T2/F.126)
386a. Five coin mould fragments, including 'two of larger diameter than a denarius, so either an antoninianus or even a small as' (Boon, pers. comm.) (T2/F.126/7)
387. Sixteen coin mould fragments, including 'four… double-sided for denarii; one of these shows part of a seated figure to l. but not enough to make identification possible' (Boon, pers. comm.) (T2/F.127)

Metal small-finds from La Plaiderie and the Bonded Store

by Heather Sebire and Philip de Jersey

The condition of many of the metal small-finds from the Bonded Store was compromised by the underlying granitic geology, creating very acidic conditions in the soil. Metal finds were in many cases very corroded and few recognisable artefacts survived, although there was much detritus from metal-working (see p. 108, below). In contrast to La Plaiderie, no Roman coins were found, which is surprising given the quantity of settlement material that was recovered; this was not considered to be a factor of the difficult lighting conditions on the Bonded Store site, since great care was taken to check spoil during the excavation. One Iron Age coin – a base silver stater of the Baiocasses dating to the mid-1st century BC – was found in a Roman context. The metal finds from La Plaiderie were generally in better condition. A small selection of those from Roman contexts is illustrated below.

Fibulae from the Bonded Store (Fig. 67)

1. Small-find 41 (context A2005). Langton Down type. Corroded copper alloy. Length 59mm, width 25mm, depth 13mm. Eight coils of spring remain inside the head. The bow is decorated with the classic 'light and shade' decorative motif
2. Small-find 298 (context C3033). Coil and shaft fragment of fibula. Copper alloy. Possibly a *Drahtfibel* derivative. Length 47mm, width 11mm, depth 22mm

Catalogue of unillustrated metal small-finds from Roman contexts at the Bonded Store

Listed by small-find number:

31. Copper alloy object, possible fibula pin. Length 41mm, thickness 1.8mm (A1203)
45. Small iron fragment (A1205)
50. Three iron fragments plus 'crumbs', very corroded. (1) Curved flat piece, maximum length 72mm, maximum width 52mm, thickness 1mm plus encrustation. (2) Round with encrustations, diameter 29mm, possibly part of fibula or brooch. (3) Square sectioned 'nail' shaft, length 33mm, width 4–5mm (A1205)
52. Iron object with square section, curved and hollow. Maximum length 16mm, diameter 4mm (B2054)
53. Copper alloy Iron Age coin attributed to the Baiocasses (DT series 344). Thickness post-treatment 3mm, weight post-treatment 3.40g. (B2054)

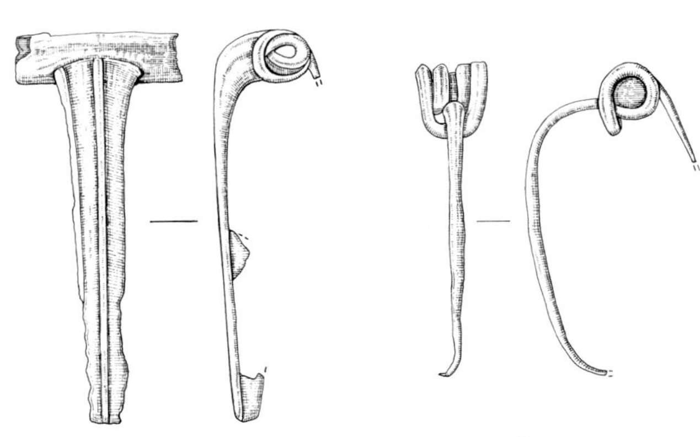

Figure 67 Fibulae from the Bonded Store. Scale 1:1.

57. Small rectangular metal object, maximum width 15mm, maximum length 18mm, thickness 11mm (A1204)
88. Iron nail, corroded. Square in section. Head diameter 13mm, length of whole nail 38mm. (C2093)
89. Iron object, corroded. Maximum length 52mm, minimum width 9mm, maximum width 18mm (C2004)
90. Iron object, possibly a nail. Length 68mm, width 5–9mm (C2093)
92. Three very small, flat metal fragments. (1) length 8mm × width 7mm. (2) length 6mm × width 3mm. (3) length 6mm × width 2mm (C2093)
94. Iron, two flat corroded joining fragments of irregular shape. Overall maximum length 77mm, maximum width 50mm (C2093)
104. Six small fragments of a copper alloy object, possibly a blade. Longest has rounded end. Length 11m × width 7mm (B3102)
105. Copper object, possibly a rivet. Maximum diameter of head 8mm (C2094)
107. Iron object, possibly a blade. Length 24mm, width 21mm, thickness 2mm (C2097N)
115. Iron ring, corroded but with metal residue. Maximum diameter 27mm, hole diameter 7mm, height 10–20mm (C2094)
131. Four fragments of copper alloy; (1) now in two pieces. (1a) maximum length 10mm, maximum width 8.5mm. (1b) maximum length 9mm, maximum width 5mm. (2) maximum length 13mm, maximum width 6mm. (3) maximum length 13mm, maximum width 6mm. (4) maximum length 14mm, maximum width 8mm (C1003)
217. Flat lead strip, folded at one end. Width 15mm, thickness 1mm, length 18mm (D2009)
244. Curved iron fragment, possibly nail, corroded onto pottery rim sherd, now separated. Nail very concreted; shaft tapers but end broken off. Length 58mm, average thickness 19mm. Pot with beaded rim of black-burnished ware, light brown fabric possibly BB2 'cooking pot' (C2094)
249. Iron nail with head, length 33mm (B1203)
254. Iron object, possibly a nail, corroded. A point protrudes through concretion. Length of encrustation 43mm, width 20mm (C2094)
269. Lead sheet folded lengthwise. Length 31mm, maximum width 10mm (D2009)
283. Lead, two fragments with oxidization. Very irregular. (1) Maximum length 19mm, maximum width 19mm. (2) Maximum length 19mm, maximum width 9mm (C3017)
285. Iron object, possibly a nail. Little metal remaining. Maximum length 75mm, maximum width 25mm (C3017)
292. Two iron objects. Encrusted concretions, very little metal remaining. (1) Concretion only with hollow. Maximum length 43mm, maximum width 28mm, maximum height 12mm. (2) Some iron remaining. Maximum length 42mm, maximum width 23mm, maximum height 1mm (C3023)
296. Six fragments of copper alloy, one semi-circular. Possibly part of fibula or brooch (C3022)
317. Many iron fragments and concretion. Largest length 65mm, width 28mm (D4109)

Catalogue of illustrated metal small-finds from probable Roman contexts at La Plaiderie (Fig. 68)

1 Pierced lead counter (T1/F.90, small-find 139)
2 Copper alloy 'foot' (T1/L4, small-find 413)
3 Copper alloy 'foot' (T2/L3, small-find 281)
4 Copper alloy finger ring (T1/F.29, small-find 9)
5 Copper alloy finger ring (T1/F.29, small-find 11)
6 Copper alloy cleaning utensil (T2/L3, small-find 256)
7 Copper alloy cauldron foot (T2/L3, small-find 262)

Miscellaneous small-finds from the Bonded Store and La Plaiderie

by Heather Sebire

In addition to the metal items described above, a number of Roman or probable Roman objects in other materials were recovered from the excavations at La Plaiderie and the Bonded Store. In the catalogue below all objects are from the Bonded Store unless otherwise stated.

Pipeclay figurines (Fig. 69.1–3)

1. Pipeclay Venus figurine, upper section only, 45mm × 36mm × 22mm, La Plaiderie (T1/F.44, small-find 130)
2. Pipeclay figurine. Fragment of a 'Dea Nutrix' figure, consisting of the right hand side of the basket chair in which the suckling matron sat. Dimensions 24mm × 12mm × 7mm (context C3003)
3. Pipeclay Venus figurine representing the lower torso and upper legs, 67mm × 39mm × 13mm (context D1007, small-find 201)

Spindle whorls (Fig. 69.4–9)

4 Ceramic spindle whorl, diameter 36mm, hole diameter 9mm (context C2003, small-find 86)
5 Ceramic spindle whorl, diameter 42mm, hole diameter 9mm (context D4003, small-find 232)
6 Ceramic spindle whorl, diameter 38mm, hole diameter 11mm (context D3012, small-find 233)
7 Ceramic spindle whorl, diameter 36mm, hole diameter 8mm (context C3011, small-find 289)
8 Ceramic spindle whorl, diameter 28mm, hole diameter 4mm (area A trench 2, unstratified, small-find 80)

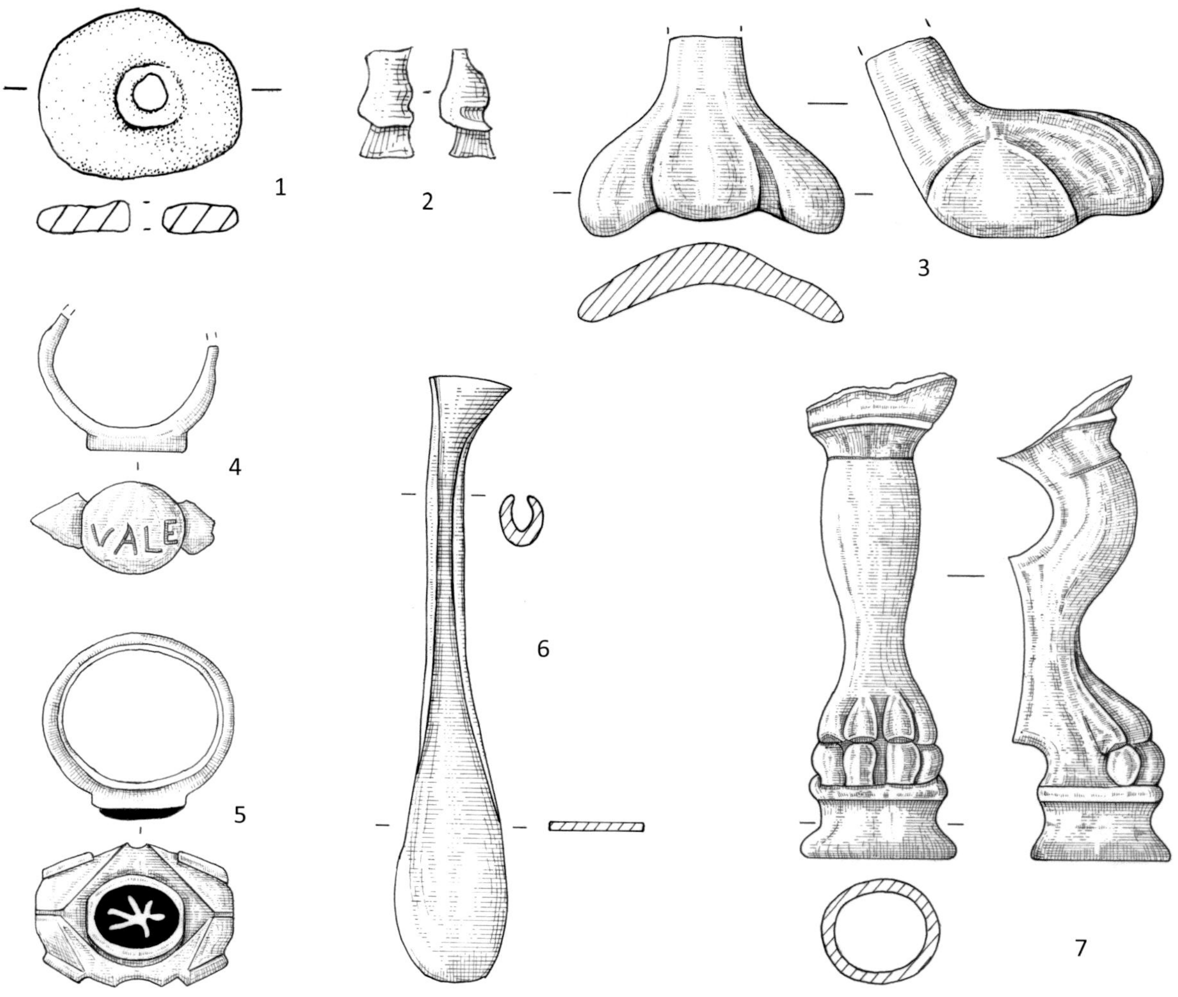

Figure 68 Metal small-finds from La Plaiderie. Scale 1:1 (nos 1–5), 1:2 (nos 6–7).

9 Ceramic spindle whorl, diameter 44m, hole diameter 9mm (context B2025, small-find 124)

Pottery object (Fig. 69.10)

10 Pottery sherd reformed into a gaming piece, 16mm × 14mm (context D4003, small-find 234)

Stone (Fig. 70.1–10)

1. Hone, 94mm × 28mm × 10mm (La Plaiderie, T1/L5, small-find 330)
2. Hone fragment, 26mm × 34mm × 27mm (La Plaiderie, T1/L3, small-find 124)
3. Hone fragment, 40mm × 27mm × 40mm (La Plaiderie, T1/L4, small-find 132)
4. Hone fragment, 24mm × 42mm × 12mm (La Plaiderie, T1/L5, small-find 418)
5. Fragment of stone tool, 56mm × 50mm × 13–32mm, possibly prehistoric but found in a Roman context (La Plaiderie, T1/F.73, small-find 122)
6. Stone rubber, 90mm × 77mm × 45mm (La Plaiderie T1/L4, small-find 419)
7. Quern fragment, 270mm × 204mm × 102mm (La Plaiderie T2/F.123, small-find 287)
8. Hone fragment, 107mm × 53mm × 15mm (context B3004, small-find 103)
9. Broken fragment of smoothed or carved igneous stone with quartz intrusion, 90mm × 50mm × 32mm (context C2094, small-find 239)
10. Stone rubber, 72mm × 65mm × 35mm (context D2009, small-find 270)
11. Lower half of rotary quern, diameter 0.40–0.45m (La Plaiderie, T1/F.90, small-find 214; see Fig. 6)
12. Small fragment of quern in conglomerate, maximum depth 70mm (context D4035, small-find 312; not illustrated)
13. Quern fragment in conglomerate, maximum depth 0.18m, maximum diameter 0.34m (context D4106, small-find 313; not illustrated)
14. Hand-shaped granite sphere, possibly a pestle, diameter approximately 60mm (context C3033, small-find 299; not illustrated)

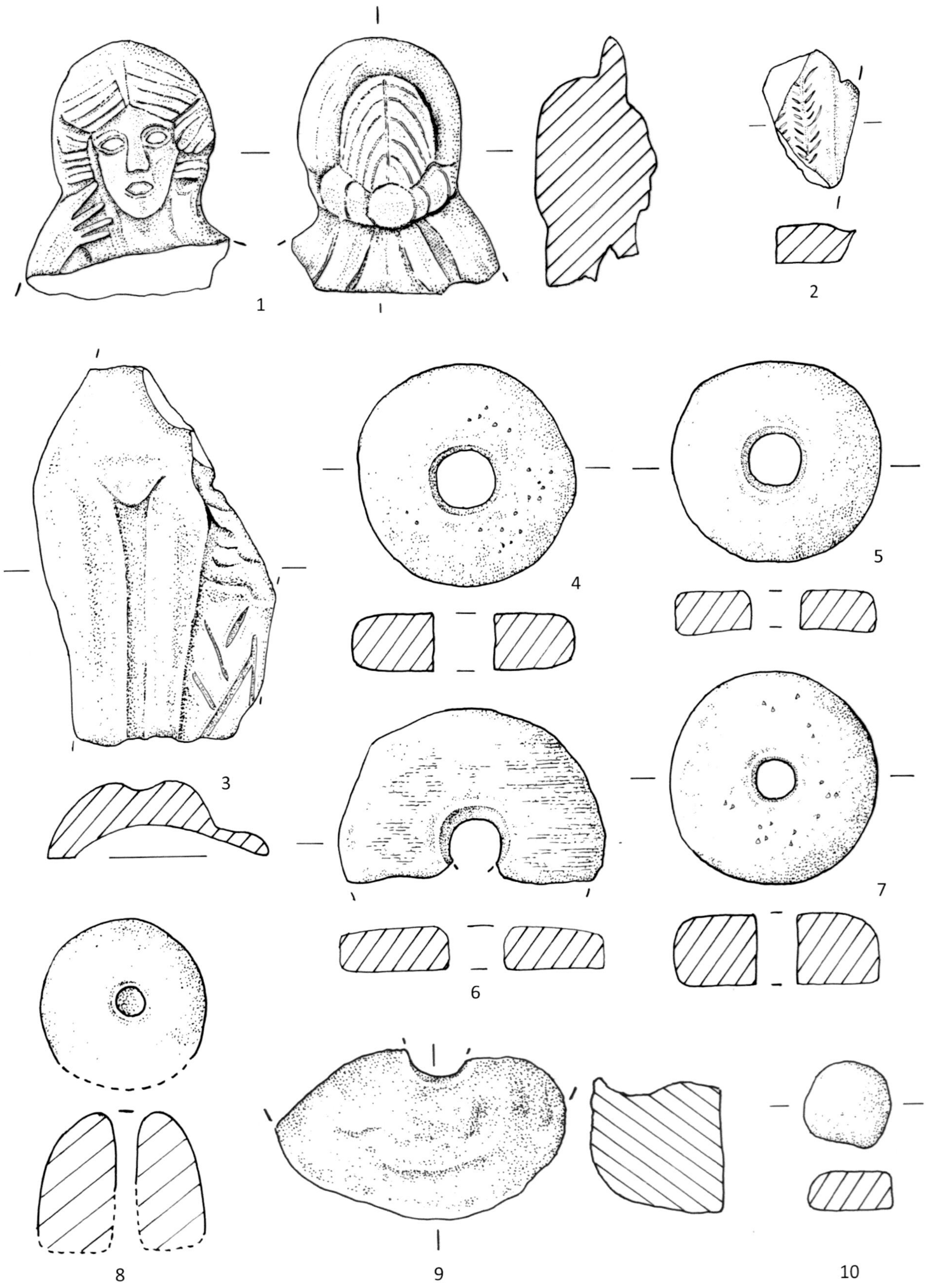

Figure 69 Miscellaneous small-finds from the Bonded Store and La Plaiderie. Scale 1:1.

Figure 70 Stone small-finds from the Bonded Store and La Plaiderie. Scale 1:2 except for no. 7, at 1:4.

15. Fragment of shale, probably from a bracelet, 84mm × 20mm (context C2003, small-find 256; not illustrated)
16. Fragments of shale, possibly from a bracelet (context B2004, small-find 127; not illustrated)

The Bonded Store glass

by Vivien Ferneyhough

The Roman glass assemblage consisted of some 66 pieces including four handle fragments, one window glass fragment and one bead. The majority of the glass is blue-green in colour with a small number of tinted-colourless and colourless fragments, together with one fragment of polychrome glass. All of the Roman glass found during this excavation appears to have been imported, as there has been no evidence to date of glass making or re-working in Guernsey.

From the unstratified glass two fragments are possibly Roman. Both are blue-green in colour with one fragment being water-worn and difficult to identify, while the other is a convex body fragment possibly from a globular unguent bottle. The Bonded Store site yielded a considerable quantity of glass, but mostly of a very small and fragmentary nature; there may therefore be some other fragments in the residual material that are Roman but have not been included in this report.

From Area A, nine fragments were recovered which are broadly dateable to the 1st to 3rd century AD. Of particular note are a fragment of ribbon handle with side ribs, probably from a 'Frontinus' type bottle or a rectangular bottle (Fig. 71.1), a fragment from a tubular base ring with concave kick (Fig. 71.2), and a fire-rounded rim fragment from a cylindrical cup or bowl with fold (Fig. 71.4).

Area B yielded 20 fragments that fall within a date range of the 1st to 3rd century AD. This assemblage contained several fragments from bowls with a horizontal fold (Fig. 71.3). A fire-rounded rim fragment, similar to that from Area A, was found in the same context and may be associated with the bowl fragments. Fragments from a bottle with a tubular folded rim dateable to the 1st or 2nd century AD were also recovered in this area (cf. Price and Cottam 1998, 191–202, fig. 1.4) together with a water-worn tubular rim fragment from a jar, re-worked as a bead (Fig. 71.5). The remaining fragments include a piece of blown window glass and two very small convex fragments, possibly from an unguent bottle. The rest are too small to be truly diagnostic, but may be from bottles or flasks.

Area C yielded 18 fragments ranging in date from the 1st to the early 4th century AD. The most notable is a rib fragment from a polychrome pillar-moulded bowl (Fig. 71.8). This type of cast bowl was being manufactured in the central and west Mediterranean from the late 1st century BC to the end of the 2nd century AD and therefore spans the Augustan, Claudian and Neronian periods (Cool and Price 1994, 14–21; Price and Cottam 1998, 44–6). However, it is well documented that polychrome pillar-moulded bowls were considered to be items of luxury glass and later became regarded as family heirlooms, being passed down through the generations after they were no longer being produced. Therefore it is possible that this fragment entered the archaeological context after the 1st century AD.

The majority of fragments found in Area C are of blue/green glass. Only three very small body fragments of thin colourless glass and one of pale green/colourless were found in this area. One fragment has a horizontal wheel-cut line and is from a cup with a date range of late 1st to 2nd century AD (cf. Price and Cottam 1998, 88–9, 91–7). A ribbed handle fragment (Fig. 71.7), probably from a square bottle, was recovered as well as a base fragment with one circle extant; both fragments are likely to be from mould-blown square bottles (for type see Isings 1971, fig. 20 no. 155). Other fragments worth mentioning are two body fragments from 'Frontinus' type bottles and a fire-rounded rim fragment from a cup or bowl.

Area D produced 21 glass fragments dateable to the late 1st, 2nd and 3rd centuries AD. Again only a small percentage of the glass is colourless and comprises three vertical fire-rounded rim fragments, one of which has a horizontal abraded line below the rim (not from the same vessel) and two body fragments; these fragments are all from cylindrical cups. The majority of fragments recovered in this area are from bottles. Worth noting is a fragment from an angular ribbon handle (Fig. 71.6) with a broad edge rib, and a diagonal folded rim fragment with handle scar; both fragments are from bottles. Among the body fragments, one from a hexagonal bottle and another from a prismatic bottle can be identified (cf. Cool and Price 1994, 179–85).

In summary, although the Bonded Store site is situated close to the historic harbour of St Peter Port, the relatively small assemblage of identifiable Roman glass from this site, and the types represented, seem to suggest that this glass was used in a domestic context rather than being part of a consignment for trade.

The author would like to thank Dr J. Price for her invaluable comments regarding dating and typology.

Catalogue of illustrated glass (Fig. 71)

Abbreviations: BG: blue/green. Br: brown. CL: colourless. G: green. OW: opaque white. PG: pale green. Y: yellow. nos 2, 3, 4 and 6 drawn by Vivien Ferneyhough.

1. BG ribbon handle fragment. Broad folded edge rib. Width incomplete. Probably 'Frontinus' or rectangular bottle (cf. Cool and Price 1994, 204–6; Allen 1998, 31–5). Second or 3rd century AD. A2003, small-find 4

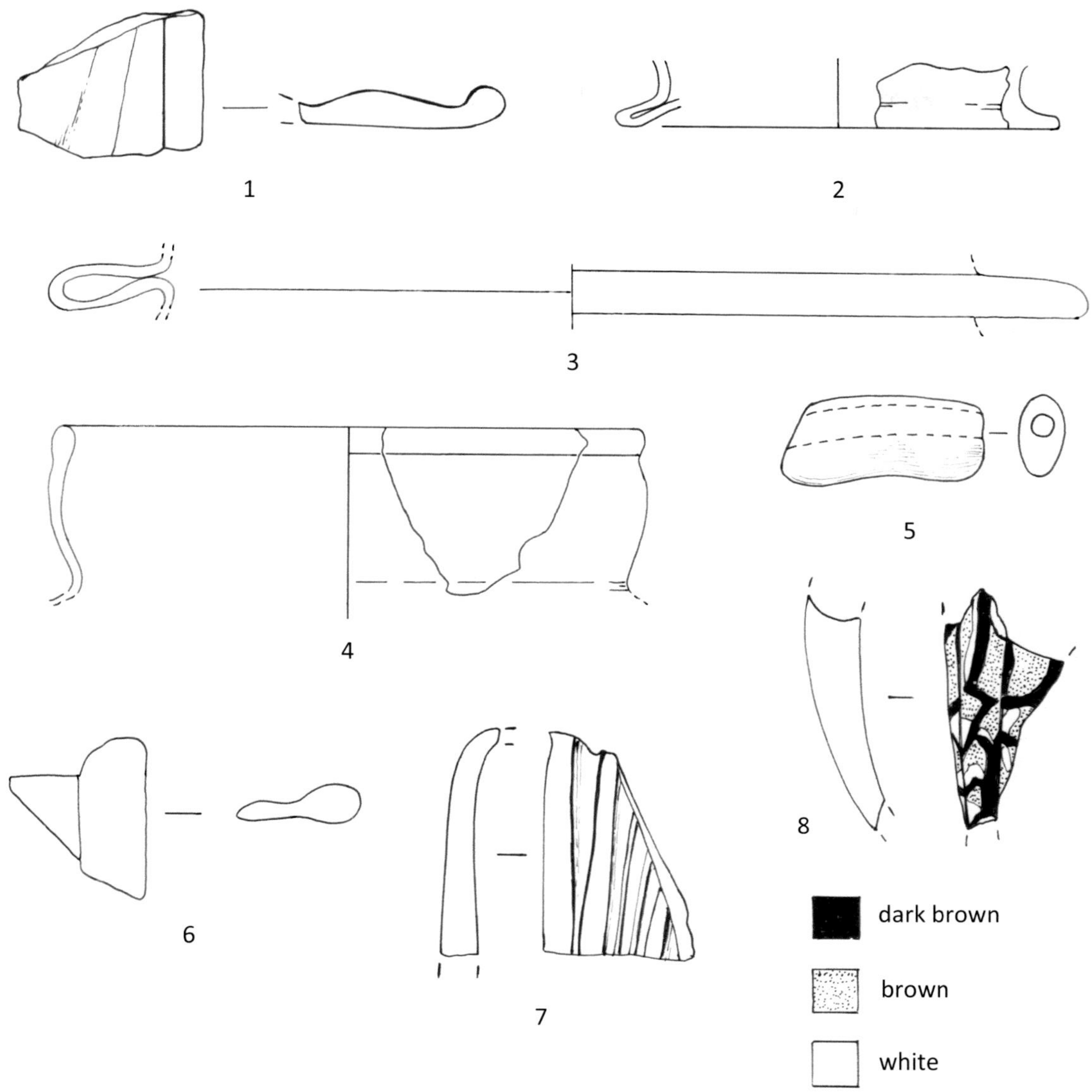

Figure 71 Roman glass from the Bonded Store. Scale 1:1.

2. BG, tubular base ring fragment with concave kick (cf. Price and Cottam 1998, 25–7), probably cup or bowl. Wear on base. Bubbly; slightly abraded. First to 3rd century AD. A2003, small-find 26
3. BG, fragments from bowl with horizontal fold (cf. Cool and Price 1994, 102, fig. 706). Thin-walled glass; small bubbles; slightly abraded. Second or 3rd century AD. B1003, small-find 15
4. BG, fire-rounded rim fragment. Cylindrical cup/bowl with fold (cf. Price and Cottam 1998, 109–10). Small bubbles; slightly abraded. Second or 3rd century AD. A2003, small-find 56.
5. BG, abraded and water-worn. Fragment of tubular rim from jar, re-used as bead. Present length 27mm. Second or 3rd century AD. B3005, small-find 106
6. BG angular ribbon handle fragment from bottle; bubbly, abraded on outer surface of edge rib. Second or 3rd century AD. D2002, small-find 209
7. BG, angular ribbed handle fragment, bottle; bubbly, slightly abraded on edge rib. Second or 3rd century AD. C1068, small-find 71
8. Y/Br glass with opaque white rods. A rib fragment of a polychrome pillar-moulded bowl. First century AD. Cf. Price and Cottam 1998, 44–6. Unstratified, small-find 81

Catalogue of unillustrated glass

Listed by small-find number:

28. BG, two very small fragments, possibly of neck; abraded. Probably Roman. A2003
29. PG/CL body fragment, possibly of unguent bottle; abraded, bubbly. A2003

33. BG convex body fragment, possibly of bottle. Abraded, bubbly, slight weathering. 8–10mm thick. Probably Roman. A2004
48. BG, three joining water-worn and abraded rim fragments. Horizontal tubular folded rim. Bottle. First or 2nd century AD. B2054
54. BG, thin fragment from tubular fold plus small fragment from body of bowl with tubular fold. Fold 1mm thick, body 1.3mm thick. Second or 3rd century AD. B1003
55. BG body fragment, probably of cup/bowl. Slightly abraded; 1.1mm thick. A2003
74. BG body fragment, cylindrical corrugated fragment from 'Frontinus' type bottle, bubbly; vertical mould seam. 1.2mm thick. Second or 3rd century AD. C1071
75. BG, two small convex body fragments. 1mm and 1.5mm thick. C1003
76. BG, small melted body fragment. Probably Roman. C1073
78. BG base fragment of mould-blown square bottle, one part circle extant. Second century AD. C1003A
79. BG, small mould-blown body fragment, possibly of 'Frontinus' type bottle. 0.9mm thick. Second or 3rd century AD. C1004
93. BG, small body fragment, thin-walled vessel, 1mm thick. C2093
99. (one piece)/ 242. (two pieces)
CL, three small body fragments, one from cup with horizontal abraded line, 0.6mm thick. Second century AD. C2094
102. G/CL thick body fragment, probably of bottle; bubbly. 4mm thick. B3004
109. BG, two body fragments, one with raised rib, possibly from bottle. C2094
111. CL small convex body fragment. 1mm thick. Possibly Roman. C2005
113. BG rim/body fragment, fire-rounded edge, cup/bowl, rim 2mm thick, body 1mm thick. Second or 3rd century AD. C2094
117. BG, very small convex fragment; abraded, 0.9mm thick. Identification of type not possible but probably Roman. B3005
130. BG body fragment of bottle or flask; bubbly and abraded. 3mm thick. B3003
202. BG lower body/concave base fragment, probably of flask/small bottle. Wear on base edge. 2mm thick. D1007
215. BG diagonal folded rim fragment with handle scar from bottle/jug. Second or 3rd century AD. D2005
216. BG body fragment of hexagonal bottle, bubbly, 3.5mm thick. Late 1st to late 2nd century AD. D2009
221. G/CL tubular base ring fragment, bubbly. Third century AD. D3003
235. BG, small fragment, possibly of neck. Probably Roman. D3004
236. BG, body fragment of prismatic bottle, abraded. 3.5mm thick. Second or 3rd century AD. D2005
242. *see 99*
259. CL vertical rim fragment of cylindrical cup with fire rounded edge. 2mm thick. Second or 3rd century AD. D1002/1004
260. CL, two joining fragments, vertical rim, fire-rounded edge, cylindrical cup. Second or 3rd century AD. D2001
263. BG body fragment. Abraded. 2mm thick. Probably Roman. A1004
265. BG small body fragment, possibly of small globular bottle. Bubbly and abraded. 1.5mm thick. B1022
266. BG body fragment from cylindrical vessel, abraded, 2mm thick. Probably Roman. D3007
267. BG, thick fragment of water-worn glass, probably Roman. Unstratified
268. BG rim fragment, fire-rounded possibly from bowl; two more small fragments of folded horizontal rim not from same bottle; pale BG bubbly fragment with convex body, straight ribbon handle and lower attachment visible, possibly a jug. Second or 3rd century AD. D4002
271. CL vertical cracked- off rim fragment of cup with cylindrical body and horizontal abraded line. 1.2mm thick. Third century AD. Plus further small body fragment of BG glass. D3003
273. BG, thin convex body fragment, possibly of globular unguent bottle. 1–2mm thick. Unstratified
274. BG body fragment of cylindrical vessel/bottle, plus two very small body fragments; CL fragment of base and base ring plus many de-vitrified fragments. Probably Roman. D2005

La Plaiderie glass

by Vivien Ferneyhough

A small quantity of Roman glass, amounting to some 11 pieces, was recovered from the Plaiderie excavations.

Catalogue of illustrated glass (Fig. 72)

1. BG bubbled glass; flared sheared rim, short neck, upper body expanding out. Unguent bottle, rim diameter 31.4mm, rim thicknesss 1.5mm. F.48, small-find 85
2. BG, slightly bubbled and seeded glass. Broad, straight ribbon handle fragment. With seven promiment ribs visible. Lower attachment of bottle. F.122, small-find 286
3. BG, fragment of base of small 'Frontinus' bottle. Concave base with FRO facing left to right embossed. Cf. Price and Cottam 1998, 209–11; Cool and Price 1994, 206. F.90, small-find 209

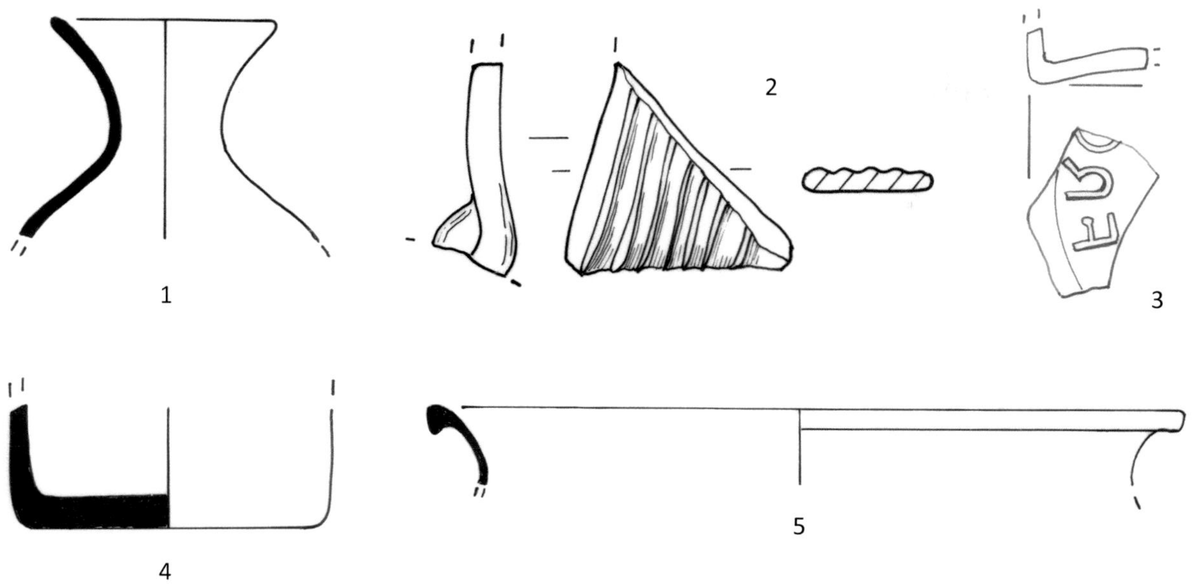

Figure 72 Roman glass from La Plaiderie. Scale 1:1.

4. CL with PG tinge, slightly bubbled glass; base of small cylindrical cup or flask. Slightly concave base with pontil mark. Base diameter 40mm, base thickness 4.5mm. Third century AD. F.44, small-find 127
5. G, fragment of rim, edge rolled out and down. Probably Roman. T2 L3, small-find 363c

Catalogue of unillustrated glass

Listed by small-find number:

121. BG, window pane. Two rounded sides and distorted corner. Possibly Roman. F.72
141. Dark blue bead, hexagonal, with two wider sides. Narrow perforation. Worn at ends. Possibly Roman. F.47
188. BG, slightly bubbled glass. Fragment of neck and shoulder from flask or jug. 2mm thick. F.85
216. G, long ovate bead. Narrow perforation. Possibly Roman. T1 L3
273. BG, fragment of base. Concave with two concentric rings and pontil mark, letter 'F' facing right between the two rings. Probably a cylindrical 'Frontinus' bottle
409. BG, bubbly, fragment of thin (1.5mm) walled vessel. F.102

Intaglios

by Tristan Arnison

1. Bonded Store, context C3017 (small-find 284) (Fig. 73.1) The intaglio is moulded in glass with a flat or slightly convex upper face; it is ovoid, 11.5mm in length and 9.5mm in width. The surface is badly pitted but despite this, the image itself is relatively clear. On the left is a small naked male figure who stands three quarters to the right but with his head in profile and his right arm bent at an angle to his body. On the right, a bearded man is depicted, either crouching or perched on a stool (not visible) in front of the smaller figure. His left leg is extended across the foreground and his right leg is shown behind it. He is somewhat round-shouldered and leans forward, raising his left forearm just above the smaller figure's head. His right arm is, however, angled downwards. There is the faint trace of a vertical undulating line that is most clearly visible in front of the smaller figure's upper thigh.

   This gem appears to belong to the type that has traditionally been interpreted as showing Prometheus creating mankind from clay. It was a device particularly popular on Italic and early Republican gems, although judging by the classicising style employed on this example, it probably only dates to the late 1st century BC. I have argued elsewhere (Arnison 2006, 67–8) that the image may in fact represent a sculptor using a plumb line to take measurements from a clay model.
2. Bonded Store, context D2005 (small-find 212) (Fig. 73.2) This intaglio is engraved on red jasper, measuring 15.5 × 11.35mm, probably dating from the late 2nd or early 3rd century AD. It portrays a *gryllos* consisting of the head of Silenus facing right, conjoined with the head of a boar facing left. Silenus's beard forms the hair of a third head, another bearded male facing downwards. The image is very similar to that on a red jasper intaglio from Silchester (Henig 1978, no. 377). It can be seen simply as an invocation of rural prosperity, although it is also possible to see

1 2

Figure 73 Intaglios from the Bonded Store. Scale 4:1.

it as having a more complex, narrative context (see Arnison 2006, 68–9).

Metal-working debris from the Bonded Store

by Chris Salter

Summary

All the material found was consistent with iron-smithing. The slag types found were typical of small-scale iron-smithing to produce or repair iron artefacts. These mainly came from three contexts, B2004, B2048 and B2054. The size and quantity of material recovered is not compatible with the interpretation of feature B2032 as a smelting furnace. While it was the right size for the base of a truncated iron-smelting furnace, one would expect to see more vitrified hearth-lining and, more importantly, dense furnace slag, usually associated with smelting as well as tap slag.

What can be inferred is that there was an iron-smithing hearth in the near vicinity, and one of its products might well have been the nails found in the hardpan concretion and soil associated with the slag. However, the absence of hammer-scale, which is usually restricted to close to the hearth and anvil, suggests either that it did not withstand the corrosive soil conditions, or that the active hearth and anvil was not in the immediate vicinity.

Smithing hearth bottoms

A number of complete or fragmented smithing hearth bottoms were found in contexts B2004, B2048, B2054 as well as C2094 (see Table 20). This type of slag is formed when the surface layer of the iron is oxidised, when the metal is heated in the hearth and falls off to react with the fuel ash and fused material from the hearth lining. Hearth bottoms often have a distinctive plano-convex cross-section and a D-shape plan, but can be very variable in form. They have to be removed from the hearth at regular intervals to prevent the formation of the slag interfering with the air flow in the hearth. Thus their size and shape gives an indication of the size of the hot zone of the hearth and the scale of the object being worked. In this case, most of the smithing hearth bottoms were relatively small (below 130g) indicating small-scale and/or low-temperature activity. One of the two heavier examples comes from B2048; the heaviest example, from context B2054, consisted of a smithing hearth bottom running into a layer of vitrified hearth lining with some flows, as well as hearth lining in the form of well-fired clay.

Other slag

The remaining material classified varied from material that was close to smithing hearth bottom in form, including fragments of dense irregular slag flow (solidified in furnace), and low-density slag often grading into flows of vitrified hearth-lining flow. All these are normal by-products of iron-smithing. Again these predominantly came from the three contexts B2004, B2048 and B2054.

Hearth lining

Vitrified hearth lining is not necessarily an indication of metal-working as it can be produced in any situation where there is sufficient fuel and air to raise the surface temperature of the walls or floor of the area to the point where the material starts to melt. However, in this case it is reasonable to consider the material to be from the area of the tuyere of the smithing hearth, as the majority of the material is associated with the iron-smithing slags.

Fired clay

Some of this material poses a problem on this site. Much of it consisted of a red sandy-clay mix looking as if it had been heated. A large area of this material formed the bed of what looked like the base of a large furnace. Initially it was thought that this could have been an iron-smelting furnace due to its size, but from the above study of the slag it is clear that this cannot be the case. It may have been the rake-out area of the smithing hearth but unfortunately due

Table 20 The Bonded Store: metalworking residues by context.

Context	Smithing hearth bottom	Slag/SHB	Slag	Low-density slag	Vitrified hearth lining	Fired clay	Fired clay + burnt bone	Iron	Concretion	Natural	Burnt bone	Charcoal	Pitch
B2003				3.3	37.9								
B2004	760.5		182.8		256.5			11.7					
B2048	691.9		91.6		297.8	188.8	19.7	189		15.9	926.2	12.4	
B2054	483.5		511.5		31			34.5		178.1		2	90.9
B3006					93.5								
B2032						323.7				516.2	76.7		
D4003			16	40.4	57.7								
D1002			19.3										
C2100				13.2									
C2104			16.8		8			55.3					
C2108										305			
A1033										2.3			
C1067				37.9									
C1073			31.4					156.4		28.9	14		
C1083									45.4				
C2094	422.5		172	22.7	136.3	50.7		670			5.8		
C1003						236							
C1005		113.6	107.1		115.2			92		138.5			
sf 307					14.7								
Total wt/g	2358.4	113.6	1148.5	117.5	1048.6	799.2	19.7	1208.9	45.4	1184.9	1022.7	14.4	90.9

to truncation of the various features by later buildings and the absence of hammer-scale is it impossible to put this in its true metallurgical context.

Concretion and natural

There was a considerable amount of iron oxide-concreted soil and rock present. Some of this contained corroded iron artefacts. For most the corrosion had gone to the point where there was only a hollow shell of iron oxide around where the original object had been. However, in many instances it was possible to identify the object, with the vast majority being small to medium-sized square nails.

Not all the material from this site was fully sorted due to the fine size of the fragments. Much of the material recorded here as 'natural' was soil and other material concreted together by iron oxides. It is likely that these oxides originated from the corroded iron artefacts from the same context.

Animal bone from the Bonded Store

by Jonathan D. Le Huray

Identification and recording

A total of 2832 animal bone fragments from the Bonded Store were examined, and an archive report compiled (held at Guernsey Museum). Each individual bone fragment was given an identification number in order to aid cross-reference between photos, measurement records, dental-ageing records and the main bone table. Teeth were identified to species, while eruption and wear were recorded following the methods of Grant (1975). All mandibles and loose teeth were recorded. Bone measurements were taken with sliding calipers according to von den Driesch (1976).

Where possible, determination of species and element was accomplished with reference to identification texts including Hillson (1992), Schmid (1972), Wheeler and Jones (1989) and Cohen and Serjeantson (1986).

Burning was observed on a number of bones during excavation and as a result it was deemed worthy to examine this feature in more detail. The presence of cut marks on bone elements was also noted during the analysis and this too was examined in more detail.

Quantification

The high level of bone fragmentation meant that an analysis of bone epiphyses to determine the minimum number of elements (MNE) and the record of skeletal parts present would be extremely biased. As a result a system of zone recording, as developed by Serjeantson (1991), was used to record the distinguishing areas or zones present on each bone fragment (Table 21). This allows the calculation of MNE to be based on the most frequent part of the bone present (Serjeantson 1996, 195).

Table 21 The Bonded Store: zoned and not zoned animal bones.

Zoned bones	*Not zoned bones*
scapula, humerus, ulna, radius, pelvis, femur, tibia, astragalus, calcaneum, metacarpal, metatarsal, phalanx 1, phalanx 2, occiput, horn core	vertebrae, small tarsals, sesamoids, patella, small phalanges, lateral metapodials, disarticulated skull parts, isolated teeth, sternum, hyoid

The minimum number of individuals (MNI) for a particular species is calculated for each bone element by dividing MNE by the number of bone elements present in the skeleton; for example, the MNI for the proximal femur is determined by dividing the MNE for the proximal femur by two. The overall species MNI is based on the highest element MNI observed. MNE for mandibles was based upon those mandibles recorded for tooth wear analysis, since mandibles are not zoned and MNE for all observed mandibles would simply represent the number of identified specimens (NISP). MNE and MNI were not calculated for isolated teeth, ribs or vertebrae.

Where observable, the state of epiphyseal fusion was recorded as fused (F), un-fused (UF), or fusing (FG) for both the proximal and distal epiphyses. This data can be used to examine age profiles of species through the percentage of un-fused early, middle and late fusing bones (e.g. Serjeantson 1996).

Results

IDENTIFICATION

Of the 2832 bone fragments examined, 1746 (61.7%) were unidentified. A further 549 (19.4%) bone fragments could not be identified to species, but could be identified to element. Of these, 132 were classified as cow/horse/deer-size (CSZ), 219 as sheep/pig/dog-size (SSZ), and 198 as ungulate (UNGUL) tooth fragments. The remaining 537 (19.0%) bone fragments were identified to species and element. The majority of these fragments (83.6%) were those species associated with animal husbandry, i.e. cow, sheep/goat and pig (see Table 22). Horse bones comprise of just two loose teeth and as a result this species was not examined in any detail. Rodent and rabbit bones were treated in a similar manner. Bird and fish bones are examined in less detail than those species associated with animal husbandry due to the difficulty in identifying them to species.

QUANTIFICATION – NISP, MNE AND MNI

An analysis of NISP produces the MNE and MNI for each bone element (see Table 23). Maximum NISPs for zones 1–4 are used to obtain proximal long bone MNEs, while maximum NISPs for zones 5–8 are used to obtain distal long bone MNEs. MNIs are calculated for each bone element and the maximum MNI observed provides the species MNI. This

Table 22 The Bonded Store: number of identified specimens (NISP) by species.

	n	*% of identified*
bird	28	5.2
cat	2	0.4
cow	273	50.8
crab	7	1.3
dog	4	0.7
fish	35	6.5
horse	2	0.4
pig	35	6.5
rabbit	1	0.2
rodent	9	1.7
sheep/goat	141	26.3
Total	537	100

produces an overall MNI of three individuals for cattle, four individuals for sheep/goat and one individual for pig. MNI figures for crab and fish bones were not calculated, while an analysis of NISP provides an MNI of one individual for cat, one for dog and three individuals for bird. This is based on the most frequent element observed. No further analysis of bone fusion data, dental recording or bone measurements took place, but raw data is recorded in the archive, held at Guernsey Museum.

BURNED BONES

Of all bone fragments examined, 540 (19.1%) were burned. Of these, 470 (87%) were unidentified, suggesting that the act of burning is related to the resulting fragmentary state of the assemblage. The 70 identified burned bones consisted of 23 cow bones, 10 cow-size bones, 1 fish bone, 5 sheep/goat bones and 31 sheep-size bones.

CUT AND CHOP MARKS

A total of 22 chop marks and 12 cut marks were observed.

GNAW MARKS

Only one case of gnawing was observed in the assemblage, on a cow-size rib.

BIRD BONES

Bird bones recovered most likely represent natural intrusion. This interpretation could be assessed through detailed analysis of the bird bones with a comprehensive reference collection in order to examine specific species.

FISH BONES

A total of 35 fish bones were identified, along with seven fragments of crab shell. Although species identification and calculations of MNI were not attempted for fish bones, an examination of maxillae and dental bones reveals that at least four species of fish are present.

Table 23 The Bonded Store: MNE and MNI data for cow, sheep/goat and pig.

	Cow		*Sheep/ goat*		*Pig*	
Element	*MNE*	*MNI*	*MNE*	*MNI*	*MNE*	*MNI*
mandible	1	1	4	2	0	0
horncore	2	1	0	0	–	–
atlas	0	0	0	0	0	0
axis	0	0	0	0	0	0
scapula	1	1	1	1	0	0
proximal humerus	1	1	2	1	0	0
distal humerus	4	2	6	3	0	0
proximal radius	0	0	5	3	2	1
distal radius	1	1	6	3	1	1
proximal ulna	6	3	5	3	0	0
distal ulna	1	1	3	2	0	0
proximal metacarpal	1	1	1	1	1	1
distal metacarpal	1	1	1	1	0	0
pelvis	0	0	4	2	0	0
sacrum	0	0	0	0	0	0
proximal femur	2	1	2	1	0	0
distal femur	2	1	1	1	0	0
proximal tibia	2	1	2	1	0	0
distal tibia	3	2	8	4	1	1
proximal fibula	–	–	–	–	0	0
distal fibula	–	–	–	–	0	0
proximal metatarsal	4	2	5	3	2	1
distal metatarsal	3	2	5	3	2	1
astragalus	8	2	4	1	2	1
calcaneum	2	1	3	1	2	1
phalanx 1	5	1	0	0	0	0
phalanx 2	6	1	1	1	0	0
phalanx 3	6	1	0	0	1	1
max MNI	3		4		1	

DOG BONES

A total of four dog bones were identified in the assemblage, comprising of one mandible, one humerus, one radius and one tibia.

CAT BONES

Two cat bones were identified in the assemblage, both of which were mandibles. One mandible was recovered from the unstratified layer of trench 3, Area D, while the other was recovered from the same context as the dog mandible

(D4004). These specimens are most likely to represent the use of this species as a household pet.

Conclusions and further study

Burning observed on a high proportion of bone fragments is related to the high level of fragmentation in the assemblage. This burning is most likely the result of cooking for meat, since the majority of burned bone elements represent elements which form the extremities of the skeleton, e.g. foot bones, skull bones and ribs.

Cut and chop marks support the interpretation of burning as the result of food preparation since the majority of bone elements with cut and chop marks are either those elements with high proportions of meat, or those elements directly connected with elements with high proportions of meat: femur, humerus, ulna and tibia; astragalus, metatarsal and pelvis.

The dog bones could represent either dogs used for hunting or simply dogs kept as pets. The association of dog and cat mandibles in the same context suggests that the dog bones represent animals kept as pets during occupation of the later phases of the site. The context in which they were found, D4004, was a disturbed layer.

Environmental finds from the Bonded Store

by James Rackham

Methods

Eight samples were submitted for environmental assessment from the excavations at the Bonded Stores.

Sample volume and weight were measured prior to processing. The samples were washed in a 'Siraf' tank (Williams 1973) using a flotation sieve with a 0.5mm mesh and an internal wet sieve of 1mm mesh for the residue. Both residue and flot were dried, and the residues subsequently refloated, to ensure the efficient recovery of charred material. The dry volume of the flots was measured and the volume and weight of the residue recorded. Two of the samples were wash-over floated in a bowl. One produced no residue at all, while the other produced a residue that was dried and sorted. The waterlogged flots were kept wet.

The residue was sorted by eye, and environmental and archaeological finds picked out, noted on the assessment sheet and bagged separately. A magnet was run through each residue in order to recover material such as hammerscale and prill. The dry flot of each sample was studied using ×10 magnification and the presence of environmental finds (i.e. snails, charcoal, carbonised seeds, bones *etc*) was noted and their abundance and species diversity recorded on the assessment sheet. A sub-sample of the waterlogged flots was scanned and the diversity and abundance of seeds, insects *etc* was noted. These, along with the finds from the sorted residue, constitute the material archive of the samples.

The individual components of the samples were then identified and the results are summarised in Tables 24, 25 and 26, below.

Results

A total of 26.5 litres of soil was processed, which washed down to leave residues of sub-rounded and angular/sub-angular granite gravel, pebbles and coarse sand, with occasional inclusions of charcoal, bone, pottery and root pseudomorphs. Two samples (3 and 5) contained preserved organic material, and one sample (3) washed down to leave a single waterlogged flot and no residue.

The samples produced a limited range of artefacts and ecofacts (Tables 24 and 25). Finds included 59 sherds of pottery, fragments of brick/tile, magnetic material, a single fragment of iron and two small sherds of glass. The majority of the pottery was recovered from the Roman deposits (samples 1 and 4) within the confines of the Roman wall, and from an undated deposit (sample 2, context 3034), although sample 1 (context C3005) contained the greatest number of pot sherds per litre. Magnetic material was recovered in varying densities from all seven residues, consisting of magnetised stone crumb with no hammerscale or prill present. The greatest densities were from a Roman deposit within the area of the Roman wall (context C3035) and from an Iron Age layer sealed by silts (context C3044).

In terms of environmental remains, the materials recovered included bone, snail shell, charcoal, charred and uncharred plant remains, and preserved wood. Most of the bone, the majority of which is burnt, calcined and unidentifiable, is associated with the later phases of activity (Table 24). A sheep/goat innominate bone was present in sample 4, and a few fragments of burnt fish bone were identified in sample 5001 (context 3021). Charcoal is present in all bar one sample (3), but generally in low densities, with only four samples (5001, 2, 4 and 5) containing fragments suitable for further analysis.

Identifiable charred plant remains averaged 2.72 items per litre, ranging from 0.2 items per litre (sample 5) to 10.6 items per litre (sample 4). Cereal grain was present in six of the eight samples and cereal chaff and weed seeds in four of them (Table 25). The cereals present are predominantly barley (*Hordeum* sp.), including hulled (*Hordeum* sp. var. *vulgare*) and six-rowed hulled barley (*H. vulgare* var. *vulgare*) (Table 26), the latter identified on the basis of lateral or 'twisted' grains being present, characteristic of that variety. The presence of wheat is indicated by wheat chaff, some of which can be identified as possible emmer-type wheat (*Triticum* cf. *dicoccum*), but the fragmented state and poor preservation of the remains precluded further identification. Other charred plant remains included a single

Table 24 The Bonded Store: finds from the processed samples in phase order.

Sample no.	Context	Phase	Sample vol. (l)	Residue vol. (ml)	Pot#/g	Mag. (g)	Fe no.	Brick/tile weight (g)	Bone (g)	Comments
6	D1008u	prehist.	2	50	–	3	–	–	–	
6	D10081	prehist.	2	50	–	2	–	–	–	
5	C3044	Iron Age	5	1200	9/4	13	1	–	2	
3	C3045	Roman	2	–	–	–	–	–	–	
1	C3005	Roman	1.5	200	9/3	2	–	–	1	
4	C3035	Roman	5	1200	15/25	15	–	162*	8	*may include some pottery
5001	C3021	C2 +	4	450	3/82	2	–	–	10	two chips of glass
2	C3034	Roman	5	1500	23/28	1	–	–	2	

Table 25 The Bonded Store: environmental finds from the processed samples in phase order.

Sample no.	Context	Sample vol. (l)	Flot vol. (ml)	Charcoal**	Wood*	Charred grain*	Charred chaff*	Charred seed*	Waterlogged seed*	Snail*	Comments
6	D1008u	2	1	0/2	–	–	1	–	–	–	indet. cereal chaff
6	D10081	2	2	1/2	–	1	–	–	–	–	indet. cereal fragment (<2mm)
5	C3044	5	34	2/3	1	1	–	–	5	–	barley, nettle, bramble, elder, goosefoot, insects, indet. calcined and unburnt bone
3	C3045	2	300	0/0	5	–	–	–	5	–	nettle, bramble, elder, goosefoot, rose/bramble-type thorns, insects
1	C3005	1.5	3	2/4	–	1	1	1	–	–	?barley, indet. cereal chaff
4	C3035	5	35	3/5	–	2	2	2	–	–	barley, barley and wheat chaff, vetch/vetchling, grasses, sedge, rose/bramble-type thorns, sheep innom., indet. calcined bone fragments
5001	C3021	4	11	4/5	–	1	–	1	–	1	barley, ?pale persicaria, Vallonia costata, much small calcined bone fragments, burnt fish bone
2	C3034	5	15	3/5	–	1	1	1	–	–	?barley, wheat chaff, indet. chaff and seed, indet. calcined and unburnt bone

* abundance: 1 = 1–10, 2 = 11–50, 3 = 51–150, 4 = 151–250, 5 = 250+
** charcoal figures as abundance > 2mm/abundance < 2mm

seed of *Polygonum* cf. *lapathifolium* (pale persicaria), two *Vicia*/*Lathyrus* (vetch/vetchling), one small *Gramineae* (grass) and one *Carex* sp. (sedge) (Table 26).

At the assessment stage only a proportion of the waterlogged flots (samples 3 and 5) were scanned, and were found to be abundant in degraded plant material and weed seeds. Wood was also abundant in sample 3. Charcoal was present in low densities in sample 5 only, which also contained a single barley grain. The suite of wood species is generally consistent in both samples with species identified including *Chenopodium* sp. (goosefoot), *Urtica dioica* (common nettle), *Sambucus* cf. *nigra* (elderberry?), and

Table 26 The Bonded Store: archaeobotanical remains from processed samples.

	Phase	*Prehistoric*		*Iron Age*	*Roman?*	*Roman*		*C2 +*	*unphased*
	context/ sample no.	*D1008/6u*	*D1008/6l*	*C3044/5*	*C3045/3*	*C3005/1*	*C3035/4*	*C3021/ 5001*	*C3034/2*
cereal grain									
Hordeum vulgare var. *vulgare*	six-row hulled barley	–	–	–	–	–	2	–	–
Hordeum sp. var. *vulgare*	hulled barley	–	–	1	–	–	2	1	–
cf. *Hordeum* sp.		–	–	–	–	1	–	–	2
cereal grain frags. (>2mm)		–	–	–	–	2	16	1	1
cereal grain frags. (<2mm)		–	+	–	–	–	+	–	+
cereal chaff									
glume bases *Triticum* cf. *dicoccum* (Schrank.) Schubl.	emmer-type wheat	–	–	–	–	–	4	–	–
glume bases *Triticum* sp.	wheat	–	–	–	–	–	4	–	4
rachis internodes *Hordeum* sp.	barley	–	–	–	–	–	4	–	–
rachis indet.		–	–	–	–	–	5	–	1
indet. chaff		1	–	–	–	1	–	–	1
wild species									
Chenopodium sp.	goosefoot	–	–	*	*	–	–	–	–
Vicia/Lathyrus (3-4mm diameter)	vetch/ vetchling	–	–	–	–	–	2	–	–
Polygonum cf. *lapathifolium* L.	pale persicaria?	–	–	–	–	–	–	1	–
Urtica dioica L.	common nettle	–	–	***	***	–	–	–	–
small indet. *Gramineae*	small grasses	–	–	–	–	–	2	–	–
Carex sp.	sedge	–	–	–	–	–	1	–	–
Sambucus cf. *nigra* L.	elderberry	–	–	**	**	–	–	–	–
Rosaceae thorns	rose/ bramble thorns	–	–	–	***	–	11	–	–
Rubus sp.	blackberry/ raspberry	–	–	**	**	–	–	–	–
indet.		–	–	–	–	–	–	–	1
total identified charred items		1	–	1	–	4	53	3	10
ditto, per litre of sample		0.5	–	0.2	–	2.67	10.6	0.75	2

\+ = frequency score between 1 and 10

Abundance scores for waterlogged remains: * = present, ** = frequent, *** = abundant

Rubus sp. (blackberry/raspberry). As only a proportion of the waterlogged flots was assessed, absolute counts were not taken at this stage, but the relative abundance of each species was recorded (Table 26).

Other plant material consisted of leaf fragments and degraded plant matter as well as frequent occurences of *Rosaceae* (rose family) thorns. The survival of the predominantly robust plant components and seeds (i.e. thorns, elder, bramble and nettle seeds) suggests that the material has suffered significant degradation with the probable loss of the more fragile elements and seeds, which undoubtedly biases the assemblages.

Discussion

Neither sample of the material from context D1008, assigned to the prehistoric period, produced much evidence of occupation or activity, and indeed very little overall, with no remains that could constitute domestic debris. No pottery or bone and only very low densities of magnetic material and charcoal, together with single fragments of indeterminate cereal grain and chaff, were present in samples 6 'upper' and 6 'lower'. This lack of evidence might suggest limited domestic activity, but charred plant remains are consistently at low density on most prehistoric sites.

Barley is the only cultigen represented by cereal grain in all of the samples, but wheat outnumbers barley amongst the cereal chaff fragments from the Roman samples. The presence of wheat chaff but no wheat grain is unusual and cannot simply be attributed to preservational bias, as experimental work has demonstrated that chaff, particularly free-threshing rachis internodes (such as those of barley), is more fragile and less likely to survive the charring process than the more substantial and robust cereal grains (Boardman and Jones 1990). The presence of wheat chaff and the absence of wheat grain may therefore be due to differential processing and storage of the barley and wheat crops. It should be noted, however, that the cereal and weed species identified are mostly represented by one or two seeds or chaff components only, and so do not constitute suitable material for making inferences with regard to crop-processing activities, broader inferences about arable husbandry regimes or the local habitat and environment.

The greatest concentration of artefacts and ecofacts is associated with the Roman deposits, with samples 1 and 4 containing, respectively, 2.67 and 10.6 identifiable charred items per litre, and the evidence suggests the activities are possibly domestic in nature. The presence of cereal grain and chaff suggests that crop-processing activities may have taken place on or adjacent to the site. However, the nature and degree of processing cannot be determined due to the low numbers of grain, chaff and weed seeds recovered. The presence of species such as blackberry/raspberry and elder could represent potentially exploited food resources, or more prosaically indicate that brambles, and probably elder, grew in the area, as thorns are frequent and it is very unlikely that they would arrive onto site as a result of collecting the fruit for consumption.

Contrary to expectation, the samples contain no apparent corroborative evidence for metal-working activities being performed on, or within the vicinity, of the site. Slag is not present in any samples, and the magnetic material recovered from the samples contains no hammerscale or prill, which is indicative of iron working. In addition, the density of magnetic material from the deposit opposite the area of the Roman slag furnace is very low.

Note: at a later stage in the excavations Dr Mark Robinson of Oxford University visited the site and took samples of the layer of silt beneath the Roman wall, in the central area of the site (trench CT3, context C3043). The following waterlogged seeds were found, with nettle seeds being the most numerous: *Chenopodium* (goosefoot), *Urtica dioica* (stinging = common? nettle), *Rubus fruticosus* (blackberry), *Verbena officinalis* (vervain), *Mentha aquatica* (water mint), *Sambucus nigra* (elder), and *Juncus* mix (reeds/rushes).

Context C4064, in trench CT4, contained rich charcoal indenting of *Quercus* (oak) and *Corylus avellana* (hazel), but no seeds. The burnt spread C3022, in trench CT3, contained a small amount of *Corylus avellana* (hazel) charcoal and some burnt bone fragments including a fish vertebra.

6

Gazetteer of Roman sites and finds on Guernsey and Herm

by Tanya Walls, Philip de Jersey and Jason Monaghan

The following Gazetteer lists all known sites and finds of Roman material from the islands of Guernsey and Herm, and the waters around them, up to and including 2015 (Fig. 74). The entries are split into three main groups:

A. Roman finds from excavated sites on Guernsey and Herm
B. Roman finds from non-excavated sites, Guernsey and Herm (land and inter-tidal)
C. Roman finds from non-excavated sites, Guernsey and Herm (underwater)

Group A, the excavated sites, are listed by date of first excavation. Groups B and C are arranged by material and then by date of discovery. There is some overlap between these three groups, particularly for sites in the inter-tidal zone (such as Cow Bay, St Peter Port) and for some locations (such as Castel parish church) which have revealed Roman evidence in a number of different forms. These sites are cross-referenced to one another. Every entry has an MGU reference that relates to the Historic Environment Record maintained at Guernsey Museum, and which in most cases will provide additional information. Where a site or find has been published, details of the most useful or significant publication are provided here. A number of briquetage sites have been included although their dating is often uncertain.

A. Roman finds from excavated sites on Guernsey and Herm

1. ***La Varde passage grave, Vale*** (MGU161 and MGU4410) (excavated 1837)
Neolithic passage grave apparently revisited during the Roman period. A number of samian sherds in the Guernsey Museum collection are thought to be from this tomb, along with several other sherds and a briquetage hand-brick. Two Roman coins, of Gallienus and Constantine, were found near La Varde in 1888.
References: Kendrick 1928, 119; Burns and Burns 1985, 656, 662.

2. ***Déhus passage grave, Vale*** (MGU153) (excavated 1837–47, 1932)
Neolithic passage grave apparently revisited during the Roman period. Two bronze rings thought to be La Tène or Gallo-Roman in date were probably found during the 19th-century excavations, as well as a rim sherd from a Roman flagon; several sherds are recorded from Collum's re-excavation of 1932.
References: Kendrick 1928, 154; Collum 1933, 79–86.

3. ***Le Creux ès Faïes passage grave, St Peter in the Wood*** (MGU190) (excavated 1840–43)
Neolithic passage grave apparently revisited during the Roman period. In addition to the prehistoric finds there were two samian sherds, one of which had been perforated and shaped into a spindle whorl or ornament. There was also a briquetage hand-brick.
Reference: Kendrick 1928, 185.

4. ***Lihou Priory, St Peter in the Wood*** (MGU228) (excavated 1841, 1978, 1990–2003)
The most recent series of excavations of the Benedictine Priory of Notre Dame de Lihou revealed two sherds of Roman amphorae, a few pieces of roof tile and an intaglio cut on a cornelian depicting a man and a goat; this is stylistically dateable to the 1st century BC – 1st century AD, although it may have been re-used in a medieval reliquary or similar object.

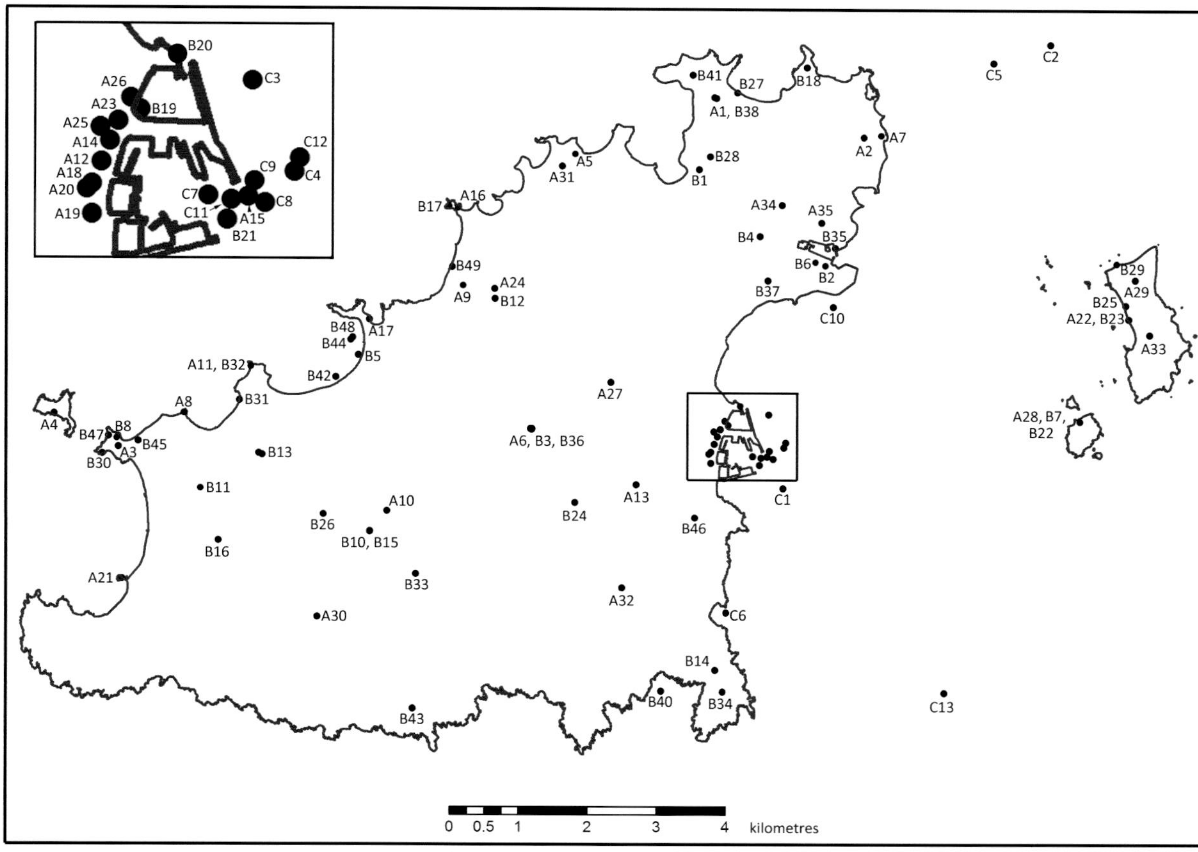

Figure 74 Location of sites listed in the Gazetteer. Sites in and around St Peter Port are shown in the inset, top left.

5. ***Pulias, St Sampson*** (MGU621) (excavated 1852)
Pottery and some briquetage were discovered in a brief examination of this site by F. C. Lukis in 1852.
Reference: Kendrick 1928, 172.

6. ***Castel Parish Church*** (MGU1364 and MGU3549) (excavated 1870s, 2000 and 2005)
This medieval parish church has fragmentary Roman tile built into the north and east walls, along with two Caen stone fragments with Roman-style lettering built into the porch. Excavations beneath the floor of the church and outside the north wall have revealed significant quantities of Roman tile; some 732 pieces have been recovered in the modern excavations and include roof, floor and wall tiles (see p. 95). There was also some unpainted Roman plaster, fragments of *opus signinum* and a few sherds of possible Roman pottery. The position of the church directly adjacent to a megalithic statue-menhir suggests a continuity of religious observance at the site, and therefore a suitable position for a Roman temple. Its commanding position with a view towards Alderney would also make it a prime military site. John McCormack (pers. comm.) has observed that it is the only church in Guernsey which originally had a square churchyard. See also Gazetteer B3.
References: McCormack 1986, 133, 136; Sebire 2005, 166.

7. ***Noirmont, Vale*** (MGU618) (excavated *c*.1912)
A kiln or salt-pan discovered during quarrying, partially excavated before it was destroyed. It consisted of a large rectangular trough with a baked clay floor. Large quantities of briquetage and sherds 'probably of the Gallo-Roman period' were recovered.
Reference: Kendrick 1928, 160–1.

8. ***Le Catioroc, St Saviour*** (MGU4347) (excavated 1958)
Briquetage site with well-preserved kiln bars and hand-bricks. One Iron Age coin was found and the site may be Iron Age or Roman in date.
Reference: Jee 1958.

9. ***Le Feugré, Cobo, Castel*** (MGU1414) (excavated 1967)
The remains of an early medieval long-house, dated by the pottery to *c*.AD 800–1150, were excavated just inland from the coast at Cobo. The finds also included a possible amphora sherd, a fragment of Roman tile and two pieces of briquetage.
Reference: Girard 1981.

10. ***Le Tranquesous, St Saviour*** (MGU254) (excavated 1976, 2014)
Iron Age and early Roman settlement discovered and partly excavated in the 1970s and again in 2014. It was occupied from *c*.80 BC – AD 50 and comprised circular

post-built houses enclosed by palisaded ditches. The site extends over a considerable area.

References: Burns 1977; Walls, de Jersey and Hughes 2014, 625–7.

11. ***Le Crocq, St Saviour*** (MGU2527 and MGU2541) (excavated?1949, 1976 and 1998)
Large quantities of briquetage are present in Guernsey Museum from an otherwise unrecorded investigation at this site in 1949. Decreasing amounts have been recovered in two excavations since then, and much of the site has now been lost to coastal erosion. See also B32.
References: Lihou 1976; Cunliffe and de Jersey 2000, 894–902.

12. ***18–20 The Pollet, St Peter Port*** (MGU543) (excavated 1980–81)
Excavations on this site revealed large quantities of medieval and post-medieval pottery. There were also five sherds of samian pottery.

13. ***King's Road, St Peter Port*** (MGU528) (excavated 1980–83 and 2005–11)
A settlement and cemetery dating from the early Iron Age through to the end of the 1st millennium BC. The presence of Roman material, including a complete samian dish stamped HONORATI, indicates a later occupation of the site.
References: Burns, Cunliffe and Sebire 1996 (1980s excavations); de Jersey 2010.

14. ***La Plaiderie, St Peter Port*** (MGU2216) (excavated 1983–85)
Roman urban settlement (this volume).

15. ***St Peter Port Pierheads*** (MGU2766) (excavated 1984–85)
Romano-Celtic vessel wrecked *c.*AD 280 following a fire on board. At the time of writing this was the most substantial sea-going vessel of the Roman era surviving outside the Mediterranean.
Reference: Rule and Monaghan 1993.

16. ***Grandes Rocques, Castel*** (MGU236) (excavated 1986)
Settlement consisting of two small apsidal-ended houses constructed with large beach pebbles, dated to the first half of the 12th century AD. Finds included a small quantity of Roman material amounting to two sherds of pottery, one of which had been modified to produce a spindle whorl, and two fragments of probable Roman glass, one from a vessel and the other a small disc, perhaps a counter.
Reference: Burns and Batt 1990.

17. ***Albecq, Castel*** (MGU224) (excavated 1995)
The excavated part of this coastal medieval settlement comprised three stone buildings set around a courtyard. There is evidence of further buildings and enclosures on the headland. Two possible Roman sherds were found here.
Reference: de Jersey 2013.

18. ***Le Riches/Lefebvre Street, St Peter Port*** (MGU542) (excavated 1996–97)
Most of the finds from this town site were medieval and post-medieval, but there were also 14 sherds of Roman pottery.

19. ***Bonded Store, St Peter Port*** (MGU541) (excavated 1996–2004)
Roman urban settlement (this volume).

20. ***Sunrise Cottage, Berthelot Street, St Peter Port*** (MGU551) (excavated 1997)
Urban site with mainly medieval and post-medieval finds, but including one Roman brick or tile fragment.

21. ***Fort Grey, St Peter in the Wood*** (MGU2528) (excavated 1999, plus several spot finds)
In addition to briquetage, this Iron Age/Roman salt-working site on the eastern side of the Fort Grey islet has yielded five sherds of possible Roman pottery and two fragments of tile.
Reference: Cunliffe and de Jersey 2000, 903–10.

22. ***Fisherman's Beach, Herm*** (MGU525, MGU2229, MGU2230, MGU3567) (excavated 1999, plus numerous spot finds)
Coastal erosion has exposed Iron Age and Roman material on the west coast of Herm below Fisherman's Cottage. Finds have been recorded since the 19th century and the site was partially excavated in 1999. More than 30 sherds of pottery have been collected and there is also a large quantity of briquetage and a few fragments of Roman tile. The Ashmolean Museum has a fragment of tessellated pavement which is recorded as having come from 'Herm' although the smudged label may in fact have once read 'Herne'. See also B23.
Reference: Cunliffe and de Jersey 2000, 911–32.

23. ***Royal Hotel, St Peter Port*** (MGU2765) (excavated 1999–2001)
Essentially an occupation site of the Early Neolithic and Bronze Age periods, but close to the Roman waterfront, and 231 pieces of Roman pottery and tile (most quite small and some water-rounded) plus 290

small scraps that were possibly Roman were found during excavations.

Reference: Sebire 2011, 245.

24. ***Route de Carteret, Castel*** (MGU518) (excavated 2000–01)
Three sherds of samian pottery were recovered from this Late Neolithic and Bronze Age occupation site, plus a spindle whorl probably fashioned from a Roman flagon base.
Reference: Walkington *et al.* 2001.

25. ***Les Canichers, St Peter Port*** (MGU2696) (excavated 2001–03)
Excavations in a garden at Les Canichers revealed part of a structure tentatively interpreted as a prehistoric cairn. The soil above the cairn contained a significant quantity of fragmentary briquetage. Also in this layer were fourteen sherds of Roman and possibly Roman pottery, and a fragment of tegula.

26. ***Savoy Hotel, St Peter Port*** (MGU3164) (excavated 2002)
Gallo-Roman deposits were identified beneath the demolished Savoy Hotel, including 68 Roman sherds and a small fragment of probable Roman glass.

27. ***St Peter Port School, St Peter Port*** (MGU3407) (excavated 2005)
A structure resembling a prehistoric cist, but associated with medieval pottery and therefore thought to have been disturbed in the Middle Ages. Amongst the finds were two sherds of samian ware and part of a flagon, and two tile fragments.
Reference: de Jersey 2009.

28. ***Jethou*** (MGU6129) (excavated 2007)
One Gallo-Roman rim sherd was found in a re-deposited context in trench A, adjacent to a midden exposure on the north coast of Jethou. See also B22.
Reference: Scarre 2016, 102.

29. ***Herm, various locations*** (excavated 2008–11)
Roman pottery was discovered during excavations undertaken by Chris Scarre at various locations in the northern part of the island. The finds are currently being studied for publication.

30. ***West of Airport, St Saviour/St Peter in the Wood*** (MGU5318) (excavated 2009–12)
Archaeological investigation in advance of the airport runway development found evidence primarily of Neolithic and Bronze Age activity, but among the finds are some 29 Roman and possibly Roman sherds and four fragments of *tegulae*.

31. ***Les Vardes Quarry, St Sampson*** (MGU6752) (excavated 2010)
Extensions to the quarry required an archaeological watching brief and a small excavation. Most of the material collected was prehistoric, but there were also two sherds of Roman greyware and three fragments probably of briquetage.
Reference: Lane and Walls 2010.

32. ***St Martin's Parish Church*** (MGU1362) (excavated 2011)
A small archaeological excavation was carried out adjacent to the west door of the church, revealing three post-medieval burials. A sherd of samian pottery was found.
Reference: de Jersey and Cataroche 2011.

33. ***St Tugual's Chapel, Herm*** (MGU 5705) (excavated 2011)
Pottery finds from excavation of part of the medieval cemetery adjoining St Tugual's Chapel included one definite and two possible Roman sherds.
Reference: de Jersey and Cataroche 2012, 426.

34. ***Le Tertre, Vale*** (MGU3812) (excavated 2014)
One small oxidized body sherd recovered during the excavation of a test-pit in the grounds of Le Tertre.

35. ***Le Maresquet, Vale*** (MGU6796) (excavated 2015)
Fragment of Roman tile found in a test-pit.

B. Roman finds from non-excavated sites (land and inter-tidal)

1. ***Vale Parish Church: brick*** (MGU1371)
Probable Roman brick has been identified within the fabric of the church, in particular inside the building in the south wall near the altar.
Reference: McCormack 2010, 720ff.

2. ***St Sampson Parish Church: brick*** (MGU1372)
John McCormack (pers. comm.) has reported that there are two small pieces of Roman brick in the south and east walls of the church.
Reference: McCormack 2010, 727.

3. ***Castel Parish Church: brick, tile*** (MGU3549) (2012)
A considerable quantity of Roman brick, tile and *opus signinum* was recovered from the spoil of a 44m trench dug for a new water pipe on the north side of the church. See also A6.

4. ***Grosse Hougue, St Sampson: pottery*** (MGU622) (1862)
A single Roman sherd recorded from a destroyed dolmen at Grosse Hougue.
Reference: Kendrick 1928, 172–3.

5. ***Vazon Bay, Castel: pottery*** (MGU2555) (19th century)
Three sherds of coarse pottery, probably Roman, were found in exposed peat deposits.

6. ***Hougue du Moustier, St Sampson: briquetage*** (MGU628) (19th century)
Briquetage hand-bricks were found when this *hougue* was quarried in the 19th century.

7. ***Jethou: briquetage*** (MGU3554) (19th century)
Some reports of two midden sites on the north coast of Jethou note that briquetage was present in these deposits when observed in the 19th century. No briquetage has been identified in more recent examination, although it may have been eroded away.
References: Kendrick 1928, 221; Scarre 2016, 88, 97.

8. ***Fort Saumarez, St Peter in the Wood: briquetage*** (MGU3634) (1928 and 1995)
Four fragments of briquetage have been found, possibly of Iron Age or Gallo-Roman date.

9. ***'Herm': pottery, briquetage, tile*** (MGU4153) (1949 and other unspecified dates)
A number of artefacts in the Guernsey Museum collection are listed as having been found in Herm, but have no precise provenance. This includes a small collection of briquetage (18 fragments) and a fragment of Roman tile which is likely to have come from the Fisherman's Beach site (MGU525, see A22).
Reference: Burns and Burns 1985, 657–9.

10. ***Field off Rue des Prevosts, St Saviour: pottery*** (MGU2252) (1970s)
One Roman sherd recovered from a field-walk.

11. ***Field at Les Arquets, St Peter in the Wood: pottery*** (MGU1939) (1978)
Two Roman sherds recovered from a field-walk.

12. ***Field at Ruette des Saumarez, Castel: pottery*** (MGU1771) (1978)
Two Roman sherds recovered from a field-walk.

13. ***Fields at La Terre Norgiot, St Saviour: pottery*** (MGU2086 and MGU2087) (1979–80)
Seventeen Roman sherds found in field-walking two adjacent fields.

14. ***Field at Jerbourg, St Martin: pottery*** (MGU1946) (1979)
One Roman sherd recovered from a field-walk.

15. ***Field at Les Prevosts, St Saviour: pottery*** (MGU1943) (1979)
One Roman sherd and two possible Roman sherds recovered from a field-walk.

16. ***Field at Les Paysans, St Peter in the Wood: pottery*** (MGU1762) (1981)
One Roman sherd recovered from a field-walk.

17. ***Grandes Rocques, Castel: pottery*** (MGU1417) (1979)
Three sherds of a samian mortarium, probably made in central Gaul in the late 2nd century AD. The soil on parts of the Grandes Rocques headland has been re-deposited and these sherds may have originated elsewhere in the island.
Reference: Sebire 1985.

18. ***Fort Le Marchant, Vale: pottery, figurine*** (MGU2223) (1982)
Eleven sherds of Roman pottery and part of a pipe clay figurine were discovered during the construction of a car park.
Reference: Burns and Burns 1985, 656, 662.

19. ***North Beach, St Peter Port: pottery, tile, coin*** (MGU2220) (1984)
Roman material was found during harbour development works in 1984. The finds comprise 16 sherds of pottery including a stamped amphora handle, three fragments of tile and a coin (*sestertius* of Marcus Aurelius, Varus or Commodus *c*. AD 161–93).
Reference: Burns and Burns 1985, 654, 659–61.

20. ***La Salerie, St Peter Port: pottery*** (MGU2221) (*c*.1985)
Eleven sherds of Roman pottery, including four samian sherds, were found in sand dredged from the main harbour, and thus probably recently re-deposited.
Reference: Burns and Burns 1985, 654–6, 657, 661–2.

21. ***Cow Bay, St Peter Port: pottery, tile*** (MGU2219) (various dates, mostly 1980s–2000s)
A large quantity of Roman pottery and tile has been collected from the beach below Castle Cornet over a period of many years. Finds include 129 sherds of Roman pottery and 19 fragments of Roman tile, including tegula, imbrex and pedalis. The material may originate from rubbish dumped overboard by ships in the harbour, or have been tipped into the sea from the Roman town. See also C7.
Reference: Burns and Burns 1985, 654, 657 – a selection only; Monaghan 1990, 64–5, 68; see also this volume.

22. ***Jethou: pottery*** (MGU6131) (1993)
A single Roman sherd was found during examination of spoil heaps created by the excavation for a swimming pool. The sherd discovered during excavation in 2007 (see A28) may have come from the same area.

23. ***Long Meadow/Fisherman's Field, Herm: briquetage*** (MGU2270) (1998)

A small collection of prehistoric pottery, Iron Age or Gallo-Roman briquetage and a rolled lead sheet were discovered during field-walking at this location, just inland from the excavated Fisherman's Beach site (see A22).

24. ***Field at Bailiff's Cross, St Andrew: pottery, tile, lead sheet*** (MGU2226) (1999)
A concentration of Roman finds collected during a field-walk, including ten Roman (or possibly Roman) sherds, and tile fragments of a variety of types (*tegula*, *imbrex*, *pedalis*, box), suggesting that a Roman building may have been nearby. A folded lead sheet which may be a *defixio* (curse tablet) was also discovered here.

25. ***Herm: pottery*** (MGU5456) (1999)
A rim sherd was found on a path from the beach on the west coast, near the cholera cemetery.

26. ***Le Neuf Chemin, St Saviour: pottery*** (MGU3302) (2001)
Two sherds of Roman pottery found in a garden.

27. ***L'Ancresse, Vale: amphora*** (MGU5453) (2003)
Amphora sherd, possibly Dressel 1A type, found during building works.

28. ***L'Ancresse, Vale: amphora*** (MGU5938) (2005)
One sherd of Roman amphora found during a watching brief on L'Ancresse Common.

29. ***Mouisonnière Beach, Herm*** (MGU3441) (2006)
Coastal erosion on the north coast of Herm exposed a buried land surface containing fired earth, burnt stones and briquetage.

30. ***L'Erée headland, St Peter in the Wood: pottery*** (MGU4363) (2008)
One Roman sherd.

31. ***Perelle Bay, St Saviour: pottery*** (MGU4872) (2008)
A rim sherd from a mortarium was found in exposed soil deposits at the north end of Perelle Bay. There were also fragments of probable briquetage.

32. ***Le Crocq, St Saviour: pottery, briquetage*** (MGU3171) (2009)
Material eroding from the low cliff south of the main site (MGU2527, see A11) includes more briquetage and a possible Gallo-Roman sherd.

33. ***La Villiaze, St Andrew: pottery*** (MGU6679) (2013)
One sherd of possible Roman pottery collected during a field-walk.

34. ***Jerbourg, St Martin: coin hoard*** (MGU2218) (before 1890)
A hoard of 68 Alexandrine tetradrachms of the late 3rd century (AD 295+) were found at an uncertain location on the Jerbourg headland. Current whereabouts unknown.
Reference: Robinson 1937.

35. ***St Sampson's Harbour, St Sampson/Vale: coins, pottery*** (MGU2217 and MGU4573) (*c.*1860)
Nine Roman coins of the 2nd century AD (Trajan, Antoninus Pius, three of Faustina I, two of Marcus Aurelius and two of Commodus) were found during the construction of the north arm of St Sampson's Harbour. Two sherds of Roman pottery were also recovered.
Reference: Burns and Burns 1985, 652, 656, 659.

36. ***Castel Parish Church: coin*** (MGU4575) (19th century)
A Roman coin found near the Castel Church; current whereabouts unknown.

37. ***Delancey, St Sampson: coin*** (MGU4572) (1880)
Coin of Hadrian (AD 117–38); current whereabouts unknown.

38. ***'near La Varde', L'Ancresse, Vale: coins*** (MGU4410) (1888)
Two Roman coins (of Gallienus, AD 253–268, and Constantine, AD 306–37) said to have been found near La Varde. Current whereabouts unknown.

39. ***'Guernsey': coin*** (MGU4576) (early 20th century)
Bronze coin of Aurelian (AD 270–275); current whereabouts unknown.

40. ***Moulin Huet, St Martin: coin*** (MGU4571) (1922)
Coin of Julia Mamea (died AD 235) found by a diver near Cradle Rock.

41. ***Chouet, Vale: coins*** (MGU5341) (1950s)
Silver antoninus of Philip I (AD 244–249) found with a second Roman coin which is now lost.

42. ***Vazon Bay, Castel: coin*** (MGU4204) (1987)
Bronze coin of the house of Valentinian (AD 364–78) found by a metal detectorist.

43. ***Le Gouffre, Forest: coin*** (MGU6683) (*c.*1990)
Chance find of follis of Constantine the Great, AD 307–10.

44. ***Vazon Bay, Castel: coin*** (MGU4414) (2000)
Dupondius of Antoninus Pius (AD 138–61) or Marcus Aurelius (AD 161–80) found by a metal detectorist.

45. ***L'Erée, St Peter in the Wood: coin*** (MGU4570) (2000)
Bronze nummus of Gratian (AD 367–75) found by a metal detectorist.

46. ***George Road, St Peter Port: coins*** (MGU5486) (*c*.2000)
Two small bronze nummi of Honorius (AD 393–423) or Arcadius (AD 383–408) were reportedly found in a garden. They are in good condition and may be more recent losses.

47. ***L'Eree, St Peter in the Wood: coin*** (MGU4196) (2008)
Dupondius of Marcus Aurelius (AD 161–180) found by a metal detectorist.

48. ***Vazon Bay, Castel: coin*** (MGU6113) (2010)
Sestertius of Hadrian, possibly RIC 611b (AD 121–22), found by a metal detectorist.

49. ***Cobo, Castel: coin*** (MGU6767) (2015)
Chance find of nummus of Valentinian I (AD 364–75). Possibly a modern loss.

C. Roman finds from non-excavated sites (underwater)

1. ***Little Russel: amphora*** (MGU5462) (1968)
An amphora spike dredged up in the Little Russel, south-east of St Peter Port.
References: Keen 1986, 139; Monaghan 1990, 65.

2. ***Little Russel 'Site B', Tautenay: amphorae*** (MGU 5403) (1970s onwards)
Fragments of amphorae dredged from the seabed off the north-east coast of Guernsey over a period of many years suggest a scattered wreck site. All but one of the rims of are of Peacock and Williams class 15 (Haltern 70), of the mid-1st century BC to mid-1st century AD, originating from Baetica (north-east Spain). The 266 pieces recovered (Table 27) include 15 basal spikes; neck and rim parts also come from at least 17 individual vessels. Necks, basal spikes and some body sherds retain traces of a pine tar lining. A second wreck clearly exists in the same area as the assemblage also includes a furrowed rim of 'gauloise' type (Peacock and Williams 55) of the 2nd century, plus part of a distinctive base and three body sherds.
References: Keen 1986, 140; Monaghan 1990, 65, 68.

3. ***Boue Penney: anchor, pottery*** (MGU5463) (*c*.1976)
A possible Roman anchor and a mortarium (second half of the 4th century AD) were discovered just to the north-east of St Peter Port harbour; they may have come from a wreck.
References: Keen 1986, 139; Monaghan 1988, 463–5; Monaghan 1990, 65, 68.

4. ***Little Russel 'Site A': amphorae, tile*** (MGU4582) (1977)
An assemblage of near-intact amphorae and more than 50 fragments were discovered some 200m outside the mouth of St Peter Port harbour. All are Peacock and Williams Class 19 (Beltran IIB) of the 1st or 2nd century AD, originating from Cadiz (south-west Spain) and suspected of containing the fish product liquamen. More remain on the seabed and it is possible that part of a wreck survives beneath an 'amphora mound'.
References: Keen 1986, 140; Monaghan 1990, 65.

Table 27 Summary of amphorae sherds from Little Russel B.

Date and/ or GMAG accession	*Body sherd*	*Base spike*	*Shoulder and lug*	*Neck and handle*	*Rim part*	*Rim whole*	*Total PW 15 (Haltern 70)*	*Gauloise type PW 55*	*Total amphorae*
1970s	0	1	0	0	1	2	4	1	5
1980s–90s	27	1	0	1	0	0	29	0	29
2009.23	0	1	0	0	0	0	1	0	1
2010.29	0	0	0	1	1	0	2	0	2
2010.276	4	3	1	0	0	0	8	0	8
2013.54	16	1	2	2	2	1	24	0	24
2015.7	99	6	12	1	4	0	122	4	126
2015.30	14	0	3	2	2	0	21	0	21
2016.122	33	1	1	0	1	0	36	0	36
2017.45	13	1	3	0	2	0	19	0	19
Total	206	15	22	7	13	3	266	5	271

5. ***La Petite Canupe: pottery, quern*** (MGU4411) (*c*.1975 and 2003)
A mortarium of the 2nd or 3rd century AD and the two parts of a rotary quern were recovered from the seabed off the north-east of Guernsey; they probably originated from a wreck although no certain traces have been identified.
References: Burns and Burns 1985, 662–4 (for mortarium, wrongly attributed to north-west coast); Keen 1986, 139; Monaghan 1990, 68.

6. ***Fermain Bay, St Peter Port: submerged wooden structure, pottery*** (MGU2222) (*c*.1980)
A submerged wooden structure which may be the remains of a pier; it is usually obscured by shingle. Gallo-Roman and medieval pottery has been found nearby, including a fragment of Syrian 'carrot' amphora, but the whereabouts of these finds is currently unknown.
References: Burns and Burns 1985, 656, 662; Monaghan 1990, 65.

7. ***St Peter Port Harbour: pottery, tile*** (MGU5449) (mostly 1980s–90s)
Over a number of years a significant quantity of Roman pottery and tile has been recovered from the harbour by divers. Around 200 pottery sherds have been collected, several of which are large pieces, and there are a few complete vessels. Some appear to have come from the Pierheads Roman ship (A15). There are also numerous fragments of tile. See also B21.
Reference: Monaghan 1990, 65, 66.

8. ***Jean Jehan: tile*** (MGU5477) (1982)
A collection of mostly post-medieval material recovered from the seabed near to the mouth of the harbour included a probable piece of imbrex.

9. ***St Peter Port Harbour: quern*** (MGU5452) (*c*.1994)
The upper portion of a Gallo-Roman rotary quern was found by a diver in the St Peter Port harbour entrance.

10. ***Belle Grève Bay: amphora*** (MGU5476) (1999)
One amphora sherd found by a diver.

11. ***St Peter Port Harbour: pottery*** (MGU5457) (2001)
Four sherds of Roman pottery were collected near the medieval wrecks in the St Peter Port harbour entrance.

12. ***St Peter Port Harbour: pottery*** (MGU5482) (2001)
Part of a Roman greyware jar found outside the harbour.

13. ***Lower Heads: pottery*** (MGU5481) (2009–10)
A fragment of *tegula* and a sherd of possible greyware dredged up near Lower Heads, off the east coast of Guernsey.

Bibliography

Abbreviations

AFEAF Association Française pour l'étude de l'Age du Fer
SFECAG Société Française d'étude de la céramique antique en Gaule

Allen, D. (1998) *Roman Glass in Britain*. Aylesbury, Shire.

Arnison, T. (2006) Two intaglios from St Peter Port, Guernsey. In M. Henig (ed.), *Roman Art, religion and society. New studies from the Roman Art Seminar, Oxford, 2005* (Oxford, BAR S1577), 67–9.

Bémont, C. (1977) Moules de gobelets ornés de la Gaule centrale au Musée des Antiquités nationales. Paris, *Gallia* suppl. 33.

Blaszkiewicz, P. (1992) La place de la Normandie dans l'Empire romaine de la fin de l'indépendance jusqu'au Ve siècle de notre ère. In M. Wood and F. Queiroga (eds), *Current Research on the Romanization of the Western Provinces* (Oxford, BAR S575), 35–61.

Blaszkiewicz, P. and Jigan, C. (1994) La céramique du Bas-Empire en Normandie. In M. Tuffreau-Libre and A. Jacques (eds), *La céramique du Bas-Empire en Gaule Belgique et dans les régions voisines. Actes de la table ronde de céramologie gallo-romaine, Arras, 8–10 octobre 1991* (Revue du Nord, Hors-Série, Collection Archéologie 4), 127–39.

Boardman, S. and Jones, G. (1990) Experiments on the effects of charring on cereal plant components. *Journal of Archaeological Science* 17, 1–11.

Bouquillon, A., Querré, G., Leclaire, A., Tuffreau-Libre, M. (1994) La terra nigra tardive à Arras (Pas-de-Calais): etudes en laboratoire. In M. Tuffreau-Libre and A. Jacques (eds), *La céramique du Bas-Empire en Gaule Belgique et dans les régions voisines. Actes de la table ronde de céramologie gallo-romaine, Arras, 8–10 octobre 1991* (Revue du Nord, Hors-Série, Collection Archéologie 4), 213–24.

Brett, C. E. B. (1975) *Buildings in the town and parish of St Peter Port*. Guernsey, National Trust.

Burns, R. B. (1977) The late Iron Age site at the Tranquesous, St Saviour's, Guernsey. *Transactions of La Société Guernesiaise* XX/2, 188–218.

Burns, R. B. (1986) Recent work on the Iron Age and Gallo-Roman period in the Bailiwick of Guernsey. In P. Johnston (ed.), *The archaeology of the Channel Islands* (Chichester, Phillimore), 89–97.

Burns, R. B. (1987) L'époque gallo-romaine. Un nouveau chapitre de l'histoire de Guernesey. In *Actes du Congrès de Caen 1987* (SFECAG), 29–37.

Burns, R. B. The Gallo-Roman site at La Plaiderie. Guernsey Museum, interim excavation report, unpublished MS.

Burns, R. B. and Batt, M. (1990) Un habitat côtier du XIIe siècle: Le Port aux Malades, Guernesey, Iles Anglo-Normandes. *Revue Archéologique de l'Ouest* 7, 111–14.

Burns, R. B., and Burns, A. G. (1985) Gallo-Roman finds from Guernsey and Herm. *Transactions of La Société Guernesiaise* XXI/5, 652–66.

Burns, R. B., Cunliffe, B. W. and Sebire, H. (1996) *Guernsey: an island community of the Atlantic Iron Age*. Oxford, Oxford University Committee for Archaeology.

Coates, D. (1991) *The ancient and modern names of the Channel Islands: a linguistic history*. Stamford, Paul Watkins.

Cohen, A., and Serjeantson, D. (1986, 2nd edn) *A Manual for the Identification of Bird Bones from Archaeological Sites*. London, Archetype Publications.

Collum, V. C. C. (1933). *The re-excavation of the Déhus chambered mound at Paradis, Vale, Guernsey*. Guernsey, La Société Guernesiaise.

Cool, H. E. M., and Price, J. (1994) *Roman vessel glass from excavations in Colchester, 1971–85*. Colchester, Colchester Archaeological Trust.

Cunliffe, B. W. (1971) *Excavations at Fishbourne 1961–1969. Vol. II: The finds*. London, Reports of the Research Committee of the Society of Antiquaries 27.

Cunliffe, B. W. (1986) The Iron Age in the Channel Islands: a review. In P. Johnston (ed.), *The archaeology of the Channel Islands* (Chichester, Phillimore), 56–67.

Cunliffe, B. W. (1987) *Hengistbury Head, Dorset. Vol. 1: The prehistoric and Roman settlement, 3500 BC – AD 500*. Oxford, Oxford University Committee for Archaeology.

Cunliffe, B. W. (1996) Guernsey and the Channel Islands in the first millennium BC. In R. B. Burns, B. W. Cunliffe and H. Sebire, *Guernsey: an island community of the Atlantic Iron Age* (Oxford, Oxford University Committte for Archaeology), 125–7.

Cunliffe, B. W. and de Jersey, P. (2000) Rescue excavations on Guernsey and Herm. *Transactions of La Société Guernesiaise* XXIV/5, 867–943.

de Jersey, P. (2009) Excavation at Les Ozouets, 2005. *Transactions of La Société Guernesiaise* XXVI/4, 551–61.

de Jersey, P. (2010) L'habitat et la nécropole de King's Road, Guernesey, et l'Âge du Fer dans les îles anglo-normandes. In P. Barral, B. Dedet, F. Delrieu, P. Giraud, I. Le Goff, S. Marion and A. Villard-Le Tiec (eds), *Actes du 33e colloque international de l'AFEAF* (Besançon, Presses universitaires de Franche-Comté), 287–300.

de Jersey, P. (2013) Excavation of a medieval settlement at Albecq, 1994–95 (unpublished archive report, available at *http://www.academia.edu/attachments/30648681/download_file*)

de Jersey, P. and Cataroche, J. (2011) Excavation at St Martin's Parish Church, 2011. *Transactions of La Société Guernesiaise* XXVII/1, 148–68.

de Jersey, P. and Cataroche, J. (2012) Excavation at St Tugual's Chapel, Herm, 2011. *Transactions of La Société Guernesiaise* XXVII/2, 381–431.

Dyson, T. (ed.) (1986) *The Roman Quay at St Magnus House, London: excavations at New Fresh Wharf, Lower Thames Street, London, 1974–78.* London, Middlesex Archaeological Society Special Paper 8.

Frere, S. S., Hassall, M. W. C. and Tomlin, R. S. O. (1992) Roman Britain in 1991. *Britannia* 23, 255–323.

Gillam, J. P. (1970, 3rd edn) *Types of Roman coarse pottery vessels in northern Britain.* Newcastle upon Tyne, Oriel Press.

Girard, P. J. (1981) The story of the excavation of the long house at Le Feugré, Cobo. *Transactions of La Société Guernesiaise* XXI/1, 94–8.

Grant, A. (1975) The animal bones. In B. W. Cunliffe (ed.), *Excavations at Porchester Castle, Vol. 1* (London, Society of Antiquaries Research Report 32), 378–406.

Hartley, K. F. (1990) The mortaria. In J. Monaghan, Pottery from marine sites around Guernsey. *Journal of Roman Pottery Studies* 3, 68.

Hartley, K. F. (1993). The mortaria. In M. Rule and J. Monaghan, *A Gallo-Roman trading vessel from Guernsey* (Guernsey, Guernsey Museum Monograph 5), 87.

Hartley, K. F. (1998) The incidence of stamped mortaria in the Roman Empire with special reference to imports to Britain. In J. Bird (ed.), *Form and fabric: studies in Rome's material past in honour of B. R. Hartley* (Oxford, Oxbow), 199–217.

Henig, M. (1978, 2nd edn) *A corpus of Roman engraved gemstones from British sites.* Oxford, BAR 8.

Hillson, S. (1992) *Mammal Bones and Teeth: an introductory guide to methods of identification.* London, Institute of Archaeology.

Holbrook, N. and Bidwell, P. T. (1991) *Roman finds from Exeter* (Exeter Archaeological Reports 4).

Huld-Zetsche, I. (1972) *Trierer Reliefsigillata Werkstatt I. Materialien zur römisch-germanisch Keramik* 9. Bonn, Habelt.

Isings, C. (1971) *Roman Glass in Limburg.* Groningen, Wolters-Noordhoff.

Jacobs, J. (1913) Sigillatafunde aus einem römischen Keller zu Bregenz. *Jahrbuch für Altertumskunde* 6, Vienna.

Jee, N. (1958) Archaeological report. *Transactions of La Société Guernesiaise* XVI/4, 313.

Keen, R. (1986) A review of Roman material from the sea off Guernsey 1860–1980. In P. Johnston (ed.), *The archaeology of the Channel Islands* (Chichester, Phillimore), 138–41.

Kendrick, T. G. (1928) *The Archaeology of the Channel Islands. Vol. I, The Bailiwick of Guernsey.* London, Methuen.

Knorr, R. (1905) *Die verzierten Terra-Sigillata Gefässe von Cannstatt und Köngen-Grinario.* Stuttgart, Kohlhammer.

Lane, D. and Walls, T. (2010) Watching brief and excavation at Les Vardes Quarry, 2010. *Transactions of La Société Guernesiaise* XXVI/5, 755–72.

Lihou, J. L. (1976) Gallo-Roman salt workings in Guernsey. *Transactions of La Société Guernesiaise* XX/1, 22–5.

McCormack, J. (1986) *Channel Island Churches.* Chichester, Phillimore.

McCormack, J. (2010) The Roman church in Guernsey: early Christianity in the Channel Islands. *Transactions of La Société Guernesiaise* XXVI/5, 720–44.

McGrail, S. (1983) Cross Channel seamanship and navigation in the late first millennium BC. *Oxford Journal of Archaeology* 2, 299–339.

Menez, Y. (1985) *Les céramiques fumigées de l'Ouest de la Gaule.* Quimper, Cahiers de Quimper Antique 2.

Monaghan, J. (1987) *Upchurch and Thameside Roman pottery: a ceramic typology for northern Kent, first to third centuries AD.* Oxford, BAR 173.

Monaghan, J. (1988) The Guernsey Maritime Trust Gazetteer 1984–88. *Transactions of La Société Guernesiaise* XXII/3, 453–65.

Monaghan, J. (1990) Pottery from marine sites around Guernsey. *Journal of Roman Pottery Studies* 3, 63–9.

Monaghan, J. (1998) Roman pottery from the Bonded Store, St Peter Port: a preliminary view. In H. Sebire (ed.), *Guernsey connections: archaeological and historical papers in honour of Bob Burns* (Guernsey, La Société Guernesiaise), 68–70.

Monaghan, J. (2011–12) Investigation of the Roman Tower and Gatehouse at the 'Nunnery' 2011. *Alderney Society Bulletin* 46, 85–97.

Monaghan, J. and de Jersey, P. (2014–15) Further evidence for Roman military activity on Longis Common. *Alderney Society Bulletin* 49, 90–6.

Moser, F., and Tilhard, J.-L. (1987) Un nouvel atelier de sigillée en Aquitaine. *Aquitania* 5, 36–121.

Oswald, F. and Pryce, T. D. (1920) *An introduction to the study of terra sigillata, treated from a chronological standpoint.* London, Longmans, Green and Co.

Peacock, D. P. S. and Williams, D. F. (1986) *Amphorae and the Roman economy: an introductory guide.* London, Longman.

Price, J. and Cottam, S. (1998). *Romano-British glass vessels: a handbook.* York, Council for British Archaeology.

Ricken, H. (1934) Die Bilderschüsseln der Kastelle Saalburg und Zugmantel 1. *Saalburg Jahrbuch* 8, 130–82.

Ricken, H. (1948) *Die Bilderschüsseln der römischen Töpfer von Rheinzabern: Tafelband.* Darmstadt, Speyer.

Ricken, H. and Fischer, C. (1963) *Die Bilderschüsseln der römischen Töpfer von Rheinzabern: Textband.* Bonn, Habelt.

Roach, R. A., Topley, C. G., Brown, M., Bland, A. M. and D'Lemos, R. S. (1991) *Outline and guide to the geology of Guernsey.* Guernsey, Guernsey Museum.

Robinson, E. S. G. (1937) A hoard of Alexandrine coins from Guernsey. *Numismatic Chronicle* series 5, vol. 17, 135–8.

Rule, M. and Monaghan, J. (1993) *A Gallo-Roman trading vessel from Guernsey.* Guernsey, Guernsey Museum.

Santrot, M.-H. and Santrot, J. (1979) *Céramiques communes gallo-romaines d'Aquitaine*. Paris, CNRS.

Sauvaget, R. (1970) Le potier Servus II de Lezouz. *Revue Archéologique du Centre* 34, 127–42.

Scarre, C. (2016) Archaeological investigations on Jethou. *Transactions of La Société Guernesiaise* XXVIII/1, 88–145.

Schmid, E. (1972) *Atlas of Animal Bones*. Amsterdam, Elsevier.

Sebire, H. (1985) A Roman samian mortarium from Grandes Rocques. *Transactions of La Société Guernesiaise* XXI/5, 720–2.

Sebire, H. (2005) *The archaeology and early history of the Channel Islands*. Stroud, History Press.

Sebire, H. (2011) Excavations at the Royal Hotel site. *Transactions of La Société Guernesiaise* XXVII/1, 190–257.

Serjeantson, D. (1991) 'Rid grasse of bones': a taphonomic study of the bones from midden deposits at the Neolithic and Bronze Age site of Runneymede, Surrey, England. *International Journal of Osteoarchaeology* 1, 73–89.

Serjeantson, D. (1996) The animal bones. In S. Needham and T. Spence, *Refuse and Disposal at Area 16 east, Runneymede* (London, British Museum Press), 194–223.

Tyers, P. A. (1996) *Roman pottery in Britain*. London, Batsford.

Vermeersch, D. (1993) La céramique à pate claire du vicus routier de Taverny (Val-d'Oise). In *Actes du Congrès de Versailles, 20–23 mai 1993* (SFECAG), 117–36.

von den Driesch, A. (1976) *A guide to the measurement of animal bones from archaeological sites*. Harvard, Peabody Museum Bulletin 1.

Walkington, H., Renouf, J. T., James, H. C. L. and Sebire, H. R. (2001). A raised beach in western Guernsey: its archaeological and geological significance. *Geoscience in south-west England* 10, 149–153.

Walls, T., de Jersey, P. and Hughes, C. (2014) Archaeology Section Report 2014. *Transactions of La Société Guernesiaise* XXVII/4, 623–30.

Warry, P. (2006) *Tegulae: manufacture, typology and use in Roman Britain*. Oxford, BAR 417.

Wheeler, A. C., and Jones, A. K. G. (1989). *Fishes*. Cambridge, Cambridge University Press.

Williams, D. F. (1973) Flotation at Sīrāf. *Antiquity*, 47, 198–202.

Williams, D. F. (1996) Roman amphorae. In R. B. Burns, B. W. Cunliffe and H. Sebire, *Guernsey: an island community of the Atlantic Iron Age* (Oxford, Oxford University Committee for Archaeology), 49–52.

Williams, D. F. and Wood, M. (1995) Autre exemple de la nouvelle forme de céramique 'à l'éponge' et étude pétrographique des tessons de cette céramique provenant de Southampton et des Iles Anglo-Normandes. In *Actes du Congrès de Rouen 1995* (SFECAG), 151–5.

Wood, M. (1989) Romano-British and Roman pottery from Jersey. *Annual Bulletin of La Société Jers*iaise 25, 175–8.

Wood, M. (1990) Céramiques inédites de la Tène finale et de l'époque gallo-romaine trouvées à Alderney et découverte récente d'amphores à Jersey et Herm (Iles Anglo-Normandes). *Bulletin de l'Association Manche Atlantique pour la Recherche Archéologique dans les Iles* 3, 47–60.

Wood, M. (1991) Céramiques romano-britanniques trouvées à Alet jusqu'en 1986 et étude des relations commerciales d'Alet au Bas-Empire. *Dossiers du Centre Régional Archéologique d'Alet* 19, 35–52.

Wood, M. (1993a) A new form of *céramique à l'éponge* from Roman Britain. *Journal of Roman Pottery Studies* 6, 119–22.

Wood, M. (1993b) Roman pottery from Bitterne Manor pipe-trench excavations of 1991. Southampton City Council, unpublished report.

Wood, M. (1994) La céramique du Bas-Empire dans les îles anglo-normandes et dans deux sites côtiers du golfe normand-breton. In M. Tuffreau-Libre and A. Jacques (eds), *La céramique du Bas-Empire en Gaule Belgique et dans les régions voisines. Actes de la table ronde de céramologie gallo-romaine, Arras, 8–10 octobre 1991* (Revue du Nord, Hors-Série, Collection Archéologie 4), 153–66.

Wood, M. (1996) North Gaulish greyware; terra nigra type ware, etc. In R. B. Burns, B. W. Cunliffe and H. Sebire, *Guernsey: an island community of the Atlantic Iron Age* (Oxford, Oxford University Committee for Archaeology), 52–5.

Appendix: pottery codes

Imported fabrics

AH	Alice Holt/Farnham Greywares
AMPH	Miscellaneous amphorae
BB1	Black-burnished ware 1
BB2	Black-burnished ware 2
BBT	Black-burnished ware type, probably part of BB2 industry, including worn/abraded sherds
BBTA	Black-burnished ware type A
BBTB	Black-burnished ware type B; coarser than the above
CC	Miscellaneous colour-coated wares
CCB	*Céramique craquelée-bleutée* (eastern Paris basin)
CF	*Céramique fumigée* (Menez 1985)
CGCC	Central Gaulish colour-coated wares, including 'black samian'
CGFM	Central Gaulish fine micaceous ware
CGWW	Central Gaulish white ware, including pipe-clay figurines
DUR	Durotrigian ware
EGGS	Miscellaneous eggshell wares
EIFL	*Eifelkeramik*
EPON	*Céramique à l'éponge*
EW	'E' ware (Tyers 1996, 145–6)
F55	Oxidised flagons; body sherds indistinguishable from Normandy amphora fabric PW55
FCB	Creamy pink/buff ware
FOX	Oxidised flagons/pitchers with reduced core; fine, slightly micaceous fabric similar to PW55
FOXO	Miscellaneous oxidised flagons
GB	Gallo-Belgic wares
GCF	Grog-tempered *céramique fumigée*, probably north Gaulish
GG	Gritty greyware; jars with grey surfaces, frequent quartz grains in sandy, fine paste
GOW	Gritty oxidised ware, fabric identical to medieval Normandy Gritty Ware (Burns 1987, 34 no. 23)
GROG	Grog-tempered ware (Romano-British)
KOLN	Cologne colour-coated wares
LEST	London-Essex stamped wares (Tyers 1996, 169–70)
MARB	Marbled ware
MCF	Miscellaneous *céramique fumigée*, distinguished from CF/SCFO *etc* by white/off-white fine micaceous fabrics
MDC	Mica-decorated thick coat (gold)
MDER	Mica-decorated early Roman ware (gold)
MDERC	Copy of MDER; a wheel-made 'local' copy of Breto-Norman MDER
MER	Coarse Merovingian/Carolingian wares (some with roller-stamp decoration)
MG	Miscellaneous greywares
MONF	Mortaria: New Forest colour-coated
MONV	Mortaria: Nene Valley
MOPIC	Mortaria: Picardy
MORH	Mortaria: Rhineland
MORHT	Mortaria: Rhineland – Taverny
MORT	Mortaria (unknown source)
MORTG	Mortaria: Gallic, possibly Breton source
MOX	Miscellaneous oxidised scraps
MR	Miscellaneous reduced scraps
MSW	Micaceous sandy ware; may be a medieval fabric
NFCC	New Forest colour-coated wares
NFGW	New Forest greywares; may be archived as AH/NF due to difficulty in distinguishing between products of the two centres
NGGW	North Gaulish greywares (undifferentiated)
NGGW1	North Gaulish greyware (finer fabric), Nord/Pas-de-Calais/Somme valley
NGGW2	North Gaulish greyware; a coarser version of NGGW1
NGGW3	North Gaulish greyware; differentiated on basis of form, including hooked-rim vessels; many Guernsey examples have an oxidised paste
NGGW4	North Gaulish greyware; off-white fabrics with *terra nigra* type finish, in H (hard) or S (soft)
NGLTN	North Gaulish late terra nigra; distinctive C3/C4 bowls (Bouquillon *et al.* 1994, 213–24)
NGSG	North Gaulish, fairly hard sandy fabric, fine mica and black inclusions, grey surfaces, often with black streaks visible on exterior
NGWO	North Gaulish wares (oxidised)
NVCC	Nene Valley colour-coated ware
OXRC	Oxfordshire red/brown colour-coated wares
PAR	Parchment ware (Romano-British)

PRW Pompeian red ware (unknown source)
PRW2 Pompeian red ware 2 (Tyers 1996, 158, fabric 2)
PRW3 Pompeian red ware 3 (Tyers 1996, 158, fabric 3)
PW3 Dressel 1A Italian amphorae
PW4 Dressel 1B Italian amphorae
PW6A Dressel 1/Pascual 1, fabric 1, Spanish amphorae
PW6B Dressel 1/Pascual 1, fabric 2, Spanish amphorae
PW10 Dressel 2–4 amphorae
PW12 Cam. 189 'carrot' amphorae
PW13 Richborough 527 amphorae (one sherd, identification uncertain)
PW15 Haltern 70/Cam. 185A Spanish amphorae
PW16 Dressel 7–11 Spanish amphorae
PW19 Beltran IIB amphorae
PW24 Oberaden 83/Dressel 25 amphorae
PW25 Dressel 20 Spanish amphorae
PW26 Dressel 23 or 49 Spanish amphorae
PW27 Pelichet 47/Gauloise 4 Gallic amphorae
PW30 Gauloise 5 Gallic amphorae
PW31 Dressel 28/Gauloise 1 amphorae
PW33 Africana I/Beltran 57 amphorae
PW38 Dressel 30 Algerian amphorae
PW46 Late Roman Palestinian amphorae
PW47 Kapitan II 'hollow foot' amphorae
PW55 Gauloise 12 'furrowed-rim' amphorae (some sherds indistinguishable from F55 flagon sherds)
QT Quartz-tempered wares, probably from various production sites in NW/northern France
QTG Quartz-tempered greywares, probably from various production sites in NW/northern France
QTW Quartz-tempered white ware; quartz inclusions larger than QTG
RC Rough Cast wares, most from Argonne/Sinzig, but see also CGCC and KOLN
RHT Rhenish wares (Trier)
SAM Terra sigillata (undifferentiated)
SAMCG Terra sigillata, central Gaul
SAMEG Terra sigillata, east Gaul
SAMSG Terra sigillata, south Gaul
SCFO Smooth *céramique fumigée* (oxidised paste) (Menez 1985), central Gaul, Armorica and many unknown centres
SCFR Smooth *céramique fumigée* (reduced paste) (Santrot and Santrot 1979), SW France, Armorica and many unknown centres
SGW Sandy greyware, probably variant of numerous north Gaulish series of fabrics, particularly NGSG
SOM & SOX Sandy oxidised micaceous ware, similar to MSW but not as hard or as micaceous
STN Sandy terra nigra; STN & STNR clearly related to north Gaulish fabrics, especially NGGW and GCF
STNR Sandy terra nigra, red paste, distinguished from STN due to distinctive paste and soapy feel
TN Terra nigra
TR Terra rubra
WNMW Western Normandy micaceous ware (Wood 1994, 160)
WW1 White ware 1, fine, hard cream/off-white paste, pink blotches on external surface, recognised only in ring-neck flagon
WW2/3 White ware 2/3, fine, fairly hard, light grey/off-white paste, some sherds with pale orange/buff surface (central Gaul?)

Local fabrics (certain and probable)

AQG Coarse quartz/granitic fabrics (local). Prehistoric to late Iron Age; includes local copies of LIA imports where not designated as LIA (Burns *et al.* 1996, 48–9, local fabrics 1, 2, 4, 5 and 6)
AQR Finer granite and quartz fabric (local and probably local). Some wheel-made, so LIA onwards. Much variation in fabric, some sherds indistinguishable from TBF series
AR Fine sandy grey/brown fabric (local?). (Burns 1977, 202–3, coarse wheel-made local pottery type IV)
TBF1 Tripod bowl fabric 1 (probably local) (Wood 1994, 161–2). Usually black but wide variation in coarseness as well as colour of TBF series
TBF1 GREY Tripod bowl fabric 1 grey (probably local) (Wood 1994, 161–2). Grey colour and finer fabric than TBF1
TBF2 Tripod bowl fabric 2 (probably local) (Wood 1994, 161–2). Grey but less proficiently made, colour more uniformly light brown/grey
VES Vesicular fabric (local?) (Burns *et al.* 1996, 48–9, fabric 3, later Iron Age)

Other coded pottery

ER Coarse early Roman pottery (various types, basically AQR and AR)
IA Coarse Iron Age pottery (various, AQG)
LIA Late Iron Age pottery (various)
MED Medieval pottery (various)
PH Prehistoric pottery (various)
PH (PMED) Post-medieval pottery (various)
BMAT Building materials
TILE Tile
BQ Briquetage